The M.A.K. Halliday Library Functional Linguistics Series

Series Editors

Chenguang Chang, Sun Yat-sen University, Guangzhou, China

Guowen Huang, Sun Yat-sen University, Guangzhou, China

This series focuses on studies concerning the theory and application of Systemic Functional Linguistics. It bears the name of Professor M.A.K. Halliday, as he is generally regarded as the founder of this school of linguistic thought. The series covers studies on language and context, functional grammar, semantic variation, discourse analysis, multimodality, register and genre analysis, educational linguistics and other areas. Systemic Functional Linguistics is a functional model of language inspired by the work of linguists such as Saussure, Hjelmslev, Whorf, and Firth. The theory was initially developed by Professor M.A.K. Halliday and his colleagues in London during the 1960s, and since 1974 it has held an international congress every year at various continents around the world. It is well-known for its application in a variety of fields, including education, translation, computational linguistics, multimodal studies, and healthcare, and scholars are always exploring new areas of application.

Jing Fang

A Systemic Functional Grammar of Chinese Nominal Groups

A Text-Based Approach

 Springer

Jing Fang (iD)
Sydney, NSW, Australia

ISSN 2198-9869   ISSN 2198-9877 (electronic)
The M.A.K. Halliday Library Functional Linguistics Series
ISBN 978-981-19-4008-8   ISBN 978-981-19-4009-5 (eBook)
https://doi.org/10.1007/978-981-19-4009-5

This Springer imprint is published by the registered company Springer Nature Singapore Pte Ltd.
The registered company address is: 152 Beach Road, #21-01/04 Gateway East, Singapore 189721, Singapore

Acknowledgements

I wish to express my deep gratitude to a group of people. Firstly, I owe a great debt of gratitude to Prof. Christian Matthiessen, who has had an immense influence on me in viewing language. From him, I learned how to approach, observe and describe a language from a systemic functional perspective. Professor Matthiessen's thought-provoking books, articles, lectures, seminar talks and presentations have been a great intellectual inspiration to me in exploring the topic of this book. Secondly, I am also greatly indebted to Dr. Canzhong Wu, who taught me about corpus linguistics and from whom I learned how to observe language in a corpus environment. Last but not least, I want to thank my family for the unfailing support and love that I received during the writing of this book.

Contents

Symbols, Abbreviations and Systemic Conventions

	System: If 'a', then 'x' or 'y'
	Delicacy ordering: If 'a', then 'x' or 'y'; if 'x', then 'm' or 'n'
	Simultaneity: If 'a', then simultaneously 'x' or 'y', and 'm' or 'n'
	Conjunction in entry condition: If 'a' and 'b', then 'x' or 'y'

(continued)

(continued)

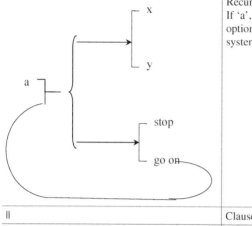	Recursive system (logical): If 'a', then 'x' or 'y', and simultaneously option of entering and selecting from the same system again
‖	Clause boundary
		Group/phrase boundary
[[ ]]	Embedded clause
[[[[ ]]]]	Further embedding: an embedded clause within another embedded clause
[ ]	Embedded group/phrase
↘	Realised by
ϕ	Omission
CONJ	Conjunction
SFL	Systemic functional linguistics
SUB	A subordinate particle (=*de* in this thesis)
MEA	A measure word in Chinese that has no equivalent in English
*	A problematic/ungrammatical example

List of Figures

List of Tables

Chapter 1
Introducing Nominal Groups

This chapter will begin with an overview of the research topic: nominal group. The term will be defined through the discussion of both 'nominal' and 'group', following which a comparison of the term 'noun phrase' with 'nominal group' will also be presented. In Sect. 1.2, I will give a review of literature focusing on nominal groups in Chinese. However, the review will not include literatures in the systemic functional linguistic field, which will be presented in Chap. 2 instead. In Sect. 1.3, the discussion will focus on the significance of nominal group in contributing to various modes of meanings as a text unfolds. Using a sample text, I will present an example analysis to demonstrate how the use of nominal groups provide resources in achieving different modes of meanings and point out a direction of a delicate text analysis model focusing on nominal groups, which can provide an additional layer of analysis to the currently dominant clause grammar. The discussion in Sect. 1.3 will give the rationale for the exploration of a grammar of nominal group to be presented in the following chapters.

1.1 Defining 'Nominal Group'

The term 'nominal group' is a term full of systemic functional linguistic (SFL) colour, which is rarely used in the literature of other grammatical models, and a corresponding term used in the latter is 'noun phrase'. Scholars working in models other than SFL conventionally regard 'nominal group' as a synonym to 'noun phrase' (e.g. Butler et al. 2007). Although by and large, these two terms are very similar in grammatical sense, the difference between the two is more than terminological. In traditional grammar, only the term 'phrase' is used to refer to the intermediate grammatical unit between clause and word, whereas in systemic functional grammar, 'group' and 'phrase' are recognised as two independent terms to stand for different grammatical organisations at the same rank. Therefore, before the definition of 'nominal group'

© Springer Nature Singapore Pte Ltd. 2022
J. Fang, *A Systemic Functional Grammar of Chinese Nominal Groups*,
The M.A.K. Halliday Library Functional Linguistics Series,
https://doi.org/10.1007/978-981-19-4009-5_1

is presented, it is necessary to first clarify the meanings of 'nominal' and 'group', respectively.

1.1.1 On 'Nominal'

In either SFL or non-SFL models, views about the notion of 'nominal' remain similar: to be 'nominal', a grammatical unit should be able to function as a noun. However, it is important to avoid confusion with 'noun' in its specific sense, as the grammatical quality of being 'nominal' can be realised by lexical items of word class other than noun, which is illustrated in the examples below:

Example 1

他们数了数, 总共有 32个。

tāmen	Shǔ le shǔ,	zǒnggòng	yǒu	sānshièr ge
they	counted	altogether	have	32 MEA
pronoun	verb	adverb	Verb	numeral + measure

They counted, and altogether, there were 32

Example 2

你想吃什么?辣的还是甜的?

nǐ	xiǎngchī	Shénme?	làde	háishi	Tiánde?
you	want to eat	what	spicy de	or	sweet de
pronoun	verb (group)	pronoun	adjective	conjunctive	adjective

What do you want to eat? Spicy or sweet?

Example 3

这些都是他最喜欢吃的。

zhèxiē	dōushì	tā	zuì xǐhuān chīde
These	all are	he	best like eat *de*
determiner	verb (group)	pronoun	Down-ranked clause + *de*

These are all his favourite food.

As shown in the examples above, a pronoun (in Example 1), a numeral + measure structure (in Example 1), an adjective + de[1] structure (in Example 2), a determiner (in Example 3) or even a down-ranked clause + *de* structure (in Example 3) can function as the same as a noun in a Chinese sentence and share the same grammatical features, such as being able to take a subject or an object[2] position, being referential and so on. This illustrates the broader sense of being 'nominal', which is adopted by the present study to define a nominal group. In other words, from a grammatical perspective, the assessment of the nominal nature of a lexical item is based on its grammatical potential, or probability, in realising a functional role in a clause which can be congruently assumed by a noun, such as the roles of subject and object in a clause. In the referential space, many nominal items share the same feature of having the potential to be identified as a referent in a given context through deixis, qualification, epithets, classification and naming. In terms of semantic representation, being nominal means that the lexical item in question has the potential to construe a thing (see further in Chap. 4), compared to non-nominal items such as verbs, prepositions and so on.

In general, 'nominal' indicates the grammatical potential of a lexicogrammatical item in realising certain functional roles in a clause (e.g. as subject or object), which can be typically fulfilled by a noun.

1.1.2 On 'Group'

It is important to distinguish 'group' from 'phrase' first. In Chinese, a *phrase* is called duǎn yǔ (短语), which literally means 'short speech', whereas a *group* is called cí zǔ (词组), which literally means 'word group'. The terminological difference in Chinese already gives some indication for the difference between the two terms. And, Halliday and Matthiessen present a more straight-forward point of view on the issue:

> A phrase is different from a group in that, whereas a group is an expansion of a word, a phrase is a contraction of a clause. Starting form opposite ends, the two achieve roughly the same status on the rank scale... (Halliday and Matthiessen 2014: 362–363)

The difference can be interpreted in this way: although phrase and group are both made up of words, they are viewed from different directions—phrase is viewed from above (thus as a contracted clause), while group is viewed from below (thus as a group of words).

It is important to point out that, although viewed as a group of words in SFL, the term 'group' should not be defined merely on the basis of the number of constituents that form a group. Rather, group should be viewed and defined on the rank scale

---

[1] de (的) is a grammatical particle in Chinese, which typically appears after a modifier in a nominal group structure to connect the modifier with the head noun.

[2] The terms 'subject' and 'object' in this chapter refer to the concepts in traditional grammar. Discussion about them in SFL will be presented in Chap. 2.

(cf. Halliday 1961). As an important part of the SFL theory, rank scale has been described as a hierarchy of order called constituency, whereby larger units are made up out of smaller ones: a clause is made up of phrases/groups; a group/phrase by words; a word by morphemes (Halliday and Matthiessen 2014).

Viewed on the rank scale, group represents the class below clause and above word. In terms of realisation, a group is made up of either one or more words. If a group is made up of more than one word, the group has a central pivot in its structure, which decides its grammatical nature: with a noun as the head of a group (elliptical or not), the group is nominal; with a verb as the head, the group is verbal; and so on.

Essentially, 'group' represents the structural nature of a class, indicating its status on the rank scale, and its constituency potential in lexicogrammar.

1.1.3   General Features of the Nominal Group

So far, I have discussed the notions of 'group' and 'nominal' in Sects. 1.1.1 and 1.1.2. When it comes to the definition of nominal group, it means that a nominal group should bear the features of both. To put it simply, a nominal group is a group of nominal words, but obviously this definition is not detailed enough to give us any clue about its general features. Therefore, it is important to introduce Halliday and Matthiessen's five principles of constituency in lexicogrammar (Halliday and Matthiessen 2014), as I will base my description of the general features of a nominal group on these principles. Altogether, they have summarised five principles of constituency in lexicogrammar, which apply to every language (Halliday and Matthiessen 2014: 9–10):

There is a scale of rank in the grammar of every language. This can be typically represented as: clause > phrase/group > word > morpheme[3]

Each consists of one or more units of the rank next below.

Units of every rank may form complexes: not only clause complexes but also phrase complexes, group complexes, word complexes and even morpheme complexes may be generated by the same grammatical resources.

There is the potential for rank shift, whereby a unit of one rank may be downranked (downgraded) to function in the structure of a unit of its own rank or of a rank below.

Under certain circumstances it is possible for one unit to be enclosed within another; not as a constituent of it, but simply in such a way as to split the other one into two discrete parts.[4]

Based on these five principles, together with the discussions above about 'nominal' and 'group', the following criteria can be established for identifying a Chinese nominal group:

---

[3] This representation applies to the case of Mandarin Chinese.

[4] Copyright©2014 from *Halliday's introduction to functional grammar* by Halliday and Matthiessen (4th edition). Reproduced by permission of Taylor and Francis Group, LLC, a division of informa plc.

- A nominal group must consist of a nominal head, which could be a noun, a pronoun, a locative[5] or a determiner. In the case of an elliptic nominal group without a head, this means that a nominal head should be recoverable.
- A nominal group may consist of one or more words.[6]
- A nominal group should be referential. Semantically speaking, this means that it must be able to represent (or refer to) a thing (including human or non-human), concrete or abstract, specific or non-specific. Grammatically, it means that one can add a deictic element before the head to test a group with a doubtful status—but this should not be considered as a rigid grammatical rule as the analysis should always be based on meaning in text rather than on rules.
- A nominal head can be expanded through different types of modification, such as qualifying, classifying, ascribing epithets and so on.
- A nominal group, same as the other types of group or phrase, must be able to play a functional part on a clause structure—for a nominal group, this is typically, but not limited to, referring to the subject or the object position in a clause.
- In terms of semantic representation, a nominal group expresses a being or a thing of any type, either concrete or abstract.

The six criteria presented involve both grammatical and semantic concerns. In this book, the recognition of a nominal group will be strictly based on these criteria listed above. In other words, a grammatical unit should at least satisfy these six criteria to be identified as a nominal group.

Based on the above six criteria, I will discuss an ambiguous case: the rank-shifted 'act clause'.

Look at the two examples below:

Example 4
这年头, 出名不是难事。

zhè niántou	chūmíng	búshì	nánshì
these years	**become famous**	not is	hard thing

Nowadays, becoming famous is not a hard thing.

Example 5
难的是不被人知道。

nánde	shì	bú bèirén zhīdào
difficult de	is	**not be known by others**

The hard thing is not to be known by others.

---

[5] Discussion about 'locative' will be presented in Chap. 4.

[6] In Chinese, a word may be made up of more than one characters.

The above two clauses (Examples 4 and 5) both contain another clause (shown in bold), which is down-ranked to function as a subject (as in Example 4) or an object (as in Example 5). As Chinese is not an inflectional language, unlike English, this type of down-ranked clauses takes on the same lexical form as a ranking clause, and its rank-shifted status is reflected by its grammatical role in another clause. In English, there is a similar type of clause, named by Halliday and Matthiessen as 'act' (Halliday and Matthiessen 2004: 438) clause. Such a clause represents an action, an event or a phenomenon, and grammatically, it functions in the same way as a nominal group. Some Chinese linguists term them as míngcíxìng jiégòu (名词性结构, *nominal structure*) and treat it at the group/phrase level (cf. Zhu 1982). If one checks against the six criteria presented earlier, this type of 'act clause', although nominal in terms of grammatical function, cannot be treated as a nominal group because it does not satisfy all the criteria of being a nominal group: there is no nominal head in the structure, the structure cannot be referred by a deictic item, and it cannot be expanded further through modification.

1.2   Reviewing the Study of Nominal Groups in Chinese

In this section, I will have a review of literature on the research of Chinese nominal groups However, this review does not cover the studies based on systemic function grammar, which will be discussed in Chap. 2 instead.

The study of the Chinese language can date back to as early as 200 B.C. with focuses on lexicology and epigraphy mainly (cf. Wang 1985; Shao 1990), but the work on nominal groups[7] happened much later. The reason is that nominal group, as well as the other topics in grammar such as syntax and morphology, was defined and recognised only in the modern linguistic history in China. As pointed out by Wang Li, one of the leading scholars in Chinese linguistics and linguistic history, there was no linguistics but only philology in the ancient Chinese history (Wang 1984). This is closely related to the fact that Chinese, as a logographic non-inflexional language, has virtually no trace of morphology, as a result of which syntactic questions have never been brought to attention (Halliday and McDonald 2004). In fact, the study of grammar was absent in the country's linguistic history till the late nineteenth century. The publication of Wéntōng (also known as Mǎshì Wéntōng, *Ma's Grammar*) in 1898 is widely regarded as the first study on Chinese grammar, which also marks the beginning of modern Chinese linguistics (cf. Wang 1984; Shao 1990).

However, the study of nominal groups did not synchronise with the modern linguistic research in Chinese. The historical reviews of Chinese language studies in the twentieth century showed that the grammatical unit of *phrase* was either not recognised or largely ignored by scholars in the first half of the century. During this

---

[7] In this section, 'the study of nominal group' by and large refers to the work on 'noun phrase' (cf. Sect. 1.3).

period, the research was under the heavy influence of Western grammatical traditions and the focus was on exploring specific grammatical rules in Chinese (cf. Shao 1990; Lu 1993). The second half of the twentieth century witnessed tremendous progress in Chinese grammatical studies with the publications of several important works (e.g. Chao 1965; Lü 1979; Zhu 1982). During this period, more and more attention was given on describing the language rather than exploring rules. When it comes to language description, it seems to be unavoidable to define grammatical units from different levels, through which a syntactic structure can be more accessible. In Chao's (1965) description of spoken Chinese grammar, he mainly focused on three levels of grammatical unit: sentence, word and morpheme, though phrase was also recognised as one of the classes. However, phrases were not discussed as a separate class and neither were they categorised as nominal, verbal, adverbial and so on. Instead, Chao described these units from a syntactic structural perspective. He argued that syntax, from the point of view of kinds of units, was not primarily concerned with expressions[8] in their capacities as lexical items, but with types of constructions into which expressions of various types enter, and a part of speech was a class of words and not of phrase. As a result, in Chao's research, phrase was not investigated as a separate grammatical class, and was classified in terms of syntactical constructions (e.g. coordinate construction and subordinate construction) rather than of functional potential. Chao's categorisation represented the predominant views shared by scholars in the 1950s and 1960s. In 1979, Lü published an important work on Chinese grammar, where he stated that 'it seems to be especially suitable in the case of Chinese to treat *phrase* as an intermediate unit between *word* and *sentence*' (Lü 1979). This was when linguists in Mainland China started to pay more attention to *phrase* (including *noun phrase*). 1980s experienced the rapid development in phrase grammar of various types with Zhu Dexi taking the lead (see Zhu 1980, 1982, 1985). On classifying grammatical units in Chinese, Zhu proposed the following points: (1) there is no simple corresponding relations between words and syntactic components; (2) same syntactic constructing principles apply to both sentence and phrase levels (Zhu 1982). Based on these two points, Zhu believed that the analysis of Chinese grammar should be based at phrase level, and the relations between morpheme and word, and between *word* and *phrase* were both compositional. In other words, it is a relation of parts and whole: a phrase is made up of words, and a word is made up of morphemes. However, the relation between phrase and sentence was different: sentence is realised by phrase, and the two share the same construction principles. Zhu has been regarded as a pioneer in promoting research on phrase-based grammar (see Shao 1990; Lu 1993). According to Zhu's definition, a group should consist of at least two words, otherwise it is not a 'word group' but only a word. This actually creates a problem of consistency because at the other three levels, in contrast, Zhu stated that a word may consist of one morpheme and a sentence may consist of only one group or even one word. So there is a clear-cut boundary between group and

---

[8] Chao uses the term 'expression' to cover either words or phrases, but not morphemes (see Chao 1965: 258).

word, but the boundary between group and sentence is in fact very ambiguous—very often the case is that a group equals a sentence. In Zhu's description, group was termed as jùfǎ jiégòu (句法结构, *syntactic construction*) and was categorised in terms of the internal structural relations between each part. Altogether, he divided group into six types (Zhu 1982: 14):

subordinate construction (typically realised by modifier + head)

verb + object construction

verb + complement construction

subject + predicate construction

coordinate construction (realised by a group of words of the same part of speech)

verb + verb construction

It is not surprising that, according to Zhu's classification, the boundary between group and sentence is very fuzzy, creating a large overlapping area, since the same constructions, such as subject + predicate construction, can also be considered as a sentence structure. Therefore, it is possible to argue that Zhu's work on groups is still a study of syntax and he tries to interpret syntax at the group level. Strictly speaking, this is not a grammar of phrase/group, as they were only used as a medium to interpret the grammar at the sentence level and the focus was always on the syntactic structure.

From 1980s till very recently, the situation of the group studies has not changed much in the Chinese linguistic field. Although some classifications of groups/phrases tend to consider both the internal construction and the external grammatical function, the dominant way to classify a group unit has been generally the same as Zhu's. In such a context, nominal groups can hardly receive much research attention since it is not often considered as a separate category in group/phrase grammar. Even in the studies with a specific focus on nominal groups, the dominant research focus is still on either the internal syntactic structure or the external roles nominal groups can play on a syntactic structure (e.g. Gu 1985; Li 1986; Liu 2006; Xiong 2008; Wang 2012; Fan 2014), and the classification within nominal groups still follow the framework similar to Zhu's.

In recent years, with the development of computational linguistics, some researchers raised doubts on the construction-based classification of groups after noticing that computers had problems in identifying nominal groups based on such classification (e.g. Zhan and Liu 1997; Zhan 1997; Qian 2010). This kind of doubts actually reflects the problems behind such classification. Firstly, the construction-based classification cannot adequately distinguish a sentence from a group/phrase since both are considered to have the same construction principles, and in practice, the only effective way to distinguish them relies on the use of punctuation marks. This leaves us an impression that, grammatically speaking, there is little difference between group and sentence in Chinese—this is in fact far from the truth. Secondly, under such classification, units of different grammatical potentials fall into the same category, as a result of which their grammatical functions tend to be overshadowed. For example, a complex of nominal groups consisting of two head nouns is put in the same category as a complex of verbal groups consisting of two verbs, simply because they both have the coordinate structure. Such classification obviously cannot reflect their different grammatical potential. Thirdly and most importantly, such a classification is purely based on form, which makes it impossible to explore any context-based meaning potentials that a group can provide, which will inevitably influence the depth of the research. For instance, some researchers work on those ambiguous constructions which are open for more than one interpretation. In fact, without a context-based perspective, such problems can hardly get resolved.

Before the end of this section, it is important to mention the work of two groups of researchers on Chinese noun phrases. One is Li and Thompson's description of Mandarin Chinese grammar (Li and Thompson 1981). In this study, they used functional terms to describe modern Chinese at all the three levels of word, phrase and sentence. In their account of phrase, noun phrase was investigated as a separate category in terms of modification, referentiality and nominalisation. This is an outstanding work in that the structural properties in the language are discussed in terms of the pragmatic situations with an eye to the context. However, as the authors stated in the preface, the grammar was explicitly designed for students and teachers of Mandarin. Therefore, judging from the linguistic theoretical perspective, many linguistics issues, such as the semantic motivations behind the grammatical choices and the grammatical strategies in realising different pragmatic purposes, remained unaddressed. The other study worth noting is Zhang Min's study of Chinese noun phrase in his book《认知语言学与汉语名词短语》(*Cognitive linguistics and Chinese noun phrase*). In this book, Zhang described the different structures that a Chinese nominal group could have and explored the semantic and cognitive motives behind the optional use of *de* on the structure (Zhang 1998). Zhang's study can be considered as one of the very limited number of studies on Chinese nominal group which based the description on meaning rather than form. However, as his study mainly focused on *de*, the description of the other parts in a nominal group only served to explain the use of *de*. Therefore, his account of nominal group was not a comprehensive one. It is obvious that more efforts are needed in exploring the Chinese nominal group.

1.3 Nominal Group and Text

As an important unit at the group level, nominal group provides rich resources for meaning making as a text unfolds. I will use a short text (Text 1) as an example to demonstrate the significant contributions that nominal groups can make to the text.

Context[9]

	Text 1: 小蝌蚪找妈妈[10] (*Little tadpoles looking for mum*) Where is our mum?
Field	The socio-semiotic function of this text is both recreating and expounding. The domain is concrete and concerned with the process in which a tadpole turns into a frog. The explanation of the process is unfolded through a narrative depicting a group of tadpoles looking for their mum
Tenor	The institutional roles are an author to the primary school students in grade 1: an adult to young children readers (around 7 years old on average). The evaluation of the experiential domain is neutral to positive
Mode	The text is monologic, written and narrative in children's language. No technical language is used in the text, and concrete scenarios are presented to demonstrate the physical change of tadpoles as they grow into frogs. The original text is multimodal with a few coloured pictures illustrating the tadpoles at different stages of growth

Text 1

小蝌蚪找妈妈

[1.1] 池塘里有一群小蝌蚪, [1.2] 大大的脑袋, [1.3] 黑灰色的身子, [1.4] 甩着长长的尾巴, [1.5] 快活地游来游去。

[2.1] 小蝌蚪游哇游, [2.2] 过了几天, 长出两条后腿。[3.1] 他们看见 [3.2] 鲤鱼妈妈在教小鲤鱼捕食, [3.3] 就迎上去, [3.4] 问: [3.5] "鲤鱼阿姨, 我们的妈妈在哪里?" [4.1] 鲤鱼妈妈说: [4.2] "你们的妈妈有四条腿, [4.3] 宽嘴巴。[5] 你们到那边去找吧!"

[6.1] 小蝌蚪游哇游, [6.2] 过了几天, 长出两条前腿。[7.1] 他们看见 [7.2] 一只乌龟摆动着四条腿在水里游, [7.3] 连忙追上去, [7.4] 叫着: "妈妈, 妈妈!" [8.1] 乌龟笑着说: [8.2] "我不是你们的妈妈。[9.1] 你们的妈妈头顶上有两只大眼睛, [9.2] 披着绿衣裳。[10] 你们到那边去找吧!"

[11.1] 小蝌蚪游哇游, [11.2] 过了几天, 尾巴变短了。[12.1] 他们游到荷花旁边, [12.2] 看见 [12.3] 荷叶上蹲着一只大青蛙, [12.4] 披着碧绿的衣裳, [12.5] 露着雪白的肚皮, [12.6] 鼓着一对大眼睛。

[13.1] 小蝌蚪游过去, [13.2] 叫着: "妈妈, 妈妈!" [14.1] 青蛙妈妈低头一看, [14.2] 笑着说: [14.3] "好孩子, 你们已经长成青蛙了, [14.4] 快跳上来吧!" [15.1] 他们后腿一蹬, [15.2] 向前一跳, [15.3] 蹦到了荷叶上。

[16] 不知什么时候, 小青蛙的尾巴已经不见了。[17.1] 他们跟着妈妈, [17.2] 天天去捉害虫。

English Translation

[1.1] In the pond, there were a group of tadpoles, [1.2] (having) big heads, [1.3] (and having) dark grey bodies, [1.4] swinging their long tails [1.5] and swimming happily.

[2] The tadpoles swam and swam. [3] After a few days, they grew two hind legs. [4.1] When they saw [4.2] Mummy Carp teaching the young carps to hunt, [4.3]

---

[9] The terms, Field, Tenor and Mode, will be introduced in Chap. 2.

[10] The text was originally written by Huizhen Fang and Lude Sheng in 1959.

they swam up [4.4] and asked, [4.5] 'Auntie Carp, where is our mother'? [5.1] Mummy Carp said, [5.2] 'Your mum has four legs [5.3] and (has) a wide mouth. [6] Go over there and find her'!

[7] The tadpoles swam and swam. [8] After a few days, they grew two front legs. [9.1] They saw [9.2] a turtle swimming in the water with its four legs swinging. [10.1] They quickly overtook him [10.2] and cried, 'Mum, mum'! [11.1] The turtle smiled [11.2] and said, [11.3] 'I am not your mum. [11.4] Your mother has two big eyes on her head [11.5] and wears green clothes. [12.1] Go over there [12.2] and find her'!

[13] The tadpoles swam and swam. [14] After a few days, their tails became shorter. [15.1] They swam to the lotus [15.2] and saw [15.3] a big frog sitting on the lotus leaf, [15.4] dressed in green clothes, [15.5] exposing a white belly and bulging eyes.

[16.1] The tadpoles swam over [16.2] and cried, 'Mum, mum'! [17.1] Mummy Frog looked down [17.2] and said with a smile, [17.3] 'Good kids, you have grown into frogs. [18] Jump on'! [19.1] With a push on their hind legs, they jumped forward [19.2] and jumped onto the lotus leaf. [20] It is not clear [[when the tail of the little frogs had disappeared]]. [21.1] They followed their mother [21.2] to catch pests every day.

Unlike a typical academic science text that is expounding in terms of socio-semiotic process type,[11] text 1 is both expounding and recreating. It is expounding as the text explains the physical changes of tadpoles as they grow into frogs. Meanwhile, the text is also recreating in that it narrates a flow of human imaginary events involving a group of tadpoles in search of their mother. Obviously, this is motivated by the purpose of the text: it aims to explain to young readers about the growing process of tadpoles. An important stylistic feature of the text is the use of personification, which is a kind of expression that gives human traits to a non-human being (cf. Dodson 2008). The use of nominal group has played an important role in realising personification. This is mainly achieved in a number of ways, including:

(1) A nominal group representing an animal (i.e. non-human) is construed as a Sayer in a verbal clause Example 6:

Example 6
[13.1] 小蝌蚪游过去, [13.2] 叫着: "妈妈, 妈妈!"
English translation:
[16.1] *The tadpoles* swam over [16.2] and *cried*, 'Mum, mum'!

(2) A nominal group representing an animal is construed as a Sayer in a verbal clause accompanied with a circumstance representing a human-only manner Example 7:

---

[11] In this book, Matthiessen's context-based registerial cartography is adopted to analyse the text type of each example text (Matthiessen 2015b). Details about the registerial cartography will be introduced in Chap. 2.

Example 7

[14.1] 青蛙妈妈低头一看, [14.2] 笑着说: [14.3] "好孩子, 你们已经长成青蛙了, [14.4] 快跳上来吧!".

English translation:

[17.1] ***Mummy Frog*** looked down [17.2] and said ***with a smile***, [17.3] 'Good kids, you have grown into frogs. [18] Jump on'!

(3) The attribute of an animal is realised by a nominal group that is construed as an attribute of human in a relational clause, as shown in Example 8:

Example 8

[9.1] 你们的妈妈头顶上有两只大眼睛, [9.2] 披着绿衣裳。

English translation:

[11.4] Your mother has two big eyes on her head [11.5] and wears ***green clothes***.

(4) A nominal group represents a name that indicates the social relationship that only exists in the human society Example 9:

Example 9

[3.5] "鲤鱼阿姨, 我们的妈妈在哪里?"

English translation:

[4.5] '**Auntie Carp**[12] (Mrs. Carp), where is our mother'?

Interpersonally, the general tone of the text sounds children-friendly. Again, the nominal group has played a significant role in achieving the interpersonal effect, which is mainly through the realisation of vocatives. When a clause is viewed as an exchange between a speaker and listener, the use of a Vocative by the speaker in addressing the listener is an important indicator of interpersonal relationship between the two parties (cf. Halliday and Matthiessen 2014: 159). In Text 1, three types of vocatives are used:

Example 10

The tadpoles speak to Mummy Carp (Example 10):

[3.5] "鲤鱼阿姨, 我们的妈妈在哪里?"

'***Auntie Carp***, where is our mum'?

Example 11

The tadpoles speak to Mummy Frog (Example 11):

[13.1] 小蝌蚪游过去, [13.2] 叫着: "妈妈, 妈妈!"

The tadpoles swam over and cried: '***Mum, Mum***'!

---

[12] In the Chinese culture, names such as 'auntie x' and 'uncle x' are commonly used in addressing a female/male adult who are senior in age than the speaker, and the addressee is not necessarily related to the speaker as a family relative. Therefore, a more conventional equivalent in the English-speaking countries would be 'Mrs' and 'Mr' instead.

Example 12

Mummy Frog speaks to the tadpoles (Example 12):

[14.1] 青蛙妈妈低头一看, [14.2] 笑着说: [14.3] "好孩子, 你们已经长成青蛙了, [14.4] 快跳上来吧!"

Mummy Frog looked down and said with a smile, '***Good kids***, you have grown into frogs. Jump on'!

Note that in Example 12, 'good kids' is a literal translation from Chinese, which is a common expression used by an adult speaker to address a child, and it indicates more of an intimacy and affectionate attitude towards the child addressee than a simple compliment.

As shown in all three examples (Examples 10, 11 and 12), the three vocatives used in the text all indicate a friendly interpersonal relationship that general child readers are familiar with—this helps amplify the children-friendly effect of the text.

Textually, nominal groups contribute to the cohesion of the text in a number of ways, such as through repetition and ellipsis. Meanwhile, as the text unfolds, the development of the story surrounding the theme of 'looking for mum' relies heavily on the indications brought by various nominal group structures.

There are three episodes in the narrative describing the process of 'looking for Mummy Frog': (1) the encounter of Mummy Carp who started giving description of Mummy Frog, (2) the encounter of a turtle who was mistaken as Mummy Frog and who gave further description of Mummy Frog, and (3) finally the finding of Mummy Frog. The description of the physical looks of Mummy Frog is introduced bit by bit in each episode through the use of nominal groups, and the connection between each episode is built through the repetition of these nominal groups in each following episode:

	Participants	Description of participants	Description made by participants
Episode 1	鲤鱼阿姨 Auntie Carp	none	四条腿，宽嘴巴 Four legs, wide mouth
Episode 2	乌龟 The turtle	四条腿 four legs	两只大眼睛，绿衣裳 Two big eyes, green clothes
Episode 3	青蛙妈妈 Mummy Frog	绿色的衣服，雪白的肚皮，一对大眼睛 Green clothes, white belly, a pair of big eyes	none

As shown above, when '鲤鱼阿姨' (*Auntie Carp*) is first introduced in the text, there is no description about her. It is clear that the information about 'Auntie Carp' is perceived as given, and in terms of lexicogrammatical realisation, this identity as given information has been presented in a nominal group structure of 'classifier (name 鲤鱼 *carp*) + head noun (social relation name 阿姨 *auntie*)', which makes the identity specific and identifiable. As '鲤鱼阿姨' *Auntie Carp* is presented as given information in its first appearance in the text, there is no need to describe this participant—it simply presents itself as it is in the text. In comparison, the other two participants in the following two episodes, '乌龟' (*the turtle*) and '青蛙妈妈' (*Mummy Frog*) are presented as new information when they are first introduced in the text, and the status of being new information and unidentified is indicated by a nominal group structure of 'numerative + measure + head noun': 一只乌龟 (*one turtle*) and 一只青蛙 (*one frog*). Later, as the story develops, these two participants become identifiable:

Participants	1st appearance as unidentifiable and new information	2nd appearance as identifiable and given information
乌龟 The turtle	一只乌龟 one measure turtle numerative + measure + noun *One/a turtle*	乌龟 turtle noun *The turtle*
青蛙妈妈 Mummy Frog	一只青蛙 one measure frog numerative + measure + noun *one/a frog*	青蛙妈妈 frog mummy Classifier (as identifier) + noun *Mummy Frog*

It is interesting to note that, through the change of the nominal group structure, the identity of '青蛙妈妈' (*Mummy Frog*) changes from unidentifiable (一只青蛙 *one frog*) to identifiable (青蛙妈妈, a literal translation is 'Frog Mummy', as *Mummy Frog* in English), which realises the key outcome of the story: the finding of the tadpoles' mother. There are no sentences in the text that directly tell the young readers that the tadpoles have found their mum successfully. Rather, it is through the match of the descriptions made by previous participants (through the repetition of nominal groups) and the change of the nominal group structure in referring to the 'frog' that such identification process is completed.

I have used sample Text 1, *Little tadpoles looking for mum*, to demonstrate the significant role that nominal groups play in achieving various functional meanings. As the analysis demonstrates, nominal groups provide abundant resources for delicate text analysis below the level of clause. It contributes to the construal of participant roles, the enaction of attitudes and the signalling of social distance, as well as the creation of texture that helps make the whole text coherent, and pushes the development of the storyline.

It would certainly be meaningful if each mode of the meanings, as demonstrated by the examples of Text 1, that a nominal group can contribute to, is analysed based on an established system network. It would then be possible to observe and examine these delicate choices below the clause level and to provide a systemic micro-text analysis as an additional layer for people interested in studying a text microscopically, which the current clause grammar alone cannot suffice—this is the rationale behind the explorations that will be presented in the following chapters.

References

Butler CS, Downing RH, Lavid-Lopez J (2007) Functional perspectives on grammar and discourse. J. Benjamins, Msterdam, Philadelphia

Chao YR (1965) A grammar of spoken Chinese. University of California Press, Berkeley & Los Angeles

Dodson JR (2008) The 'powers' of personification: rhetorical purpose in the 'book of wisdom' and the letter to the Romans. De Gruyter

Fan C (2014) The phasehood analysis of Chinese nominal phrases and NP ellipsis. Theor Pract Lang Stud 4:1359–1369. https://doi.org/10.4304/tpls.4.7.1359-1369

Gu J (1985) Mingci duanyu 名词短语 [About noun phrase]. Zhongxue yuwen 中学语文 [High School Chinese]:36–39

Halliday MAK, Matthiessen CMIM (2014) Halliday's introduction to functional grammar. Routledge, London

Halliday MAK (1961) Categories of the theory of grammar. Word 17:242–292

Halliday MAK, Matthiessen CMIM (2004) An introduction to functional grammar, 3rd edn. Arnold, London

Halliday MAK, McDonald E (2004) Metafunctional profile of the grammar of Chinese. In: Caffarel A, Martin J, Matthiessen C (eds) Language typology: a functional perspective. John Benjamins, Amsterdam, pp 305–396

Li P (1986) Mingci duanyu de jiegou gongneng he yingyong. 名词短语的结构功能和应用 [The structure, function and application of noun phrases]. J Guangxi Normal Univ 1

Lü S (1979) hanyu yufa fenxi weiti. 汉语语法分析问题 [Analysing Chinese grammar]. The Commercial Press, Beijing

Lu J (1993) xiandai hanyu jufalun. 现代汉语句法论 [Syntax of modern Chinese]. The Commercial Press, Beijing

Liu D (2006) Mingci duanyu jufa jiegou diaocha kuangjia. 名词短语句法结构调查框架 [The framework of the syntactic structural research of noun phrases]. Hanyu xuexi 汉语学习 [Chinese studies] 1

Li CN, Thompson SA (1981) Mandarin Chinese: a functional reference grammar. University of California Press Ltd., London

Matthiessen CMIM (2015) Register in the round: registerial cartography. Funct Linguist 2(1):9. https://doi.org/10.1186/s40554-015-0015-8

Qian X (2010) Yi 'de' zi jiegou wei hexin de zuichang mingci duanyu shibie yanjiu. 以"的"字结构为核心的最长名词短语识别研究 [The recognition of the longest noun phrases with a 'de' structure]. Jisuanji gongcheng yu yingyong 计算机工程与应用 [Comput Eng Appl] 18

Shao J (1990) hanyu yufaxue shigao. 汉语语法学史稿 [History of Chinese grammar]. Shanghai Education Press, Shanghai

Wang L (1984) wangli wenji: zhongguo yufa lilun. 王力文集: 中国语法理论 [Collected works of Wang Li: the theory of Chinese grammar]. 第一卷 [vol.1]. Shandong Education Press, Jinan

Wang L (1985) xiandai hanyu yufa. 现代汉语语法 [Modern Chinese grammar]. The Commercial Press, Beijing

Wang H (2012) The syntactic structure of Chinese nominal phrases. PhD Thesis, Northwestern University, Evanston, Illinois

Xiong Z (2008) Yuyin jiegou yu mingci duanyu neibu gongneng fanchou. 语音结构与名词短语内部功能范畴 [Phonetic structures and the internal function of noun phrases]. Zhongguo yuwen 中国语文 [Chinese language] 6

Zhan W (1997) Mianxiang ziran yuyan chuli de xiandai hanyu cizu benwei yufa tixi. 面向自然语言处理的现代汉语词组本位体系 [Prase-based grammatical system of modern Chinese in natural language processing]. Yingyong Yuyanxue 应用语言学 [appl Linguist] 4:100–105

Zhan W, Liu Q (1997) ci de yuyi fenlei zai hanying jiqi fanyi zhong suoqide zuoyong yiji nanyichuli de wenti. 词的语义分类在汉英机器翻译中所起的作用以及难以处理的问题 [The significance and challenges of the semantic categorisation of words in Chinese–English machine translation]. In: Chen L, Yuan Q (eds) Yuyan gongcheng 语言工程 [Language projects]. Tsinghua University Press, Bejing, pp 286–291

Zhang M (1998) Cognitive linguistics and Chinese noun phrase. China Social Sciences Press, Beijing

Zhu D (1980) xiandai hanyu yufa yanjiu. 现代汉语语法研究 [Research on the grammar of modern Chinese]. The Commercial Press, Beijing

Zhu D (1982) yufa jiangyi. 语法讲义 [Notes on grammar]. The Commercial Press, Beijing

Zhu Y (1985) Modality and modulation in English and Chinese. MA Thesis, University of Sydney

Chapter 2
Methodology

In this chapter, I will introduce the methodological issues involved in this research. First, I will discuss the relations between theory and language description (Sect. 2.1). Then, I will give the rationale for adopting a systemic functional theoretic framework (Sect. 2.2). In Sect. 2.3, the fundamental dimensions of SFL theory will be introduced, and the metalanguages to be used in this research will be explained. Also in this section, I will review the descriptive work that has been done in the SFL field with a particular focus on Chinese. In Sect. 2.4, I will introduce the process of data collection and categorisation, as well as the computational tool being used in some sample text analysis. In a word, this chapter explains why and how a text-based systemic functional approach is adopted in the study.

2.1 Theory and Language Description

In their review of the language descriptive works in the twentieth century, Matthiessen and Nesbitt noticed a prominent disjunction between theory and description in linguistics, and they continued to argue that this view of relationship between theory and linguistic description cannot help linguists cope with the new challenges in describing languages in the twenty-first century (Matthiessen and Nesbitt 1996). Considering the dominant theoretical trend of the time (especially in 1960s and 1970s), it seems to be understandable that linguists, reference grammarians in particular, were trying to move away from theory in their descriptive work. However, in reality, freedom from theory in description is simply an illusion (Matthiessen and Nesbitt 1996). To illustrate the unrealistic nature of this attitude, Halliday made the following comment (Halliday 1992, after Matthiessen and Nesbitt 1996: 64):

© Springer Nature Singapore Pte Ltd. 2022
J. Fang, *A Systemic Functional Grammar of Chinese Nominal Groups*,
The M.A.K. Halliday Library Functional Linguistics Series,
https://doi.org/10.1007/978-981-19-4009-5_2

> There is no such thing as theory-free engagement with language, whether one is actively inter-
> vening in the linguistic practices of a community or systematically describing the grammar
> of a particular language. The linguist who claims to be theory-free is like the conservative
> to claims to be non-political: they are both saying, to be impartial is to leave things as they
> are—only those who want to change them are taking sides.

It is not hard to anticipate the potential problems one may face in conducting a theory-free language description. The immediate headache will be the explicitness and accessibility of the description itself. Without using metalanguage, which a theory is able to provide, it is impossible to describe linguistic features clearly. Other problems, such as consistency and comprehensiveness, are also highly predictable. Many sophisticated language phenomena cannot be easily described and analysed without using theoretical terms. A non-theory-based language description is destined to be limited in the amount of information that can be handled and the depth of the exploration that can be achieved. Therefore, it is obvious that a separation from theory cannot produce a good description. Then, the next relevant question to consider would be: which theory should be adopted?

2.2   Introducing the SFL Framework

2.2.1   The Rationale

For the present description of Chinese nominal groups, systemic functional linguistic (SFL) theory will be adopted as the framework. There are mainly three reasons for adopting an SFL approach. First of all, in the SFL model, there is an ontological distinction between theory and description, which enriches the potential for inter-preting a wide range of language phenomena. Systemic linguistics draws the line between theory and description in such a way that theoretical assumptions are very general and all the categories of particular languages belong to the domain of description (Caffarel et al. 2004). As an applicable linguistic model, SFL constitutes the synthesis position bringing theory and application together in dialogue (Matthiessen 2012). This systemic view on the relationship between theory and language descrip-tion ensures that the theory being adopted is not developed to address a limited number of descriptive categories of a particular language only; rather, this view indi-cates that SFL theory is an extravagant modal powerful enough to serve as a semiotic engine for descriptions of any human language. In fact, this has been evidenced by the SFL descriptions of a number of languages apart from English, such as the works of French (Caffarel et al. 2004), Japanese (Teruya 2004, 2006), Tagalog (Martin 2004), Thai (Patpong 2006), Oko (Akerejola 2005), Bajjika (Kumar 2009), Korean (Park 2013) and so on (see further in Mwinlaaru and Xuan 2016). Secondly, as a very comprehensive theory, SFL is able to provide enough resources to facilitate the descriptive work in the present study. Having reviewed the literature on Chinese nominal groups (see Sect. 1.2), one can see that many accounts put the structural construction as the central concern—in other words, the semantic motivation behind these constructions remain uninvestigated, which reflects the problems of the theories which these descriptions are based upon. In contrast, the SFL model is context-based and focuses on meaning. This ensures that an SFL-based description will not view nominal groups as an isolated context-free grammatical unit. Instead, an SFL-based description will go far beyond the syntactic structural concerns and will allow for interpretations from three different metafunctional perspectives (i.e. ideational, interpersonal and textual metafunctions of a nominal group). The meaning potentials that a nominal group can realise, which have been heavily ignored by previous works but are essential in interpreting nominal groups, will be brought to focus under an SFL framework. Thirdly, unlike many other linguistic theories which parsimoniously focus on a limited number of linguistic categories, systemic functional linguistics is widely known as an extravagant theory, which allows the description to focus on a grammatical unit at any level from clause to morpheme. This makes a description being able to achieve complexity and consistency at the same time as one can view the same language phenomenon both from above and from below on the same map. This will allow for various possibilities and potentials in the description. For example, under the SFL framework, one can investigate how semantic motifs are realised by nominal groups and at the same time look at how the selections of head nouns serve the semantic motivations. All of these descriptions will draw upon the general system networks developed in SFL. Therefore, before the explorations in detail, it is necessary to give an overview of the fundamental dimensions of the SFL theory.

2.2.2   Overview: The SFL Theory

Systemic functional linguistics is a theory of language developed by Halliday in 1960s, mainly under the influence of the work of J. R. Firth. SFL approach views language as multidimensional semiotic space where resources of language are functioning in the context of situation and culture and are mapped in system networks based on their meaning potentials. Table 2.1 summarises the main theoretical dimensions of SFL along which language is organised (adapted from Caffarel et al. 2004: 19)[1]:

In the remainder of this section, I will briefly introduce the basic aspects of each of these five dimensions, which the current description of nominal groups will draw upon.

---

[1] Copyright©2004 from *Introduction: systemic functional typology* by Alice Caffarel, J.R. Martin and Christian M. I. M. Matthiessen in *Language typology: a functional perspective*. Reproduced by permission of John Benjamin Publishing Company.

Table 2.1 Dimensions of language and their ordering principles

Dimension		Regions within dimension
Global	Stratification	Context/semantics/lexicogrammar/phonology (graphology)/phonetics (graphetics)
	Instantiation	Potential (system) ← subpotential I instance type → instance (text)
	Metafunction	Ideational (logical and experiential)/interpersonal/textual
Local	Rank	Semantics: variable according to register and metafunction Lexicogrammar: clause/group–phrase/word/morpheme Phonology: tone group/foot/syllable/phoneme
	Axis	Paradigmatic (system)/syntagmatic (structure)

2.2.2.1 Stratification

As a complex semiotic system, language has various levels. This fact is acknowledged by SFL. Figure 2.1 shows SFL's STRATIFICATION² map:

As shown in Fig. 2.1, the level of context is the first on the hierarchy of the stratification system, which provides cultural and situational settings where language can unfold. Below the stratum of context, the linguistic system is organised into four levels or strata: semantics, lexicogrammar, phonology/graphology and

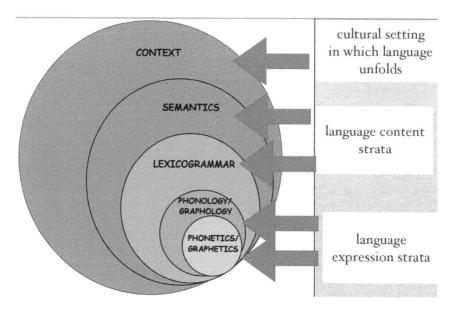

Fig. 2.1 Stratification (Matthiessen 2007b)

---

² It is an SFL tradition to present the name of a system in all capitals.

phonetics/graphetics. Among them, the systems of meaning and wording (semantics and lexicogrammar) are the strata of content, which allow the meaning potential of a language to expand, whereas the systems of composing and sounding (phonology/graphology and phonetics/graphetics) are the strata of expression, which interface with the biological environment (i.e. the human body) to realise abstract meaning and wording.

The relationship among the strata in the linguistic system is called **realisation**: semantics is realised by lexicogrammar, and lexicogrammar is realised by phonology/graphology (Halliday and Matthiessen 2014).

Perhaps it is necessary to take more efforts to discuss **lexicogrammar** here. This term, unlike others such as semantics and phonology that are widely used in the general linguistic field, often appears in SFL descriptions only. Outside SFL, lexicon and grammar are usually treated as two distinct terms representing two separate modules. In SFL, however, lexicogrammar represents the stratum that includes lexis and grammar in one system with lexis being the most delicate part of grammar (Halliday 1961; Hasan 1987; Matthiessen 1995, 1999). Halliday and Matthiessen present a more detailed interpretation of lexicogrammar (Halliday and Matthiessen 1999):

> ...grammar, as used in systemic theory, is short for 'lexicogrammar'. The lexicon, or 'lexis' as it is more properly known, is not a separate component, but simply the most 'delicate' end of the (unified) lexicogrammar...Lexis and grammar are not two different phenomena; they are different ways of looking at the same phenomenon (p. 5).

2.2.2.2 Instantiation

The dimension of **instantiation** is concerned with the two perspectives of viewing language: language as **system** and language as **text**. The system of a language is 'instantiated' in the form of text and the relationship between the two is a cline—the cline of instantiation (see Fig. 2.2, adapted from Halliday and Matthiessen 2014: 28). As shown by this cline, there are intermediate patterns between the instance pole and the potential pole. On the 'instance' end is the individual texts in context, which represents the delicate samples of single texts. Through observation, we may be able to identify patterns or some recurrent features that some sample texts all share, and then, we are able to group them as a **text type**, which is located somewhere in the middle of the cline. However, the same area taken by 'text type' can also be achieved from the other direction: when one moves alone the cline from the 'potential' end towards the 'instance' end, we will get into the same middle area on the cline but the interpretation taken 'from above', which is based on **register**. A register is thus a functional variety of language, the patterns of instantiation of the overall system associated with a given situation type (Halliday and Matthiessen 2014: 29). To sum, if these intermediate patterns are viewed from the instance pole, i.e. from below, one can identify them as text types. In contrast, if viewed from the system pole, i.e. from above, they can be described as registers.

The cline of instantiation works as a perfect methodological guidance in the description of a grammar: quantitative study of texts will help identify patterns that

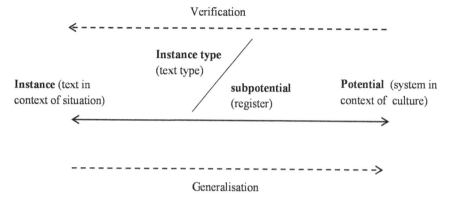

Fig. 2.2 Cline of instantiation

they all share, which in turn may develop into system; at the same time, to test a tentative system that has been developed, it is always necessary to put it back into texts for verification (see Fig. 2.2). As Halliday and Matthiessen have stressed, writing a description of a grammar entails constant shunting between the perspective of the system and the perspective of the instance (Halliday and Matthiessen 2014: 30).

2.2.2.3   Metafunction

In systemic functional interpretation, the entire architecture of language is arranged along three functional lines, which is termed as metafunctions (Halliday and Matthiessen 2014; Matthiessen 1995). Halliday calls these three metafunctions the ideational, interpersonal and textual metafunctions.

The **ideational** metafunction provides resources for construing human experiences. This is realised through naming things, modelling our experience of the world into categories and so on. It can be distinguished into two parts, with the **experiential** metafunction encoding the experiences and the **logical** metafunction showing the relationships between these experiences.

The **interpersonal** metafunction provides resources for enacting roles and social relationships. This is typically realised through encoding ideas about obligation and inclination and expressing attitude. As Halliday and Matthiessen point out, if the ideational function of the grammar is 'language as reflection', interpersonal function is 'language as action' (Halliday and Matthiessen, 2014: 30).

The **textual** metafunction provides resources for constructing a text. This is realised by presenting ideational and interpersonal meanings as information and organising these meanings into a coherent and linear text.

It is important to note that meanings are **simultaneously** organised along the three functional lines. point of view (see further Sect. 2.2.2.5), this means a simultaneous selection of three strands of meaning in the system network. At the same time, as an integral component within the overall SFL theory, metafunctionality applies to lexicogrammar systems at all ranks (see further Sect. 2.2.2.4). At the clause rank, the three metafunctions generate three distinct structures combined into one. At the group rank, in comparison, the metafunctionality is represented in a single structural line with each element in the structure making partial contributions to one or more metafunctional meanings (see further Chap. 3).

2.2.2.4 Rank

Rank is the dimension along which language resources are distributed into hierarchical units, similar to the systems of all other orders—physical, social and biological (Caffarel et al. 2004). According to the five principles of constituency in lexicogrammar presented in Sect. 1.1.3, rank orders grammatical units on a scale from highest to lowest. The highest unit on the rank scale is clause, and there is no separate rank for a sentence, as organisation beyond the clause and clause complex is taken to be semantic (see further Matthiessen 1995). The second highest on the rank scale is group/phrase. A review of the language descriptive work reflects that most of the accounts are primarily concerned with these two highest ranks (cf. Matthiessen 2007a). As Matthiessen points out, if we want to understand how the grammar is organised as a resource according to functional principles, the way into the grammatical system is 'from above'—the interpretive view is clause-based rather than word- or morpheme-based (Matthiessen 1995: 76).

In Sect. 1.2, I reviewed the work on Chinese nominal groups based on non-systemic theories and pointed out that most of these accounts did not distinguish between groups and phrases, and in many cases, the term 'phrase' was used to cover both. In contrast, SFL recognises that 'groups' and 'phrases' are organised in quite different ways. A group is a group of words, whereas a phrase is like a reduced clause. By reflecting the difference between the two types, a systemic description of Chinese nominal groups is able to solve the chronic problem of differentiating a group from a clause caused by the construction-based classification (see the discussion in Sect. 1.2).

SFL studies of Chinese have shown that English and Chinese share the same number of units on the rank scale as well as the way of distributing meanings across these ranks (see Halliday and McDonald 2004; Li 2003, 2007). However, as Halliday and McDonald point out, unlike English, the lowest rank with implications for clause grammar in Chinese is the group rather than the word due to the derivational structure of the latter (Halliday and McDonald 2004). Table 2.2 presents an example of a Chinese clause analysed in terms of rank[3]:

---

[3] The use of conventions here follows Halliday and McDonald (2004: 319).

Table 2.2 Example of rank

Clause	Carrier	Circumstance		Process			Attribute		
Group	Nominal group	Adverbial group		Verbal group			Nominal group		
Word	Noun	Adjective	APART	verb	PV	ASP	NUM	MEA	NOUN
	冰	慢慢	的	变	成	了	一	滩	水

2.2.2.5   Structure and System

Linguistic resources are organised along two axes, the paradigmatic and the syntagmatic. Matthiessen presents very clear definitions of the two organising modes when he discusses the grammatical organisation of language (Matthiessen 1995):

> The fundamental mode of organisation is the organisation of the grammatical resources into options (alternative strategies, choices) available for realising meanings. In fact, the grammatical resources form a set of inter-related options, what the speaker can do grammatically to express meanings. This mode of organisation is called **paradigmatic**. These options are realised by means of the other mode of organisation, structures and items, or wordings—called the **syntagmatic** mode of organisation (p. 12).

So structure is the syntagmatic ordering in language, the structural specification that realises options. In contrast, System refers to the paradigmatic ordering in language, a set of interrelated options to realise meanings. Halliday and Matthiessen (2014: 22) have explained the two terms in plain language: Structure is the ordering of patterns in *what goes together with what*, whereas System is the ordering of patterns in *what could go instead of what*. Structure, being the expressive mode of organisation, is secondary in relation to System (i.e. paradigmatic organisation), as the latter represents the meaning potential of language. In SFL, grammatical resources are considered in terms of both System and Structure, but the former is more global as it is freed from structural placement. For instance, in lexicogrammatical descriptions of language, an SFL account often focuses more on system, or **system network**, which is a network of systems, than on structure. This again reflects one of the fundamental features of SFL that contrasts it with formal grammar: SFL is very much concerned with meaning and meaning potential, rather than form. Figure 2.3 (adapted from Matthiessen 2007b) shows the MOOD system network of English (paradigmatic organisation) and its structural representation (syntagmatic organisation):

As the example in Fig. 2.3 shows, the paradigmatic MOOD system network provides a set of options with an entry condition, such as 'major clause' as the entry condition for FREEDOM. Then, the options in the system network contribute to the formation of a syntagmatic structure. For example, the configuration of Subject ^ Finite is the syntagmatic structure of a declarative clause, which is the result of the selections on the system network.

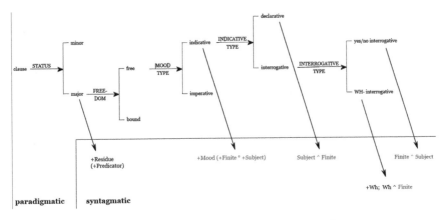

Fig. 2.3   English MOOD system network and its syntagmatic representation

2.3   The SFL Description of Chinese: A Brief Review

Since Halliday published the first edition of his *Introduction to Functional Grammar* in 1985, a number of works have been conducted on the SFL description of English as well as other languages including Chinese (see further in Matthiessen 2007a). In this section, I will briefly review the SFL-based descriptive work in Chinese in recent years.

Since the late 1970s with China's opening up to the outside world, SFL has become influential among the Chinese linguists. As a result, a significant number of publications have been made by the Chinese scholars in the field of SFL, covering a wide range of areas such as theory introduction (e.g. Shen 1987), discourse analysis (e.g. Huang 2001), coherence and cohesion (e.g. Zhang 2003), translation studies (e.g. Huang 2006) and lexicography (e.g. Chang 2017), to name a few. It is worth noting that most of these works were based on the study of English rather than Chinese. In the field of SFL study of Chinese, in contrast, the contributions have been limited and the credit mainly goes to the overseas-based scholars of Chinese. Among them, the earliest and also the most prescriptive contributions came from Halliday himself. Halliday's accounts of modern Chinese grammar date back to his early publication in the 1950s (cf. (Halliday 1956; Halliday and Ellis 1951 [2006]). His work on the lexicogrammar of Chinese resumed in 1980s with publications on grammatical metaphor (Halliday 1984). During that period, under Halliday's supervision, a number of Chinese scholars also produced a series of MA thesis at Sydney University describing Chinese from SFL perspectives, each focusing on a particular dimension such as transitivity (Long 1981), modality and modulation (Zhu 1985), circumstances (Tsung 1986) and clause complex (Ouyang 1986). Following this productive period, the first two decades in the twenty-first century have witnessed further development in SFL-based linguistic description of the Chinese language. For example, McDonald and Li expanded the description focus to cover all the three metafunctions of Chinese in general (cf. McDonald 1998; Li 2003, 2007). Furthermore, Halliday and McDonald (2004) presented a metafunctional profile of Chinese grammar. This account is very important in that it not only gives a very insightful overview of the language from the perspectives of rank and metafunction, but also presents the descriptive potential of the language by describing the clause systems in detail. More recently, new typological work on Chinese were added to the field, such as Yang (2011) on grammatical metaphor, Yang (2014) on non-material clauses and Yang (2021) on modality, to name a few. In a word, their work has set a good example for any future SFL accounts of Chinese.

All the above-mentioned works have been unfolded with a focus on clause, which is understandable since this is the rank at which the three metafunctions are integrated into a single syntagm. However, this does not mean that the grammatical potentials at other ranks, group/phrase in particular, can be ignored, as these units are the integral parts that make up a clause. In fact, ignoring these intermediate structural units means some important aspects of meanings will be missing. As Halliday and Matthiessen argue, 'describing a sentence as a construction of words is rather like describing a house as a construction of bricks, without recognizing the walls and the rooms as intermediate structural units' (Halliday and Matthiessen 2014: 362). Unfortunately, the descriptive work at the level of group/phrase within SFL field is far fewer than clause, especially in the case of languages other than English. In Matthiessen's review of systemic functional descriptions of language since 1970s, only one account, Sutjaja's PhD thesis (Sutjaja 1988) is listed as the work on nominal group of a language other than English (see further Matthiessen 2007a, b: 796). In the case of Chinese, the work at group/phrase level is quite blank indeed as most attentions are given to the clause or text. In fact, only a small number of work gives special attention to nominal groups, such as Fang (2008) on the experiential meaning of Chinese nominal groups, Fang (2012) on logical resources of Chinese nominal groups and Li (2017) on an overview, Zhang and Li (2017) on the use of 之 in Chinese nominal groups. And among these limited number of studies, many approached the nominal group from a single metafunctional perspective, instead of a comprehensive and full metafunctional description. This fact gives the current author a strong motivation to fill in the gap.

2.4 Methodological Issues

2.4.1 Texts Used in This Book

As the present study is text-based, it is essential to have a further discussion of **instantiation**, one of the fundamental dimensions in SFL theory (see Sect. 2.2.2.2), which provides theoretical basis for adopting a text-based approach. Then in Sect. 2.4.1.2, I will introduce the details of data collection in this study.

2.4.1.1 Locating 'Text' on the Cline of INSTANTIATION

As Matthiessen points out, the evidential or empirical basis of any work involving language is text in context (Matthiessen 2009: 52). There has been a long tradition for systemic functional linguists to use texts and corpus for language investigations and descriptions (cf. Wu 2009). This SFL tradition can be explained and justified by the fundamental theoretical dimension of instantiation. As explained in Section 2.2.2.2, the dimension of **instantiation** is concerned with the two perspectives of viewing language: language as **system** and language as **text**. And, the system of a language is 'instantiated' in the form of text. When observing language, one can choose to view it from the instance end by investigating a particular text, that is, an instantiated text. It is also possible to move along the cline of instantiation to analyse a group of texts to find some recurrent patterns or features that belong to a particular text type or register. Or one can explore the overall systemic potential of the language from the system end. Whichever stance is taken, it is essential to base the investigation on text in context, as the systemic potential can only be represented and realised by the textual instances of the language. Figure 2.4 (Matthiessen 2015b: 4) shows how the cline of Instantiation is related to the overall systemic potential and how it intersects with the hierarchy of Stratification—this figure is based on Halliday's Stratification-Instantiation matrix (see Halliday 2002).

Figure 2.4 provides three important methodological indications on language description. Firstly, it shows that systemic selections are instantiated in texts and it is possible to observe the frequencies of the systemic selections made by texts. In this way, we can generalise the systemic features by accumulating instantial profiles of texts, provided that we get large enough samples of texts. In fact, this indication is also supported by Halliday's view (Halliday 1991a: 42):

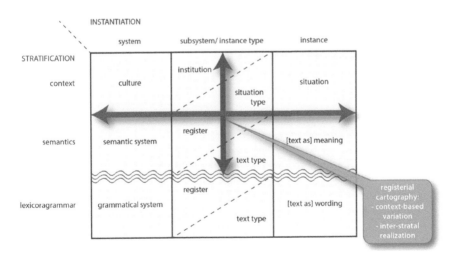

Fig. 2.4 Systemic potential and textual instance

Frequency in the text is the instantiation of probability in the system. A linguistic system is
inherently probabilistic in nature.

Secondly, as Fig. 2.4 shows, to approach a grammatical system of a language,
which is on the system pole of the INSTANTIATION cline, and located at the lexicogrammar level on the STRATIFICATION system, the entry point is each individual
text, which is on the instance end of the INSTANTIATION cline. To analyse a text,
its immediately environment, i.e. its text type/register features, must be considered
(Halliday 1991b). As Fig. 2.4 shows, text type/register is located somewhere between
instance and system. In the process of data collection, if enough texts are collected
to cover a wide range of registers/text types, then the analysis of these texts can
help support the description of the systemic potential of a language (cf. Matthiessen
2009). Based on a table of context-based register typology initially developed by
Jean Ure, Matthiessen sketches a map—or in his own term, 'registerial cartography'
(see Fig. 2.5, adapted from Matthiessen et al. 2008). This effort is significant in
that this map is flexible and takes into account all the three contextual variables
(Field, Tenor and Mode). As Matthiessen explains, the development of the map
starts with Field, more specifically field of activities, and Tenor and Mode values
can be added when they are needed (Matthiessen 2015a). As the texts used in this
book will be introduced according to Matthiessen's text typology, it is necessary to
give an overview of the mapping of the field of activities, reflecting the contextual
parameter of Field. As the diagram in Fig. 2.5 shows, the parameter of Field, or in
Matthiessen's term **socio-semiotic process**, is presented topologically as a circle of
eight sectors, including expounding, reporting, recreating, sharing, doing, recommending, enabling and exploring (see Matthiessen 2015b). Explanations about each
activity type are presented below (Matthiessen 2015b: 6):

expounding: contexts where natural phenomena such as cold fronts are explained to
help readers or listeners as part of the construction 'knowledge' about general classes of
phenomena.

reporting: contexts where the flow of particular human events are chronicled to help readers
or listeners construct keep up with or review events.

recreating: contexts where the flow of particular human imaginary events are narrated to
achieve some kind of aesthetic effect.

sharing: contexts where personal values and experiences are exchanged to help interactants
relate to one another for example by calibrating their sense of moral values in a work place.

doing: contexts where people are engaged in a joint social activity, using language to facilitate
the performance of this activity.

enabling: contexts where a course of action is modelled semiotically and made possible
through instruction.

recommending: contexts where a course of action is advised for the benefit of the addressee.

exploring: contexts where public values and ideas are put forward and debated.

In Fig. 2.5, (Matthiessen 2007b) provides guidance in data collection, ensuring the
texts being collected are context-based representation of different fields of activity.
Using this map, when a text is selected for further analysis, we can characterise it

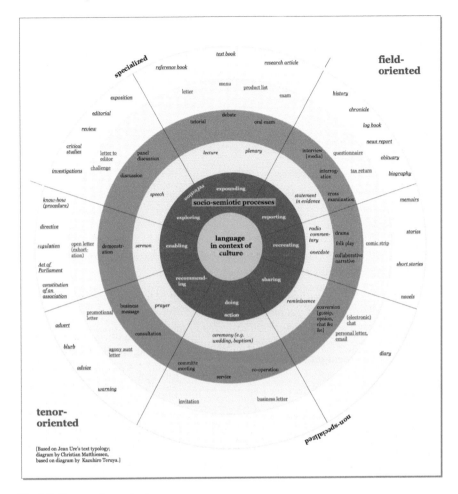

Fig. 2.5 Text typology wheel

by referring to its context of situation and relate the choices in lexicogrammar to the semantic systems.

Thirdly, the cline of instantiation also provides clues on testing the validity of the system networks being proposed. When moving along the cline of instantiation from the system end to the instance pole, we can check if the proposed system network is able to reflect the potential selections being realised by instantial texts. This is usually done by manual analysis of a reasonable number of sample texts covering various text types.

2.4.1.2 Data Collection

As the discussion in 2.4.1.1 indicates, although the focus of the present study is
the nominal group, the observation is still based on text. This is a major difference
between an SFL-based description and a description based on formalist approaches,
as in the latter language is typically studied in a 'vacuum'—free from text and context.
The potential problem of a context-free description can be illustrated by a simple
example:

> **Example 1**
> 晚会的神秘嘉宾突然出现, 给大家带来了出乎意料的精彩表演。
> The mysterious guest of the evening appeared all of a sudden, who brought
> everyone <u>an unexpected wonderful performance</u>.
> **Example 2**
> 开场前一直不被看好的胡悦, 给大家带来了出乎意料的精彩表演。
> Hu Yue, who had been seen as unpromising before the show, brought everyone
> <u>an unexpectedly wonderful performance</u>.

As the above examples illustrate, the nominal group 出乎意料的精彩表演 (*unex-
pected/unexpectedly wonderful performance*) has different connotations in different
contexts: in Example 1, 出乎意料 (*unexpected*) functions as a qualifier modifying
the head 表演 (*performance*), whereas in Example 2, 出乎意料 (*unexpectedly*) is a
metaphorical comment adjunct sub-modifying the Epithet 精彩 (*wonderful*). As a
non-inflectional language, Chinese does not reflect this context-based grammatical
difference in form—the difference can only be interpreted through meaningful text
in context.

As discussed in Sect. 2.4.1.1, to explore the systemic potential, one needs to get
large enough samples of text for observation. To this end, two corpora are used in this
research: a working corpus of 180 texts covering different text types and a reference
corpus for general observation of lexicogrammatical potentials of Chinese nominal
groups. Figure 2.6 illustrates how the two corpora work on the cline of instantiation:

As demonstrated in Fig. 2.6, the reference corpus, which is immense in size, is
used to observe the systemic potentials of the nominal groups, and to examine all the

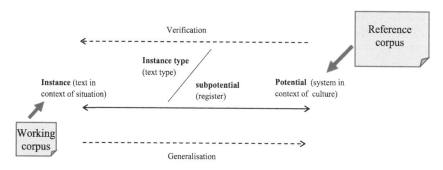

Fig. 2.6 Corpora on the cline of instantiation

possible patterns that the nominal group may have in realising metafunctional meanings. In comparison, the working corpus is a much smaller corpus of limited number of texts, which are used to verify the potential patterns that have been observed in the reference corpus and to closely analyse how these systemic potentials are realised in the instantial texts.

2.4.2 Reference Corpus

The Chinese Web 2017 (zhTenTen17) simplified corpus is used as the reference corpus of this study. This is a cleaned corpus established on the basis of the Internet content retrieved in 2017 from domains in the Mainland China, Hong Kong and Taiwan. Foreign languages other than Chinese have been filtered (see further information about the TenTen corpus family in Jakubíček et al. 2013). As Chinese language is based on characters (i.e. tokens) which could be either a morpheme or a word, the texts in a Chinese corpus also need to be tokenised to define the word boundary. The tokenisation of the Chinese Web 2017 corpus has been processed by Stanford Core NLP Tools (Pipeline v.2) and are tagged in terms of part of speech. Some further details about the corpus are listed in Table 2.3:

The reference corpus is available for observation and analysis via Sketch Engine (http://www.sketchengine.eu), a powerful online corpus tool for text analysis, corpus linguistics, lexicographical research, translation studies, and so on (see Kilgarriff et al. 2014). With the use of 'Word Sketch', a key function on Sketch Engine, researchers can examine the grammatical and collocational behaviours of any word in many languages including Chinese. As the Chinese Web 2017 corpus has been tagged in terms of part of speech, one can search a word, which could be used as both noun and verbs, and observe its use in texts as either noun or verb. The collocation search will mean that we can examine both the most and least common collocative structures where a noun functions as the head of a nominal group. And, a concordance search will ensure that we can then further investigate the textual and contextual environment of the nominal group being searched. Figure 2.7 gives an example of a concordance search of the word 愤怒 (*angry* or *anger*) when it is used as a noun and is used in a coordinative structure where another noun is connected with it as a parallel item:

Table 2.3 Information about the reference corpus	Counts	
	Tokens	16,593,146,196
	Words	13,531,331,169
	Sentences	667,201,792
	Paragraphs	280,848,826
	Documents	40,233,300

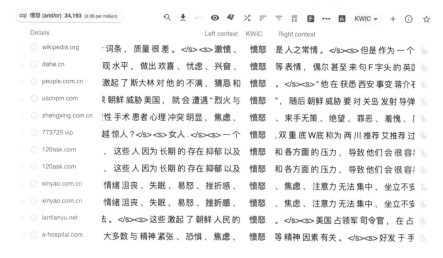

Fig. 2.7 Concordance search of '愤怒' (*anger*) when used as a noun in a coordinative structure

Another important function that Sketch Engine provides is 'visualisation', through which the collocative potential of a noun can be illustrated in an easily accessible manner. Figure 2.8 gives an example show some common collocative patterns of 愤怒 (*anger*) when it is used as a noun in a coordinative nominal group structure when another noun is used as a parallel collocate. As shown in Fig. 2.8, different frequencies of each collocate with the searched item 愤怒 (*anger*) are illustrated as different sizes of word circles, with the most frequently collocated word being the largest, and the least being the smallest.

With the powerful search functions provided by Sketch Engine and the huge size of the reference corpus (with 1.3 billion words in total), it is possible to observe all the potential modification environment of nouns of different types, as well as the grammatical environment when a nominal group functions in a clause of a paragraph of a text. And, this lays the foundation for the development of the system networks of each functional element within a nominal group structure. As Halliday and Matthiessen (2014: 51) point out, the corpus is fundamental to the enterprise of theorising language, and with the size of a corpus as such, it becomes possible to explore the probabilistic nature of a grammatical system such as the one of Chinese nominal groups. However, even with the support of computational tools like Sketch Engine, the grammatical systems which we describe need to be validated by analysing authentic instances of text, which justifies the need for another corpus.

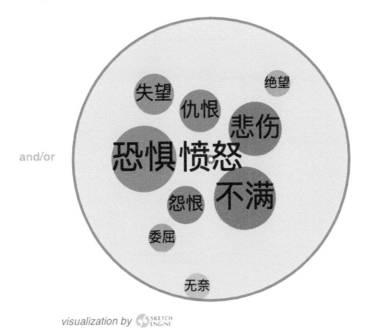

visualization by ⓢ SKETCH ENGINE

Fig. 2.8 Visualised common collocative patterns of 愤怒 (*anger*) as a noun in a coordinative structure

2.4.3 Working Corpus

Texts from Chinese textbooks used by schools in China were collected to form the major part of the working corpus. Most of the texts were retrieved from the Chinese textbooks published by the People's Education Press (http://www.pep.com.cn), a specialised publisher directly under the Ministry of Education of the People's Republic of China, which undertakes the overall tasks of compiling and publishing teaching materials for school education. All these texts are used by the public primary and secondary schools across China, either as model texts for in-class study or supplementary texts for after-class reading. Therefore, it is reasonable to assume that the quality of the texts is guaranteed, since they are used as model texts for Chinese language teaching purpose.

Altogether 162 texts have been collected from the Chinese school textbooks, with a total word count of 244,306 characters, ranging from Semester 2 of Year 1 to Semester 2 of Year 12. However, the number of texts being selected from each year is not maintained at an even level. For example, only two texts are selected from Year 1 and only five from Year 12. In fact, a large part of the collection is made of texts from the 'middle' years, Year 4 to Year 8 in particular. This reflects the different emphasis of each year's textbook: for Year 1, the textbook aims to teach students individual characters as well as pronunciations (in the form of pinyin), and these are taught word by word out of a text; in comparison, as the students move onto senior high school years, the Chinese textbooks become more and more focused on

Table 2.4 Number of texts from each grade

Grade	Text count
12	5
11	8
10	11
9	11
8	15
7	16
6	21
5	22
4	26
3	13
2	12
1	2

ancient Chinese literature, and the number of modern Chinese texts are reduced. It is in the middle years of schooling that many modern Chinese texts are included in the Chinese textbooks. Table 2.4 lists the number of texts being collected from each grade:

Two selection criteria are adopted in selecting these texts: text typological features and lexical density.

In perspective of Matthiessen's text typology theory (Matthiessen 2015a and b) the overall socio-semiotic type of a textbook is expounding. However, each individual text within a textbook may represent a different text type. Altogether the texts being collected in this study fall into six types on the 'text typology wheel': recreating, sharing, expounding, exploring, reporting and recommending. However, the coverage of text types in each year does not display an even pattern. Figure 2.9 shows the profile of text type selections in each grade's textbook:

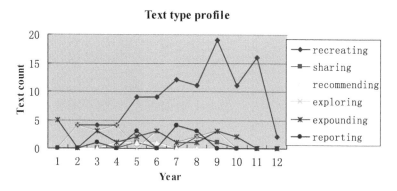

Fig. 2.9 Text type profile of the working corpus

Generally speaking, the selections of text type in these textbooks are quite limited. As shown in Fig. 2.9, recreating texts seem to predominate most of the years, and the predominance starts to decrease after Year 4 with some other text types being introduced into the textbooks. At around Year 9 and onwards, exploring texts become another major text type in these textbooks. It is also interesting to note that in the first two years of primary school, only recreating texts are included; whereas in the senior years, Year 10 to Year 12, exploring and expounding texts are the major selections. Table 2.5 lists all the detailed socio-semiotic process types of the texts in Archive A.

In terms of lexical density, it is not surprising to see an increasing tendency along the years: as the year goes up, the texts tend to be more lexically dense (see Fig. 2.10):

As can be seen from Fig. 2.10, after Year 6, there is a significant increase in average lexical density from well below 1500 words to over 2000 per text. Another noticeable increase occurs in Year 10 when the texts in average are more than 3000

Table 2.5 Detailed text types in the working corpus

Text type	Detailed socio-semiotic process type
Recreating	Short story, poem, travel notes (prose), novel, drama, myth, memoir, reporting literature
Sharing	Travel notes (diary), letter
Recommending	Advice
Exploring	Written speech, exposition, review, investigation, essay
Expounding	Research article, explanation, taxonomic investigation
Reporting	Biography, history, obituary, news story

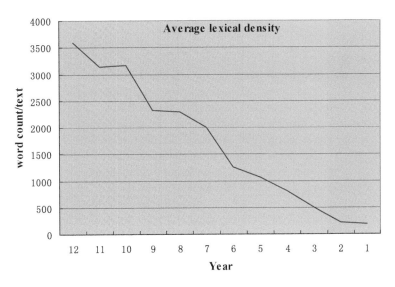

Fig. 2.10 Average lexical density of texts and school year

Table 2.6 Additional texts in the working corpus

Text type	Text count	Detailed semiotic type
Enabling	7	Recipe, contract, product instruction, legal document
Doing	10	Invitation, public notice, letter of commendation, offer letter
Reporting	37	News report

words long. However, it is also worth noting that, apart from its close correlation with the year, the lexical density of these texts may also be related to text type. For example, poems, which belong to the recreating category, are generally shorter than a research article, which falls into the type of expounding.

As some type of texts, which could be relevant for analytical purposes, were not available in the school text collection, additional texts were collected from various sources, including published books, legal documents, newspapers, documents retrieved from government Websites, so that the texts in the working corpus can cover all the text types.

Altogether 54 texts of around 80,000 words, which are texts other than those from textbooks, were collected to be included in the working corpus, with 10 texts as doing, 7 enabling and 37 reporting texts.

Table 2.6 gives the details of the additional texts being collected:

2.4.4 How to Use This Book

2.4.4.1 Presentation of System Networks and a Trinocular Vision

In Sect. 2.2.2.5, I have introduced two grammatical organisation modes, namely *System* and *Structure*. In the following chapters, my exploration will cover both but with a focus on the former by developing systems and system networks reflecting the potential choices in terms of functional categories in a nominal group structure. The presentation of these systems and system networks will follow the SFL conventions where applicable, reflecting both simultaneous and non-simultaneous selections. A list of systemic conventions which this book uses in presenting the system networks has been given (see p. xi) with example figures illustrating each organisation being provided. It is important to note that the presentation of realisation of each choice in a system network is not always available, for sometimes, the realisation is very straightforward and does not become the focus for the discussion at hand. For example, the Thing is typically realised by a noun, which is widely accepted as a general realisation feature. In this case, the discussion of the system of THING will focus on some more significant features, such as the modification potential, the measurability and so on.

The development of each system and system network is based on the observation of the collected data. A trinocular vision is adopted where possible in probing these data. According to Halliday (1978), any language phenomenon or category can be viewed from three angles based on the system of STRATIFICATION, which he later named 'trinocular vision' (Halliday 1996): from above, from roundabout and from below. Although the focus of the current study is on the lexicogrammatical selections in realising the three strands of meaning of nominal groups, the description of the system networks will involve semantic and contextual concerns from above, as well as discussions on categories below the rank of group. This trinocular vision is particularly relevant in exploring systems in the logical, experiential, interpersonal and textual domains. When introducing each major selection in a system, the semantic motivation behind the selection will be discussed, and where relevant, how it can be realised by items down the rank scale will also be examined. Undoubtedly, the most important and also challenging part is to observe the nominal groups 'from roundabout': how to find the patterns through the observation of examples and generalise them; how to identify the problems of the current system after testing it through the examples; how to fit the highly marked instances into the existing systems; and so on. The trinocular vision is inevitable as each stratum is related to the other strata and their relationship, namely 'realisation', means that any effective lexicogrammatical description should include aspects of the other strata. Figure 2.11 illustrates how the nominal groups will be approached trinocularly in the current study:

From above:

- Context: Different text types, tenor relations
- Semantics: Things, attitudes, references

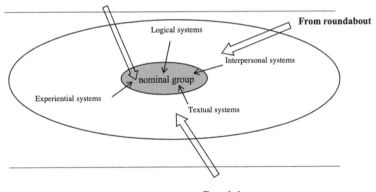

Fig. 2.11 Trinocular vision of the nominal group

2.4.4.2 Presentation of Chinese Examples

There are two ways by which examples of Chinese are presented in this book. Firstly, a large part of the selected samples, such as clauses and paragraphs and short texts, will be presented in Chinese characters, and then a literal English translation will be provided. If the example is used to illustrate a nominal group of a particular category, the nominal group in the example, together with the corresponding part of the English translation, will be highlighted. A literal translation makes sure that the original structural organisation in the Chinese examples will be maintained as much as possible in the English translations. Where the translation is too literal to convey the connotation, a second translation, which is more meaning-focused and serves the purpose of explanation, will be presented. Examples:

Example 3
Nominal group being highlighted in a sentence.
写文章解决了[["写什么"]]的问题后, 还要解决[["怎么写"]]的问题。
On writing, after solving the **problem** of [['what to write']], one also needs to solve the **problem** of [['how to write']].

Example 4
Chinese example being presented with two lines of English translation.
因为 "灼人"表示 像 火 一样 烫 人
because '**burning people**' means fire-like burning (literal translation)
because 'burning' means as hot as fire (idiomatic translation)

When a grammatical item under discussion is not translatable because there is no equivalent grammatical item in English, it will be presented in the English translation as a conventional abbreviation to indicate its actual location in the nominal structure (see further in the list of *Symbols, abbreviations and systemic conventions* on pp. xi). Example 5:

Example 5
我买了五条鱼, 吃了两条, 还有几条?
I bought five fish, ate two MEA, how many MEA left?
Secondly, sometimes when the selected example is presented to illustrate the position of each functional element in a structure, interlinear glossing will be used in the presentation. The basic principles of interlinear glossing, a literal, word-for-word translation approach will be adopted for illustrating this kind of examples, as shown below.

Example 6

这	是	我	新买	的	一	辆	蓝色	轿车
Zhè	shì	[[wǒ	Xīnmǎi]]	de	yí	liàng	lánsè	jiàochē
This	is	I	Newly bought	SUB	one	MEAS	blue	sedan
This is a blue sedan that I newly bought								

Example 6 uses four lines of transcription: the first line is the orthographic presentation in Chinese characters, the second line is the phonetic transcription in *pinyin*, the third line is a word-by-word gloss in English, and the fourth line is an English translation of the whole clause. Please note that, depending on the actual needs in the discussions, there might be some differences in the arrangement of the lines of transcription.

It is also important to emphasise that, in the third line of word-by-word gloss, translation equivalence is achieved at the word level. This means that more than one Chinese character could be aligned with one English word, as many Chinese words are compounds which are made up of more than one characters. Of course, a one-to-many correspondence is also possible for some monomorphic Chinese words may be glossed as more than one word in English.

Additionally, as the second and the third lines show, some labels may be needed in phonetic transcription and word-level glossing. Generally speaking, there are two types of labels being used: general grammatical labels and SFL symbols and conventions. The former includes the symbols being used to represent the general grammatical categories in terms of word class, such as *de* in Fig. 2.9 being labelled as 'SUB', representing a subordinating particle. The latter refers to the notational specifications that are conventionally used in systemic functional linguistics. For example, the '[[…]]' in Fig. 2.9 is an SFL structural symbol for rank-shifted clauses. All the general grammatical labels being used in this study, as well as all the SFL symbols and conventions, are listed at the beginning of this book (see page xiv).

2.4.4.3 Presentation of Texts in Case Studies

Case studies are included in Chaps. 3, 4, 5 and 6, where the metafunctional resources of the nominal group are explored. These case studies, though focusing on nominal groups, are based on texts functioning in various context of situations (see Halliday and Hasan 1976). As the study of the nominal group will be text-based, it is essential to present the context where a text is used in the case study. This is achieved by providing an analysis of the register in terms of Field, Tenor and Mode, using Matthiessen's text typology model (see discussions in 2.4.1.1). This means that, when a text is presented in a case study, it will first be characterised in terms of the type of field of activity where the text is used, of the relationship between the author and the anticipated readers, the general tone of attitude about the subject matter, and of the kind of the text that is being made (as written or spoken, and as monomodal or multimodal, etc.). Case studies are used to demonstrate how the analysis of nominal groups in terms of each metafunction can be carried out in a text environment, based on which directions for future research projects will be pointed out.

References

Akerejola ES (2005) A text-based lexicogrammatical description of Oko: a systemic functional approach. PhD thesis, Macquarie University, Sydney

Caffarel A, Martin JR, Matthiessen CMIM (2004) Introduction: systemic functional typology. In: Caffarel A, Martin JR, Matthiessen CMIM (eds) Language typology: a functional perspective. John Benjamins Publishing Company, Amsterdam/Philadelphia, pp 1–76

Chang C (2017) Defining English idioms in a bilingual learner's dictionary: applications of systemic functional linguistics in lexicography. In: Webster J, Peng X (eds) Applying systemic functional linguistics: the state of the art in China today. Bloomsbury, London & New York, pp 321–334. https://doi.org/10.5040/9781474220170.ch-020

Fang J (2008) Exploring experiential meanings of the Chinese nominal group. In: Matthiessen CMIM, Harke M, Wu C (eds) Proceedings of ISFC35: voices around the world. Macquarie University, Sydney

Fang J (2012) Exploring the logical resources of Chinese nominal groups: a systemic functional approach. In: To boldly proceed: papers from the 39th international systemic functional congress. UTS, Sydney

Halliday MAK (1956) Grammatical categories in modern Chinese. Trans Philol Soc 55(1):178–224

Halliday MAK (1961) Categories of the theory of grammar. Word 17:242–292

Halliday MAK (1984) Grammatical metaphor in English and Chinese. In: Hong B (ed) New papers in Chinese language use. Contemporary China Centre, Australian National University, Canberra, pp 9–18

Halliday MAK (1978) Language as social semiotic: the social interpretation of language and meaning. University Park Press, Baltimore

Halliday MAK (1991a) Corpus linguistics and probablistic grammar. In: Aijmer K, Altenberg B (eds) English corpus linguistics. Routledge, London, pp 30–43

Halliday MAK (1991b) The notion of 'context' in language education. In: Le T, McCausland M (eds) Interaction and development: proceedings of the international conference. Language Education, University of Tasmania

Halliday MAK (1996) On grammar and grammatics. In: Hasan R, Cloran C, Butt D (eds) Functional description: theory in practice. John Benjamins Publishing Co., Amsterdam/Philadelphia, pp 1–38

Halliday MAK (2002) Computing meanings: some reflections on past experience and present prospects. In: Huang G, Wang Z (eds) Discourse and Language Functions. Foreign Language Teaching and Research Press, Shanghai, pp 3–25

Halliday MAK, Ellis J (1951 [2006]) Temporal categories of the modern Chinese verb. In: Webster J (ed) Studies in Chinese language: volume 8 of the collected works of M.A.K. Halliday. Equinox, London & Oakville

Halliday MAK, Matthiessen C (1999) Construing experience through meaning. Cassell, New York

Halliday MAK, McDonald E (2004) Metafunctional profile of the grammar of Chinese. In: Caffarel A, Martin J, Matthiessen C (eds) Language typology: a functional perspective. John Benjamins, Amsterdam, pp 305–396

Halliday MAK, Matthiessen CMIM (2014) Halliday's introduction to functional grammar. Routledge, London

Hasan R (1987) The grammarian's dream: lexis as most delicate grammar. In: Halliday MAK, Fawcett R (eds) New developments in systemic linguistics: theory and description. Pinter, London, pp 184–211

Huang G (2001) Yupian fenxi de lilun yu shijian 语篇分析的理论与实践 [Theory and practice of discourse analysis: a study in advertising discourse]. Shanghai Foreign Education Press, Shanghai

Huang G (2006) Fanyi yanjiu de yuyanxue tansuo 翻译研究的语言学探索 [Linguistic explorations in translation studies]. Shanghai Foreign Education Press, Shanghai

Jakubíček M, Kilgarriff A, Kovář V, Rychlý P, Suchomel V (2013) The TenTen corpus family. In: 7th international corpus linguistics conference CL

Kilgarriff A, Baisa V, Bušta J, Jakubíček M, Kovář V, Michelfeit J, Rychlý P, Suchomel V (2014) The sketch engine: ten years on. Lexicography 1(1):7–36. https://doi.org/10.1007/s40607-014-0009-9

Kumar A (2009) Moodand the, transitivity me in Bajjika in a typological perspective: a text-based description. PhD thesis, Macquarie University, Sydney

Li ES-h (2003) A text-based study of the grammar of Chinese from a systemic functional approach. PhD thesis, Macquarie University, Sydney

Li ES-h (2007) Systemic functional grammar of Chinese: a text-based analysis. Continuum, London & New York

Li ES-h (2017) The nominal group in Chinese. In: Bartlett T, O'Grady G (eds) The Routledge handbook of systemic functional linguistics. Routledge, London and New York, pp 338–353. https://doi.org/10.4324/9781315413891

Long R (1981) Transitivity in Chinese. MA thesis, University of Sydney

Martin JR (2004) Metafunctional profile of the grammar of Tagalog. In: Caffarel A, Martin JR, Matthiessen CMIM (eds) Language typology: a functional perspective. John Benjamins Publishing Company, Amsterdam/Philadelphia, pp 255–304

Matthiessen CMIM (1995) Lexicogrammtical cartography: English systems. International Language Sciences, Tokyo

Matthiessen CMIM (1999) The system of TRANSITIVITY: an exploratory study of text-based profiles. Funct Lang 6(1):1–51

Matthiessen CMIM (2007a) Surveying a language In *LING319 lecture slides* (unpublished). Macquarie University, Sydney

Matthiessen CMIM (2007b) The 'architecture' of language according to systemic functional theory: developments since the 1970s. In: Hasan R, Matthiessen CMIM, Webster J (eds) Continuing discourse on language. Equinox, London, pp 505–561

Matthiessen CMIM (2009) Ideas and new directions. In: Halliday MAK, Webster J (eds) Continuum companion to systemic functional linguistics. Continuum, London & New York, pp 12–58

Matthiessen CMIM (2012) Systemic functional linguistics as appliable linguistics: social accountability and critical approaches. DELTA: Documentação de Estudos em Lingüística Teórica e Aplicada 28(special issue):437–471. https://doi.org/10.1590/S0102-44502012000300002

Matthiessen CMIM (2015a) Register in the round: registerial cartography. Function Linguist 2(1):9. https://doi.org/10.1186/s40554-015-0015-8

Matthiessen CMIM (2015b) Modeling context and register: the long-term project of registerial cartography. Letras 15–90. https://doi.org/10.5902/2176148520205

Matthiessen CMIM, Nesbitt C (1996) On the idea of theory—neutral descriptions. In: Hasan R, Cloran C, Butt D (eds) Functional descriptions: theory in practice. John Benjamins Publishing Company, Amsterdam/Philadelphia, pp 39–84

Matthiessen CMIM, Teruya K, Wu C (2008) Multilingual studies as a multi-dimensional space of interconnected language studies. In: Webster J (ed) Meaning in context. Continuum, London & New York, pp 146–221

McDonald E (1998) Clause and verbal group systems in Chinese: a text-based functional approach. PhD thesis, Macquarie University, Sydney

Mwinlaaru IN, Xuan WW (2016) A survey of studies in systemic functional language description and typology. Funct Linguist 3(8):1–41. https://doi.org/10.1186/s40554-016-0030-4

Ouyang X (1986) The clause complex in Chinese. MA thesis, University of Sydney, Sydney

Park K-h (2013) The experiential grammar of Korean: a systemic functional perspective. PhD thesis, Macquarie University, Sydney

Patpong P (2006) A systemic functional interpretation of Thai grammar: an exploration of Thai narrative discourse. PhD thesis, Macquarie University, Sydney

Shen J (1987) Halliday gongneng yufa daolun jieshao [Introduction to Halliday's 'introduction to functional grammar']. 外国语言学 [Linguistics Abroad] 1(2):17–24

Sutjaja IGM (1988) The nominal group in Bahasa Indonesia. PhD thesis, University of Sydney, Sydney

Teruya K (2006) Systemic functional grammar of Japanese. Continuum International, Sydney

Teruya K (2004) Metafunctional profile of the grammar of Japanese. In: Caffarel A, Martin JR, Matthiessen CMIM (eds) Language typology: a functional perspective. John Benjamins, Amsterdam/Philadelphia, pp 185–254

Tsung T (1986) Circumstantial elements in Chinese. MA thesis, University of Sydney, Sydney

Wu C (2009) Corpus-based research. In: Continuum companion to systemic functional linguistics. Continuum, London & New York, pp 128–142

Yang Y (2011) Grammatical metaphor in Chinese: a corpus-based study. Funct Lang 18(1):1–28. https://doi.org/10.1075/fol.18.1.01yan

Yang G (2014) Range characteristics in non-material clauses in Mandarin Chinese. Linguist Human Sci 10(2):83–102. https://doi.org/10.1558/lhs.v10i2.28555

Yang S (2021) A systemic functional study of modality in modern Chinese. The M.A.K. Halliday library functional linguistics series. Springer Nature, Singapore

Zhang W, Li M (2017) A functional study of Zhi 之 in the Chinese nominal group. Engl Lang Teach 10(11):173–182. https://doi.org/10.5539/elt.v10n11p173

Zhang D (2003) Yupian xianjie yu lianguan lilun de fazhan ji yingyong. 语篇衔接与连贯理论的发展及应用 [The development of the theory of coherence and cohesion and its application]. Shanghai Foriegn Language Education Press, Shanghai

Zhu Y (1985) Modality and modulation in English and Chinese. MA Thesis, University of Sydney

Chapter 3
Logical Resources of Chinese Nominal Groups

3.1 Introduction

In the previous chapter, I have introduced the fundamental dimensions of SFL theory, which provides a theoretical framework for the current study of Chinese nominal group. Among the five theoretical dimensions being discussed (see Sect. 2.2.2), it seems to have become a convention for an SFL description of a language to draw upon the dimension of metafunctions in setting up the framework, and the current account in this book is no exception. In the following four chapters, the description will be presented along the lines of metafunctions: I will start from investigating the logical metafunction in this chapter, followed by experiential in Chapter 4, and interpersonal in Chapter 5 and finally textual in Chapter 6.

Logically speaking, nominal groups can be approached from two perspectives: complexing and logico-semantic relations, similar to the situation at clause rank. In Sect. 3.2, I will investigate the complexity of Chinese nominal group, and then take the next step to interpret nominal group complex from the perspectives of both s and logico-semantic type. Then in Sect. 3.3, I will take a closer look at nominal group simplex, the predominant type in complexing. Detailed discussions will be presented in terms of the modification structure, types of expansion, types of embedding within a nominal group, and the affordance of expansion. After the discussion of the above mentioned, a case study will be presented in Sect. 3.4 with an aim to demonstrate how, through a logical lens, the resources of the nominal groups can contribute to the overall complexity of a text.

3.2 Nominal Group Complexing

When observing the complexity of nominal groups, it is helpful to view it both from above and from below along the rank scale: when viewing it in the clause

© Springer Nature Singapore Pte Ltd. 2022
J. Fang, *A Systemic Functional Grammar of Chinese Nominal Groups*,
The M.A.K. Halliday Library Functional Linguistics Series,
https://doi.org/10.1007/978-981-19-4009-5_3

environment, we examine the functional role that a complex of nominal groups plays in the clause structure; when viewing it from the word level, we examine lexico grammatical realisation of such a complex. So, a nominal group may enter into a **nominal Group Complex** by working with another group, typically another nominal group, to function as one element in a clause (see Example 1, Example 2 and Example 3). In terms of realisation, this means that a nominal group complex is made up of two or more nominal groups and each of them has its own Head.

Example 1
风把太阳永生不灭的宣言带到了全世界: 喜马拉雅山的最高峰, 太平洋中的小岛, 古老宁静的小村落, 繁华的现代都市 ——世界上一切它想去的地方, 夕阳都喷上了红光烈焰。

The wind brings the declaration that the sun is eternal to **the whole world: the summit of Himalaya, the small islands in the Pacific, the peaceful old villages and the busy modern cities**—in everywhere it wants to visit, the setting sun sprays its red light and roaring flames.

Example 2
梅花雀、小黄雀, 还有小杜鹃已经在选好的枝丫间开始做窝了。
The waxbill, the little siskin, as well as the little cuckoo have started building nestles in their chosen twigs.

Example 3
蓝色的小河里有一群快乐的鱼和虾。
In the blue creek, there were a group of happy fish and shrimps.

As shown in Example 1, Example 2 and Example 3, the parts highlighted in bold are complex of nominal groups, where more than one nominal group work together to play a participant role (as a part of circumstance in Example 1, as subject/participant in Example 2 and as object/participant in Example 3) in a clause. It is interesting to note that, in Chinese, the nominal groups within a group complex may be connected with a conjunction as in Example 2: 还有 (*as well as*) is used to link each group. However, it is also common for each group to be presented without any conjunction, but to still form a group complex as in Example 1. Also, as demonstrated in Example 3, the nominal heads in a nominal group complex may share the same set of modifiers— the situation is somewhat similar to the elliptical structure in clauses where, when the same subject is functioning in two clauses, the subject can be omitted in the second clause that comes after the first one. In Example 3, as the Things represented by the two nominal heads, 鱼 (*fish*) and 虾 (*shrimp*), share the same attribute 快乐 (*being happy*) and can be measured in the same manner (by 'group'), it becomes possible for them to enter into a complex structure with two heads jointly modified by the same set of modifiers.

For a nominal group complex with multiple head nouns, whether the heads can be jointly modified by a single set of modifiers depends on the Thing type (see Sect. 3.4) which determines the modification potential of a noun. For example:

Example 4

不论是亲密的朋友还是仇敌，都怀着最深的敬意在他的遗体前哀痛的埋下
了头。

Close friends or enemies, with the deepest respect, all sadly bowed their heads
in front of his body.

亲密的	朋友	还是	仇敌
Close	Friends	Or	Enemies
Premodifier	Noun 1	CONJ	Noun 2
Nominal group 1		CONJ	Nominal group 2
Nominal group complex			

As shown in Example 4, the modifier in the structure, 亲密的 (*close*), is functioning within the first nominal group only, and the second nominal group of the
complex contains no modifying elements. The semantic distance between the head
nouns of the two groups, 朋友 (*friend*) versus 仇敌 (*enemy*), has provided a strong-
enough indication that they cannot be jointly modified by the only modifier, 亲密
的 (*close*). Therefore, it is impossible to interpret this structure as a nominal group
complex with two head nouns being jointly modified by the same modifier.

Compared with nominal group complex, it is more common to see a nominal
group taking a functional position on its own in a clause structure, in which case it is
a **nominal group simplex** (see Example 5). In terms of realisation, a nominal group
simplex is made of only one nominal group, which has only one Head.

Example 5

鹰的眼睛炯炯发亮，羽毛颜色与狮子皮毛相近，爪子形状也与之相同。

The eagle's eyes are bright and shiny,‖ **the colour of its feathers** is similar to
that of a lion's fur, ‖ and **the shape of its claws** is also like that of a lion. ‖‖

As shown in Example 5, there are three nominal groups in the sentence that is
made up of three clauses. Each single nominal group functions as subject in a clause,
and each of them has only one nominal head. In fact, the term 'nominal group' and
'nominal group simplex' may often refer to the same grammatical unit—it is a matter
of perspectives of viewing the unit, as the term 'nominal group simplex' indicates
that the complexing status, compared to a nominal group complex.

3.2.1 Nominal Group Complex: Taxis and Logico-Semantic Type

Let us take a further look at the logical complexity of a nominal group complex.
Same as a clause complex, from a logical perspective, a nominal group complex
can also be interpreted in terms of taxis and logico-semantic type. The former refers

to the degree of interdependency of each group unit within the complex, whereas the latter refers to the fundamental semantic relations between each unit within the complex.

3.2.1.1 Taxis

In a nominal group complex, one may find such a structure where each group and/or phrase within the complex are taking equal status, and any of these group-level unit can stand alone and serve the same function as the whole group complex. In terms of taxis, this type of structure is **paratactic**. In Chinese, groups and phrases within a nominal group complex can be linked paratactically either with or without a conjunction.

Sometimes, one may also see another type of structure where groups and phrases within a complex do not take equal status, with one of them serving as the dominant group and the others as dependent ones. Under such circumstances, only the dominant group can stand alone and serve the same function as the whole complex. In terms of taxis, this type of structure is **hypotactic**. In Chinese, the dominant group and the other dependent units in a hypotactic nominal group complex can be connected either with or without conjunctions.

For the purpose of a clear representation of the logical structure, I follow the SFL convention to label each group/phrase within a nominal group complex according to their tactic relations (see Table 3.1):

Below are some examples of a nominal group complex being analysed in terms of tactic relations (Example 6 and Example 7):

Example 6
教育、医疗、住房、养老, 这些民生问题该不该市场化?

Education, health, housing, aged care, these welfare issues should or not be commercialised?

Should these welfare issues, education, health, housing and aged care, be commercialised?

1	1	教育 education
	2	医疗 health
	3	住房 housing
	4	养老 aged care
2		这些民生问题 these welfare issues

Table 3.1 Conventions of tactic relations

	Group 1	Group 2	Group 3
Parataxis	1 (initiating)	2	3
Hypotaxis	α (dominant)	β	γ

Example 7

除了内在特征，一部艺术作品，例如一部小说、一首长诗或一部戏剧作品，
还可能有其它有趣的因素。

Except internal features, <u>an artistic work, such as a novel, a long poem or a play</u>,
may also have other interesting elements.

α		一部艺术作品 an artistic work
β	1	例如一部小说 such as a novel
	2	一首长诗 a long poem
	3	或一部戏剧作品 or a play

As shown in Example 6 and Example 7, nominal group complexes may also
display a similar complex pattern that clause complexes have. However, unlike clause
complexes, in Chinese nominal group complexes, parataxis is highly unmarked
whereas hypotaxis is less common. When two nominal groups form a group complex
in Chinese, conjunctions are often optional in connecting the groups, as the taxis
status can be realised through implicit logico-semantic relations.

3.2.1.2 Logico-Semantic Relations

From a logico-semantic perspective, one can investigate what type of semantic relations that the groups enter into to form a complex. In the Chinese nominal group
complex, three types of expansion are found to relate one group with another, and
unlike the case of the clause complex, there is no projecting type in a nominal group
complexing.

The type of expansion can be further categorised into elaboration, extension and
enhancement. In the case of the Chinese nominal group complex, an elaborating
group presents the complexity of the thing by explaining, exemplifying or particularising it. In comparison, an extending group construes the experiential complexity
of the thing by adding something new. For enhancement, a group is used to enhance
the meaning of another group of the same complex by qualifying it in terms of
sequence of time. Table 3.2 sets out each type and subtype of expansion as well as
the SFL conventions for each category:

Examples of each type and subtype of expansion are presented below:

Example 8

Elaboration: appositive

胡杨，维吾尔语称作 "托克拉克"，即 "最美丽的树"。

Huyang, in Uyghur is called 'toghraq', viz. 'the most beautiful tree'.

Example 9

Elaboration: exemplifying

Table 3.2 Types of expansion

Type of expansion	Subtype
Elaboration =	Appositive
	Exemplifying
	Particularising
Extension +	Additive
	Alternative
	Subtractive
Enhancement ×	Sequential

中国内陆的几个大城市, 例如西安和太原, 教育也比较发达。

(In) some big cities in inland China, such as Xi'an and Taiyuan, the education there is also advanced.

Example 10

Elaboration: particularising

一个最基本的原因就是俄罗斯的人口, 尤其是富人, 一直在向莫斯科等大城市聚集。

One of the most fundamental reasons is that the Russian population, especially the rich people, are moving towards big cities like Moscow.

It should be noted that the use of structural conjunctions, such as 即(viz) in Example 8, 例如(such as) in Example 9, 尤其 (especially) in Example 10, is often a strong indicator for an elaborating relation between two groups, and such relation is often hypotactic through the use of these conjunctions.

Example 11

Extension: additive

莎士比亚是英国16世纪最伟大的诗人、剧作家。

Shakespeare was Britain's sixteenth century greatest poet, playwright.

Shakespeare was the greatest British poet and playwright in the sixteenth century.

Example 12

Extension: additive

除了辣椒, 茄子和西红柿也是夏天常见的蔬菜。

Except chillies, eggplants and tomatoes are also common vegetables in summer.

Example 13

Extension: alternative

传统教学也好, 远程教学也好, 都需要包括老师、学生和教材三个要素。

Whether (it is) traditional teaching (or) correspondence education, (both) need to include the three factors of the teacher, the student and the teaching materials.

In the case of alternative extension, a nominal group complex of this type often appears in an emphatic structure, where each nominal group within the complex represents one of the alternatives.

Example 14
Extension: subtractive
全班同学除了他都到齐了。
<u>The whole class except him</u> were there.

Note that in Example 13 the conjunction 除了 (*except*) may mark an additive extension and may also be used to indicate a subtractive extension.

Example 15
Enhancement: sequential
事故发生后, <u>先是妇女和小孩, 接着是现场工作人员</u>, 都出现了类似的症状。

After the accident, it was <u>first the women and children, and then the working staff on the site</u>, that all showed the symptoms of the kind.

In terms of Chinese nominal group complex, the relation of enhancement is highly marked. As shown in Example 15, the logico-semantic relation of enhancement is realised by the collocated use of conjunctions: 先是 (*first*)…, and 接着 (*then*). In fact, conjunctions like these, which show a sequence of time, as well as others which mark the other circumstantial relationships such as location, condition, reason or cause (see further Halliday and Matthiessen 2014), can rarely be used to link two nominal groups. Rather, circumstantial conjunctions of this kind are more often used to connect two clauses. I may quote Halliday and Matthiessen's (2014) view to explain this from a semantic perspective:

…enhancing relationships are essentially between figures as a whole, and only rarely can they be interpreted as holding between particular elements of a figure (pp. 563).

As nominal groups typically realise participant roles, which only represent some elements of a figure, it is not surprising that, based on Halliday and Matthiessen's explanation, it is uncommon to see an enhancing relationship between to nominal groups.

Similarly, the fact that no projecting relations are found between nominal groups may be explained in the same manner: as a projection essentially requires either a mental or verbal process to be involved, it is a relationship typically found among clauses and verbal groups, rather than nominal groups. However, when a mental or verbal process are packed into a nominal form through grammatical metaphor, the part of nominalisation does play the essential role in realising the projecting relationship between two clauses. This can be illustrated by the following examples:

Example 16
|||土豆网做出了<u>一个艰难的决定</u>: || 融资1.62亿美元。|||
|||The Tudou.com made **a hard decision**: || to be financed of USD 162 million.

Example 17

‖他的结论, < < "中国还没有那样好的小说家" > > , 让许多人不能接受。‖

‖ **His conclusion**, <<'There is no such a wonderful novelist in China'>>, can hardly be accepted by many. ‖

Note that in Example 17, the logico-semantic relationship between the two clauses is elaborating, as the interrupting clause helps explain part of the other clause. However, the relationship between the nominal group 他的结论 (*his conclusion*) and the clause 中国还没有那样好的小说家 (*There is no such a wonderful novelist in China*), is more of a projecting one, as the nominal group here is simply a nominalised verbal process and the clause is the content of this verbal projection.

I have now discussed the logical meaning of the nominal group complex by means of both taxis and logico-semantic relations. Table 3.3 sets out examples of different types of logico-semantic relations with a combination of parataxis or hypotaxis in Chinese nominal group complexes:

Theoretically speaking, in terms of the logical complexity, the potential for a nominal group complex to expand is no less than any other unit in the language. However, the use of nominal group complexes in Chinese is less common than the use of nominal group simplexes (i.e. a simple nominal group), and the expansion of the former is pervasively realised through extension, either hypotactically or paratactically. Examples:

Example 18

Paratactic extension

<u>风把太阳永生不灭的宣言带到了全世界</u>: <u>喜马拉雅山的最高峰</u>, <u>太平洋中的小岛</u>, <u>古老宁静的小村落</u>, <u>繁华的现代都市</u>。

<u>The wind brings the declaration that the sun is eternal to the whole world</u>: <u>the summit of Himalaya</u>, <u>the small islands in the Pacific</u>, <u>the peaceful old villages</u> and <u>the busy modern cities.</u>

1		全世界: the whole world
= 2	1	喜马拉雅山的最高峰 the summit of Himalaya
	+ 2	太平洋中的小岛 the small islands in the Pacific
	+ 3	古老宁静的小村落 the peaceful old villages
	+ 4	繁华的现代都市 the busy modern cities

Example 19

Hypotactic extension

除了内在特征, 一部艺术作品, 例如一部小说、一首长诗或一部戏剧作品, 还可能有其它有趣的因素。

Table 3.3 Examples of different types of nominal group complexes

Expansion type	Subtype	Parataxis	Hypotaxis
Elaboration	Appositive	胡杨, 维吾尔语称作 "托克拉克", 即 "最美丽的树"。Huyang, in Uyghur is called **'toghraq', viz. 'the most beautiful tree'**	
	Exemplifying		中国内陆的几个大城市, 例如西安和太原, 教育也比较发达。**Some big cities in inland China, such as Xi'an and Taiyuan,** the education there is also advanced
	Particularising		一个最基本的原因就是俄罗斯的人口, 尤其是富人, 一直在向莫斯科等大城市聚集。One of the most fundamental reasons is that **the Russian population, especially the rich people,** are moving towards big cities like Moscow
Extension	Additive	画一个红人, 一只蓝狗, 一间紫房子。。。Draw **a red man, a blue dog, and a purple house**…	除了辣椒, 茄子和西红柿也是夏天常见的蔬菜。**Apart from chillies, eggplants and tomatoes** are also common vegetables in summer
	Alternative	传统教学也好, 远程教学也好, 都需要包括老师、学生和教材三个要素。**Traditional teaching or correspondence education,** (both) need to include the three factors of the teacher, the student and the teaching materials	我们要记住的是友情, 而不是仇恨。What we must remember is **friendship, rather than hatred**
	Subtractive		全班同学除了他都到齐了。**The whole class except him** were there
Enhancement	Sequential	事故发生后, 先是妇女和小孩, 接着是现场工作人员, 都出现了类似的症状。After the accident, it was **first the women and children, and then the working staff on the site,** that all showed the symptoms of the kind	

Except internal features, <u>an artistic work, such as a novel, a long poem or a play,</u> may also have other interesting elements.

α		一部艺术作品 an artistic work
$= \beta$	1	例如一部小说 such as a novel
	+ 2	一首长诗 a long poem
	+ 3	一首长诗或一部戏剧作品 or a play

3.2.2 Nominal Group Simplex

Nominal group simplex, i.e. simple nominal group, refers to the choice of developing one nominal group only, and the entry condition is to have a single nominal head, typically a noun. In Chinese, the simple nominal group is much more common than the nominal group complex. Same as the latter, a nominal group simplex can also be logically analysed in terms of taxis and logico-semantic relations. Viewed through a logical lens, a simple nominal group may be interpreted as a structure where a group of elements expand a nominal head through modification.

3.2.2.1 Taxis

In terms of taxis, only one type of relation is found between the head of a nominal group and its modifiers: all the modifying elements are dependent on the head, which forms a hypotactic relation. For example:

Example 20
那个高度融合统一的很亮的灰白色的线, 总是在前边吸引着你。

That highly amalgamated bright grey line is always attracting you at the front.

那个	高度融合统一	的	很亮	的	灰白色	的	线
That	highly amalgamated	de	Bright	de	Grey	de	Line
Modifier 4	Modifier 3	SUB	Modifier 2	SUB	Modifier 1	SUB	Head
ε	δ		γ		β		α

As can be seen in Example 20, if one ignores the different experiential aspects of the Thing (being realised by the head noun) that each modifying element represents, the nominal group structure can be viewed as a univariate one by simply looking at all the functional elements as modifiers in general. The head of the nominal group, marked as α, is the only part that can stand alone, and therefore is independent. All the other elements in the nominal group, marked as β, γ, δ and so on, are the ones that depend on the Head. Another feature about the Chinese nominal group is that a subordinating article, 的 (de), is commonly used to connect modifiers and the Head. In Example 20, altogether three 的 (de) are used to link the three modifiers β, γ, δ with the Head α. Therefore, logically speaking, 的 (de) can be interpreted as a hypotactic conjunction functioning within a simple nominal group to connect modifiers with the Head. However, it is also important to note that not all the hypotactic relations in a Chinese nominal group have to be marked by the use of 的 (de), as it depends on the experiential function of each modifying element in relation to the Thing. Discussions about this will continue in Chapter 4.

In terms of sequencing, the sequence of modifiers in a Chinese nominal group is always regressive, which means that the modifiers are sequenced from right to left, starting from the Head in an increasing order of expansion. This is a structural difference between nominal groups of Chinese and English, as an English nominal group can expand in both ways, in a regressive sequence where premodifiers such as Epithet and Classifier come before the Head, and also in a progressive sequence where modifiers (typically qualifiers) are sequenced from left to right starting from the Head. Being able to expand in both ways makes an English nominal group more flexible in structure; thus, it is more capable of packing various types of experiential properties of the Thing into the group structure. In comparison, as all the modifiers come before the Head, a Chinese nominal group tends to have less flexible expansion potential than its English counterpart. If judged purely from a logical perspective, the univariate structure can expand again and again following the sequence of $\alpha \rightarrow \beta \rightarrow \gamma \rightarrow \delta \ldots$, awkwardness will increase accordingly as the expansion continues. See the example below, which is expanded from the previous one:

Example 21
那个总是在你前面的让你着迷的高度融合统一的很亮的灰白色的线*

That highly amalgamated bright grey line which is always in front of you and attracts you.

那个	的	总是在你前面	的	让你着迷	的	高度融合统一	的	很亮	的	灰白色	的	线
That	de	Always in front of you	de	Attracts you	de	Highly amalgamated	de	Bright	de	Grey	de	Line
Modifier 6	SUB	Modifier 5	SUB	Modifier 4	SUB	Modifier 3	SUB	Modifier 2	SUB	Modifier 1	SUB	Head
η		ζ		ε		δ		γ		β		α

Table 3.4 Examples of modifiers of different expansion types

	δ	γ	β		α
Elaboration	一束 A bunch of	美丽 Beautiful	芬芳 Aromatic	的 de	鲜花 Flowers
			[[卖车]] Selling cars	的 de	工作 Job
Extension		我的 My	第一辆 First		汽车 Car
Enhancement			三十多年前 More than thirty years ago	的 de	事 Event
			花园里 In the garden	的 de	百合花 Lilies

With all the modifiers coming before the Head, a nominal group as such is very unnatural in Chinese, and a more congruent realisation in lexicogrammar will instead be one or two clauses.

3.2.2.2 Logico-Semantic Relations in a Simple Nominal Groups

In terms of logico-semantic relations, I will investigate the relationship between the nominal Head and its modifiers. Generally speaking, the logico-semantic relations between them fall into two types: expansion and projection.

Expansion

Same as in a nominal group complex, three different types of expansion can be found in a simple nominal group, namely elaboration, extension and enhancement. Different modifying elements within a nominal group may have different types of expansion to the Head. Examples in Table 3.4 illustrate how these items form different logico-semantic types with the Head in a nominal group—the items in bold belong to the relevant type of expansion as set out in the table:

In terms of elaboration, if a modifier elaborates the Head, there could be two possible subtypes of the elaboration: one is as an intensive attribute, and the other as an opposition. As in the first example shown in the table above, the modifiers of 美丽 (*beautiful*) and 芬芳 (*aromatic*) elaborate the Head by presenting the attributes of the Thing 鲜花 (*flowers*). In the second example of elaboration, the relation between the modifier 卖车 (*selling cars*) and the Head 工作 (*job*) is appositive, as the latter simply refers to the former.

In terms of extension, there are no categories of additive, alternative or subtractive found in the case of simple nominal group. The only category is possession, which represents the relation of ownership and various kinds of association with the Head. As can be seen in the example above, the modifier 我的 (*my*) represents a relation of ownership, whereas 第一辆 (*first MEA*) represents an abstract association of both quantity and measure with the Thing 汽车 (*car*).

In terms of enhancement, the modifiers can form various kinds of circumstantial relations including time and location, as shown in Table 3.4. In fact, the relation of circumstantial enhancement is not limited to the spatio-temporal categories. The enhancement may also be realised through other types of relation such as manner, cause and conditions. In most cases, this is realised by an embedded clause which functions as a qualifier in the nominal group. In Chapter 4 when experiential resources are under focus, the logico-semantic relations between an embedded clause as a qualifier and the Head will be discussed.

Projection

Unlike in a nominal group complex, where expansion is the only type of logico-semantic relation, in a simple nominal group complex (i.e. a nominal group simplex), projection is found as the other option. If the logico-semantic relationship between a nominal Head and its modifier is projecting, then one can be certain of two things: on the one hand, the Head is realised by a noun which either represents a metaphorical, nominalised version of a mental or a verbal process or by a noun representing the name of a phenomenon, a fact or a verbiage; and on the other hand, the modifier is realised by a rank-shifted embedded clause which represents the content of the projection. Examples:

Example 22
科学家提出了发展 "绿蓝白"三色农业的构想。

Scientists introduced the concept of developing 'green, blue and white' triple-colour agriculture.

[[发展 "绿蓝白"三色农业]] [[Developing 'green, blue and white' triple-colour agriculture]]	的 de	构想 Concept
`β		α

Example 23
她要我记住她盼望我用功读书的话。

She wants me to remember her words that she hopes me to study hard.

[[她盼望我用功读书]] [[She hopes me to study hard]]	的 de	话 Words
'β		α

Example 24
因为古人有 "无过雷池一步" 的话, 后人就 以 "雷池" 表示不可超越的界限。

As the ancient Chinese had such a saying 'don't get yourself one step beyond leichi', afterwards people use 'leichi' to refer to the unsurpassable limit.

[['无过雷池一步']] [[Don't get yourself one step beyond leichi]]	的 de	话 Words
'β		α

Example 25
孙中山先生看到周围的风景优美, 地势也很开阔, 就表示了身后要埋葬在这里的愿望。

After seeing the beautiful scenery and the broad and open view, Mr. Sun Yat-sen had expressed his wish to be buried here when he died

[[身后要埋葬在这里]] [[Be buried here when he dies]]	的 de	愿望 Wish
'β		α

Example 26
然而一百年后的今天, 我们必须正视黑人还没有得到自由这一悲惨的事实。

However, today after a whole century, we have to face the miserable fact that the black haven't been freed.

[[黑人还没有得到自由]] [[The black haven't got freedom]]	这 This	一 One	悲惨 Miserable	的 de	事实 Fact
'ε	δ	γ	β		α

The Heads of the Examples 23 and 24, 话 (*words*) are realised by nominalised verbal processes: in Example 23, the Head projects an indirect locution, whereas in Example 24 a direct locution being marked by punctuations. Note that mode of

Table 3.5 Types of head nouns (locutions and ideas)

Types of Head nouns with projecting potential		Examples		
		Locutions	Ideas	
			desirative	cognitive
Proposition	Statement	抗议 remonstration, 公告 announcement, 论点 argument, 话 words, 谎言 lie, 借口 excuse, 解释 explanation, 结论 conclusion, 感叹 exclamation, 承诺 promise		想法 idea, 假设 supposition, 理念 thinking, 信念 belief, 概念 concept, 观点 view, 回想 recollection, 回忆 memory, 看法 opinion, 感悟 reflection, 感想 reflection, 体会 feeling, 猜想 assumption
	Question	疑问 doubt, 问题question, 讨论 discussion, 辩论 debate		
Proposal	Offer	建议 suggestion, 暗示 implication, 提示 indication, 意见 opinion, 劝告 persuasion	愿望 wish, 决心 determination, 念头intension, 理想 ideal, 意愿 inclination, 心愿 wish, 心声 aspiration	
	Command	要求 requirement, 命令 order, 请求request, 告诫warning, 呼声 demand, 呼吁 request		

the quotation, whether direct or indirect, does not influence the hypotactic relation between the Head and the embedded clause. In Examples 22 and 25, the Heads 构想 (*concept*) and 愿望 (*wish*) are nominalised mental processes: although both are proposals, 构想 (*concept*) is an offered type, whereas 愿望 (*wish*) is a commanding type. The Head in Example 26, 事实 (*fact*), is different from all the other four in that it is neither a nominalised sensing nor a nominalised saying. Rather, this is simply a **fact noun** which projects, and the embedded clause represents the content of the projection. Based on the discussion up to now, I can summarise the type of Head nouns which have projecting potential in the tables (see Tables 3.5 and 3.6):

Table 3.5 sets out different types of Head nouns that have the potential to project locutions and ideas. As can be seen, some of the examples are simply the names of phenomena or verbiages which could construe a participant role in a mental or a verbal process, like 念头 (*intention*), 想法 (*idea*) as phenomenon in a mental process) and 话 (*words*), 呼声 (*demand*) as verbiage in a verbal process. Other examples in the table are the names of nominalised mental or verbal processes, in other words, the names of macrophenomena, such as 感悟 (*reflection*) and 劝告 (*persuasion*). It is also interesting to note that, as Chinese is a highly non-inflectional language, these names of nominalised processes bear the same lexical forms as the verbs that congruently

Table 3.6 Types of head nouns (fact)

| | | fact nouns | |
		simple fact	Meta fact
Proposition	Statement	事实 fact, 事情 matter, 情况 circumstance, 事 matter, 新闻 news, 消息 message, 现实 reality	经验 experience, 教训 lesson, 道理 principle, 原理 principle, 现象 phenomenon, 总结 summary
	Question	谜 mystery, 问题 question	
Proposal			规定 regulation, 规矩 rule, 原则 principle, 规则 rule

construe these processes. Therefore, words such as 要求 (*requirement/require*) and 假设 (*supposition/suppose*) can be used as either nouns or verbs.

In general, most of the locution nouns are nominalisations of verbal processes, whereas the majority of the idea nouns are names of phenomena in mental processes. And further under the category of ideas, two types of sensing are sub-categorised: desirative and cognitive, both of which congruently have the ability to project. It is important to note that Chinese nouns also provide resources for naming another two types of sensing, namely emotion and perception (for the subtypes of sensing, see further Halliday and Matthiessen 1999, 2014), such as 悔恨 (*regret*) and 品味 (*taste*). However, nominalisations of these two types of mental process generally lack the projecting potential and the logico-semantic type between these Head nouns and their modifiers is typically expansion.

The Head nouns in Table 3.5 are also categorised in terms of the potential speech functions that they realise: as either propositions or proposals. For idea nouns, the desirative type falls into the category of proposal, and the cognitive type conflates with proposition. Examples:

Example 27
Idea noun: desirative + proposal
她那种[[要求增强独立行动能力]]的强烈愿望, 都使我们备受鼓舞。
Her strong **desire** [[to increase independence]] greatly encouraged us.

Example 28
Idea noun: cognitive + proposition
[["男大当婚, 女大当嫁"]]的传统观念依然存在。
The traditional **idea** that [[Men and women should get married when they grow up]] still exists.

In terms of nouns of locutions, categories of proposition and proposal can be categorised further into two subtypes, respectively: as statement and question, and as offer and command. The sub-categorisation of proposition nouns is based on the potential speech function of whether to give or request information; the sub-categorisation of proposal nouns is based on the speech function of whether to offer or command goods and services. Examples:

Example 29

Locution noun: proposition: statement

[[公众对反腐满意度达7成]]的结论靠谱吗?

Is the **conclusion** [[that 70% of the public are satisfied with the anti-corruption campaign]] reliable?

Example 30

Locution noun: proposition: question

写文章解决了[["写什么"]]的问题后, 还要解决[["怎么写"]]的问题。

On writing, after solving the **problem** of [['what to write']], one also needs to solve the **problem** of [['how to write']].

Example 31

Locution noun: proposal: offer

[[要求延期审理此案]]的提议未获得通过。

The proposal [[to adjourn the case]] was not approved.

Example 32

Locution noun: proposal: command

红四团接到了 "29日早晨夺下泸定桥"的命令。

The red regiment No.4 received the **command** that 'The Luding Bridge must be conquered on the morning of 29th'.

In terms of modality, the degree of obligation and inclination under the 'proposal' type of Head nouns can be expressed in either one or both of the following two ways: (i) by the use of the Head noun in which the sense of modality is part of the semantic meaning of the word itself, such as 建议(*suggestion*, low obligation), 要求 (*request*, median obligation) and 命令 (*command,* high obligation); (ii) by the use of modifiers, typically realised by adjectives, to intensify the degree of modality, e.g. 强烈要求 (*strong request,* high obligation), 强烈愿望 (*strong desire,* high inclination).

Table 3.6 sets out the third type of Head nouns that can project, the fact nouns. They can be further categorised as either names of simple facts or of metafacts, which are the facts resulting from subjective judgement on the simple facts. Examples of the metafact nouns, such as 经验 (*experience*), 教训 (*lesson*) and 道理 (*principle*), represent the results of complicated mental process of analysing, evaluation, reflection and summarising based on past human experiences. Fact nouns can also be categorised in terms of the potential speech function that they may realise: either as a proposition or a proposal. All the simple fact nouns tend to realise propositions by stating a fact or presenting a question. There are also a small group of fact nouns which are inherently modulations, which indicate various degrees of obligation and inclination to do things. Examples:

Example 33

Fact nouns as modulation: high obligation

[["离职人员不发放奖金"]]的规定是否有效?

Is the **regulation** that [['the staff leaving their job positions should not receive the bonus payments']] effective?

Example 34

Fact nouns as modulation: median obligation

多年来我们一直秉承[["客户利益至上"]]的原则。

For many years, we have been sticking to the **principle** that [['the interest of the clients must be put in the first place']].

3.2.2.3 Complexity of a Simple Nominal Group

The logical structure of a simple nominal group could be as complicated as that of a clause complex. In this section, the discussion of the complexity of the simple nominal group will be based on the following three situations: (a) the nominal groups with sub-modification, (b) the nominal groups where Head and Thing are not conflated and (c) the nominal groups being modified by embedded clauses.

Nominal Groups with Sub-modification

As being discussed, a nominal group can be interpreted as a univariate structure where a group of modifiers expand[1] the Head. The complicated case lies in that this univariate structure may be repeated in multiple layers. For instance:

Example 35

浙江大学文化遗产研究中心开始筹建。

The Zhejiang University Research Centre for Cultural Heritage starts to be established.

浙江	大学	文化	遗产	研究	中心
Zhejiang	University	Cultural	Heritage	Research	Centre
γ		β			α
γβ	γα	ββ		βα	
		βββ	ββα		

---

[1] Here the word 'expand' does not represent a logico-semantic type.

Within the logical structure of the nominal group in Example 35, sub-modification occurs where certain elements within the group do not modify the Head noun directly, but function to modify a subhead such as 文化遗产 (*cultural heritage*) modifies 研究 (*research*) in the example above. Such structural representations, which are often studied in constituency analysis in non-SFL research, reflect the logical complexity of a nominal group in construing the order of modification.

Nominal Groups with Head and Thing not Conflated

The example nominal groups that I have discussed so far share a common feature: the Head and the Thing map into one lexical item. In other words, the noun that functions as the Head also represents the Thing. However, there is another type of nominal group in Chinese where the Head and Thing are not conflated. Look at Example 36:

Example 36
你所了解的只是<u>真实情况的一部分</u>。

What you have known is only **a part of the truth.**

真实		情况	的	一部分
True		Situation	de	One part
ββ		αβ		
β				
	Thing			Head

In Example 36, the head and thing are realised by two separate items: a **Facet** is selected to take the head position, which represents a partitive relation to the Thing. It is also worth noting that the adjective modifier 真实 (true) does not modify the Head, but the Thing, which in turn expands the head through another layer of modification. Compare:

Example 37
这只是他名下资产的很小的一部分。

This is only a small part of the properties under his name.

他名下 Under his name	资产 Property	的 de	很小 Very small	的 de	一部分 A part
Sub-modifier βγ	Sub-Head αγ				
γ			β		α
	Thing				Head

In Example 37, the rank-shifted prepositional phrase 他名下 (*under his name*), which comes before the Thing, functions as a sub-modifier modifying the sub-Head (i.e. the Thing), whereas 很小 (*very small*), which precedes the Head but follows the Thing, modifies the Head.

This seems to represent a general situation where a modifier only modifies the Thing when it appears both before the Thing and the Head. However, if a modifier is selected to come before the Head but after the Thing, it serves the Head directly. In fact, this 'special' structural feature is simply another example reflecting the regressive sequence of modification in a Chinese nominal group, and the complexity lies in that there are more than one layer of modification and all of the layers presents the same kind of regressive pattern within their local sub-structures. This is the general logical feature of the nominal groups with sub-modifications. However, compared with those where Thing and Head are conflated, the nominal groups with separate representations for the Thing and the Head tend to be more complicated. This is because that the Thing, being the most basic experiential class in relation to which it is construed as a being, provides the biggest potential for modification compared with any other elements that could be selected in the same nominal group. This underlines the fact that all the other elements in the group, whether or not taking the Head position, can only construe the qualities that are not as basic as the Thing in its own right. Therefore, when the Thing becomes a sub-Head in a regressive modification structure, all the modifiers preceding it serve for the Thing only, which in turn serves as a modifier to the Head.

I have assumed so far that a nominal group in Chinese always contains a Thing, whether conflated or dissociated with the Head. In fact, this does not reflect the complete picture. Very similar to English, in most cases there is a Head in a Chinese nominal group, but there may be no Thing. From a logical perspective, when a nominal group is considered as a structure which can be expanded repeatedly through modification of some primary class of things, there must be a Head in the structure to make modification possible. Sometimes, functional elements other than Thing may be selected as Head. Examples:

Example 38
Measure as head:
我买了五条鱼, 吃了两条, 还有几条?

I bought five fish, ate two MEA, how many MEA left?

Example 39
Deictic as head:
你的在这儿, 我的在那儿。

Yours is here, and mine is there.

As illustrated in Examples 38 and 39, in an elliptical nominal group where the Thing is missing, another element on the structure can function as Head. More detailed discussion about nominal ellipsis will be presented in Chapter 6.

Nominal Groups Modified by Embedded Clauses

I have had a brief discussion of the nominal group modified by embedded clauses
in Sect. 2.2.2, where a logico-semantic relation of projection is investigated. In this
section, I will explore the logical complexity of the embedded clauses functioning in
the nominal groups: although only a premodifier in a nominal group, an embedded
clause may present a logical structure more complex than a ranking clause, as in the
examples below.

Example 40
Nominal group with an embedded clause simplex
月球登陆给我们提供了一个[[研究它和我们星球遥远过去]]的好机会。

The moon landing provides us with a good opportunity [[**to study the remote
history of the moon and the earth**]].

Example 41
Nominal group with an embedded clause complex
本法所称合同是[[平等主体的自然人、法人、其他组织之间设立、‖变更
、‖终止民事权利义务关系]]的协议。

A contract in this law refers to an agreement [[**establishing, ‖modifying ‖and
terminating the civil rights and obligations between subjects of equal footing,
that is, between natural persons, legal persons or other organisations**]].

Example 42
Nominal group with further embedding: simplex
对合同格式条款有两种以上解释的，应当作出[[不利于[[提供格式条款]]一
方]]的解释。

Where there are two or more kinds of interpretation of the contract terms, <u>an
interpretation [[**unfavourable to the party [[supplying the standard terms]]**]]</u>
shall be preferred.

Example 43
Nominal group with further embedding: complex
[[外国合营者在履行[[法律和协议、合同规定]]的义务后‖分得]]的净利润可
按外汇管理条例汇往国外。

The net profit [[**that the foreign side in a joint venture receives ‖ after fulfilling
its obligations [under laws and various agreements and contracts]]]**, may be
remitted abroad in accordance with the foreign exchange regulations.

Examples 40–43 illustrate the complexity of different types of nominal groups involving embedded clauses. As can be seen, the degree of complexity can be influenced by two logical structural features: the embedded clause complexity and the existence of further embedding. In the former case, the embedding is realised by a clause complex containing more than one clause. In the latter, there are more than one layer of embedding in the structure, which is actually a type of sub-modification realised in the form of further embedding. Both features may be selected simultaneously in an embedding structure, as a result of which the complexity will be greatly increased. It is interesting to note that nominal groups with complicated logical structures are often found in formal written texts such as legal documents.

3.3 The Logical System: Modification

So far I have investigated the logical resources of the nominal group in Chinese in terms of group complexity, tactic relations, logico-semantic relations and the logical complexity of the simple nominal group. Based on the discussions above, I present a logical system of modification in Fig. 3.1:

As shown in Fig. 3.1, from a logical perspective, we can interpret a nominal group in Chinese as a regressive expansion of the nominal head. This expansion is realised by repeated modification of the head. Taxis is not open for selection because the tactic relation between a head and its modifiers is always a hypotactic one. However, the logico-semantic relation between the head and its modifiers can be selected between expansion and projection. It has to be stressed that such modification can recur again and again to realise a theoretically endless regressive structure of a nominal group, though in reality, it is not common to find a long recurrent modification structure in a Chinese nominal group as an overlong modification structure brings awkwardness. Apart from the potential to develop a regressive modification structure repeatedly, the other simultaneous selection in terms of modification is to either have further modification (i.e. sub-modification) or not. The selection of sub-modification within an existing modification structure may significantly increase the logical complexity of the nominal group, which will in turn contribute to the overall complexity of the text.

3.4 Case Study

In the previous sections, I have explored the logical resources of the nominal group in Chinese. It is important that the theoretical description can be applied to the practical text analysis. For this purpose, a case study will be presented in this section.

The nominal groups will be extracted from two texts, a written speech and a school regulation. The context information for the texts is presented below (see Table 3.7):

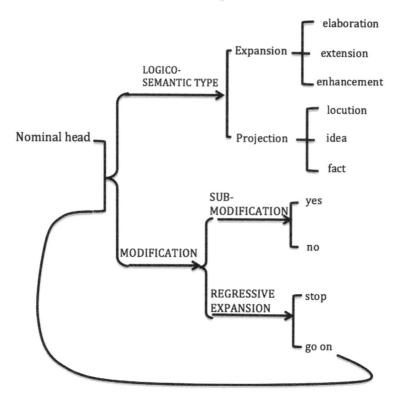

Fig. 3.1 Logical system of modification for the nominal group

Based on the contextual information, it is reasonable to assume that Text 1 is more accessible than Text 2 in terms of logical complexity, as the former is delivered orally to school-aged audience, whereas the latter is in writing for educated adults. With such contextual difference in mind, it would be interesting to investigate how the use of nominal group will contribute to the achievement of the difference.

Altogether 81 nominal groups (including nominal group complex) are extracted from Texts 1 and 71 from Text 2. Then, they are analysed and compared in terms of logical complexity—mainly four aspects are examined: in terms of group complexity, nominal groups are identified either as nominal group complex or nominal group simplex; and in terms of the complexity in nominal group simplexes, the analysis focuses on whether sub-modification exists in the structure, the total number of modifying elements in a nominal group, and whether a down-ranked clause is used as a modifying element. The counts and percentages for each category are listed in the table (see Table 3.8):

As Table 3.8 demonstrates, both texts show some similar tendencies in the use of nominal groups. For example, most of the nominal groups are group simplexes and nominal group complexes only make a very small proportion of the total instances, the case of which is found in both texts. Also, in terms of modification in the nominal

Table 3.7 Context of Texts 1 and 2

	Text 1 不骂人，不打架 No brawls, no fights	Text 2 关于处置学生打架斗殴等事件的应急预案 Plan for dealing with school fights
Field	The socio-semiotic function of this text is recommending and the situation type is that of advice. The domain is concrete and concerned with advising audience not to brawl or fight with others at school	The socio-semiotic function of this text is enabling and the situation type is that of regulation. The domain is concrete and concerned with what teachers must do in dealing with school fights
Tenor	The institutional roles are a teacher to the primary school students; an adult to children (generally under 12). The speech was delivered on campus during school hours. The speaker acts as an adviser with authority, providing guidance to the young audience on what can be done and what cannot be done	The institutional roles are the school administration committee to the primary school teachers; a policy-making authority to its staff members. The school administrative committee is in a position of power, which develops the regulation for the teachers to follow in dealing with incidents of school fights. Both the writer and the readers are adults
Mode	The text is monologic, spoken and constitutive of its contextual situation	The text is monologic, written and constitutive of its contextual situation

Table 3.8 Logical complexity of Texts 1 and 2

			Text 1 Number of instances/total (%)	Text 2 Number of instances/total (%)
Nominal group complex			7/81 (8.6)	9/71 (12.7)
Nominal Simplex	Sub-modification (incl. embedded clause)		0/74 (0%)	7/62 (11.3)
	Number of modifiers	Without modification (head noun only)	33/74 (44.6)	19/62 (30.6)
		1 modifier	35/74 (47.3)	39/62 (62.9)
		2 modifiers	3/74 (4.1)	4/62 (6.5)
		> 2 modifiers	3/74 (4.1)	0/62 (0)
	Down-ranked clause (embedded clause) as a modifier		6/74 (8.1)	8/62 (12.9)

group simplexes, the predominant types are simple nominal groups with either one modifying element or without a modifier at all—again, such distribution patterns apply to both texts. Nominal groups with two or more modifying elements only make a small proportion of the total cases in both texts. This echoes the point that is presented in Sect. 3.3: although in theory the logical system of MODIFICATION enables a nominal group to expand repeatedly, in practice it is not common to find a long recurrent modification structure in a nominal group. In the case of Chinese nominal groups, it seems that a structure with more than two modifiers could become marked. Given that the two texts are supposed to serve two highly different groups of audience and are delivered in different modes, the similarities found here indicate that the logical complexity of a text cannot be effectively demonstrated by the nominal group complexing status and the number of modifications in the nominal groups. Similarly, the use of down-ranked clauses as a modifier in a nominal group may not be an effective indicator for logical complexity, either. As Table 3.8 shows, there is not a noticeable difference between the two texts in the use of embedded clauses as modifiers, though Text 2 contains slightly more nominal groups that are modified by rank-shifted clauses than Text 1.

Despite the similarities found in the use of nominal groups in the two texts, some differences are worth noting. The two texts are found to be noticeably different in the use of sub-modification in nominal groups. As Table 3.8 shows, no sub-modification structures are found in the nominal groups used in Text 1, which is a spoken text delivered to primary school children. In comparison, there are seven nominal groups in Text 2 that have sub-modification in the structure. Example:

Example 44

Nominal groups with sub-modification in Text 2

根据我校的安全保卫工作条例

Literal translation: According to *our school's safety and security work regulation*
Translation: According to *the school's regulation on safety and security work*

我校的	安全	保卫	工作	条例
Our school's	Safety	Security	Work	Regulation
γ	β			α
	ββ		βα	
	ββ 1	ββ 2		

Note that in Example 44, another nominal group structure is embedded in the overall structure: the head 条例 (regulation) is modified by 工作 (work), which is in turn modified by 安全 (safety) and 保卫 (security) through sub-modification.

We have found that there are a few instances where an embedded clause functions as a modifier to the Head, which seems to be similar in both texts. However, some further examination shows that, although both texts use rank-shifted clauses as modifiers in nominal groups, the levels of complexity are different. In Text 1, none of these nominal groups has sub-modification in the structure and the embedded clauses are generally simple clauses functioning a modifier without further embedding to the Head. Example:

Example 45

Nominal group with embedded clause in Text 1

一个[[爱骂人‖爱打架]]的同学不可能受到大家的尊敬和喜爱

A student [[who verbally and physically abuses people]] will not be respected or liked by others.

In comparison, in Text 2, among the eight nominal groups with embedded clauses, four of these instances have further embedding in the embedded structure. Examples:

Example 46

nominal groups with embedded clause with further embedding in Text 2

Example 46a

对[[有 [[发生打架斗殴]]可能]]的苗头要及时报告.

Regarding signs [[showing the possibility [[that fighting might happen]]]], one must report immediately.

Example 46b

对校园发生打架斗殴现象的安全应急预案进行修改.

to amend the security emergency plan [regarding the phenomenon of [fighting happening on campus]]

It has been discussed in Sect. "Nominal Groups with Head and Thing Not Conflated" that when more than one layer of embedding are found in the modification structure, as demonstrated in Examples 46a and 46b, it is in fact a kind of sub-modification, as the embedding at the lower level sub-modifies an element in the higher-level embedding. Based on the discussion so far, it seems that sub-modification is a strong indicator of the logical complexity of a nominal group, which in turn contributes to the complexity of a text.

To sum up, this case study has provided some implications on the contributions of the nominal groups to the overall complexity of a text. Based on the discussion, I would like to present the following hypotheses, which could be tested by future projects based on a larger sample size. First of all, nominal group complexity, that is, whether to develop a simplex or a complex of nominal group, does not guarantee an impact on the complexity of the logical structure of a nominal group. In other words, from a logical perspective, a nominal group complex may not necessarily be more complicated than a nominal group simplex. Secondly, the number of modifiers to the nominal Head also has limited impact on the logical complexity. In other words, one cannot rely on the number of modifying elements in a nominal group to effectively evaluate the logical complexity, as more modifiers do not guarantee increased complexity of the nominal group. Similarly, the use of an embedded clause as a modifier could be found in texts of varying complexity, and therefore is not an identifying feature exclusive to the syntactically complex texts. Last but not least, sub-modification is an important indicator when a nominal group is structurally complicated. To put it in another way, sub-modification is closely related to the logical complexity of a nominal group, making it less likely to feature in a syntactically simple text. And, this complexity could be further enhanced when an embedded clause is used in the sub-modification structure. To test the validity of the above statements, studies involving experiments might be needed to assess the impact of various logical features of the nominal groups on the overall syntactic complexity of a text.

3.5 Summary

In this chapter, the logical resources of Chinese nominal group are investigated in four aspects. On group complexity, both nominal group complex and simplex are discussed. On tactic relations, the relationship between each group within a complex, and the relationship between each modifier and the nominal Head within a simplex are examined. On logico-semantic relations, I have explored the relationship between each group within a nominal group complex, and between each modifier and the Head in a simplex. Based on the above discussion, the complexity of a simple nominal group is investigated in terms of three logical features: nominal groups with sub-modification, nominal groups with Head and Thing not conflated and nominal groups modified by embedded clauses. The logical system of MODIFICATION is presented in Sect. 3.3, which summarises all the potential logical choices to realise a nominal group. Finally, a case study is conducted to illustrate how different logical selections may contribute to the complexity of a nominal group, thus increase the complexity of a text in general.

References

Halliday MAK, Matthiessen C (1999) Construing experience through meaning. Cassell, New York
Halliday MAK, Matthiessen CMIM (2014) Halliday's introduction to functional grammar. Routledge, London

Chapter 4
Experiential Resources of Chinese Nominal Groups

4.1 Introduction

In the previous chapter, I have explored one part of the ideational resources, the logical resources of the Chinese nominal group. In this chapter, I will continue to investigate the other part of the ideational resources, namely the experiential resources of the Chinese nominal group. Compared with the logical description, which focuses on the relationship between each element within the group, an experiential account aims to look at how the nominal group provides resources to construe participant roles in a human experience.

The description in this chapter will be unfolded in a few steps. First, the experiential structure of the nominal group will be presented in Sect. 4.2, where each functional element on the structure will be introduced and be given an overview. Then in Sect. 4.3, the most important system in this dimension, the System of THING TYPE, will be presented and discussed, which will be followed by an investigation of its subordinating systems in Sects. 4.4–4.7, covering Classifiers, Epithets, Qualifiers and Measure. Finally, a case study will be presented in Sect. 4.8, after the general discussion of the experiential resources, to illustrate how the description can be applied in text analysis.

4.2 Experiential Structure of the Chinese Nominal Group

I have discussed in Chap. 3 that a nominal group can be viewed logically as a repeatable expansion of the nominal head through modification. In comparison, when the same nominal group is viewed through an experiential lens, it becomes a configuration of functional elements, representing different experiential aspects of the Thing. I can use an example to illustrate the experiential structure of a Chinese nominal group.

© Springer Nature Singapore Pte Ltd. 2022
J. Fang, *A Systemic Functional Grammar of Chinese Nominal Groups*,
The M.A.K. Halliday Library Functional Linguistics Series,
https://doi.org/10.1007/978-981-19-4009-5_4

As the example shows, from an experiential perspective, a nominal group is no longer viewed as an expansion of the head, but a configuration of functional elements representing different aspects of the Thing, in terms of its classification, its quality and attribute, its quantity and its position in the referential space, which all help construe participant roles in an experiential process.

If one compares the experiential structure of the Chinese nominal group with its English counterpart, it becomes obvious that the two share many common features. For example, in terms of realisation, both use the same lexical resources: The Thing and the Classifier are typically realised by nouns, the Epithet by adjectives and the Qualifiers typically by rank-shifted clauses or groups. However, there are also two significant differences between the two. One is a structural difference: all the functional elements in the experiential structure of the Chinese nominal group, including the Qualifier, come before the Thing; whereas in English, a Qualifier may come on the either side of the Thing in the structure. The other difference is that, in Chinese, the Measure becomes compulsory when a non-possessive Deictic and/or a Numerative is selected; whereas in English there is no such an equivalent case and measure words are not recognised as a distinct functional category.

In the following two sections, I will interpret the experiential structure from two perspectives: first, some general tendencies of the functional elements along the structure will be discussed in Sect. 4.2.1; and then an overview of the metafunctional potential of each element will be given in Sect. 4.2.2.

4.2.1 Experiential Structure: Some General Tendencies

As shown by the example in Table 4.1, in a Chinese nominal group, there can be as many as 7 types of functional elements in the experiential structure: Thing, Classifier, Epithet, Measure, Numerative, Deictic and Qualifier. The Thing represents the primary class of experience. Selections can then move through sub-classification and epithets, e.g. car, sedan car, blue sedan, a blue sedan, this blue sedan and so on. As it moves on, the properties become more instantial. This is also a move in stability through time, from properties that are stable through time to properties that are more transient (see Fig. 4.1).

Table 4.1 Experiential structure of a Chinese nominal group

我买	的	这	一	辆	蓝色	的	轿	车
wǒ mǎi	de	zhe	yī	liàng	lánsè	de	jiào	chē
I buy		this	one	Measure	blue		sedan	car
Qualifier	de	Deictic	Numerative	Measure	Epithet	de	Classifier	Thing
Rank-shifted clause	SUB	Determiner	Numeral	MEA	Adjective	SUB	Noun	Noun
This blue sedan that I bought								

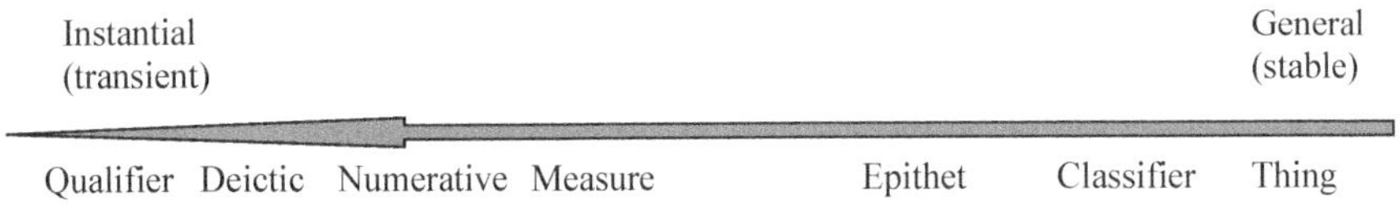

Instantial   General
(transient)   (stable)

Qualifier Deictic Numerative Measure   Epithet   Classifier   Thing

Fig. 4.1 Experiential move of nominal group in time and space

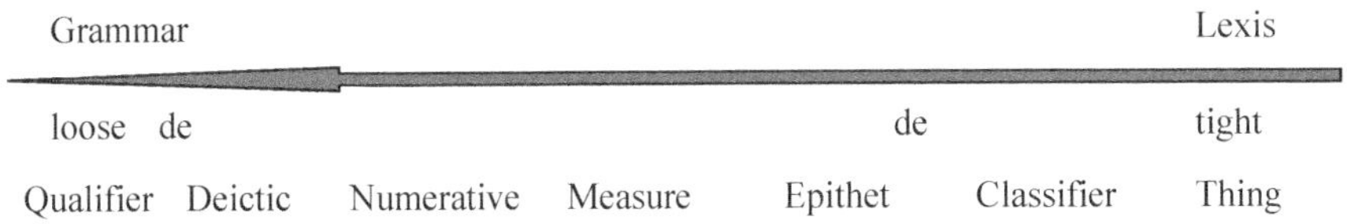

Grammar   Lexis

loose   de   de   tight

Qualifier Deictic   Numerative   Measure   Epithet   Classifier   Thing

Fig. 4.2 Move from lexis to grammar

The organisation of the functional elements of a Chinese nominal group also shows another move, the move from lexis to grammar: as the experiential structure of the nominal group develops, it tends to depend more on the grammatical organisation of the structure. This also indicates the level of integration of the each functional element with the Thing, and 的 (*de*), a hypotactic structural marker, is an important indicator on this move. In an unmarked structure of a nominal group in Chinese, *de* usually follows Qualifier and sometimes if the properties that an epithet represents are transient and loosely related to the Thing, a *de* may also be used between the Thing and the Epithet or even the Classifier. On the other hand, if the qualities being construed represent some subclasses of the Thing, the functional element construing these qualities is usually more integrated with the Thing and the structural organisation tends to be lexical (see Fig. 4.2). For example, in Chinese the boundary between a compound noun and a nominal group sometimes can be ambiguous, as the former usually can be interpreted as the latter of a structure of Classifier + Thing. So 轿车 (*sedan car*) can either be interpreted as a nominal group of Classifier (*sedan*) + Thing (*car*), or a compound noun 轿 (*sedan*) + 车 (*car*). It is interesting to note that *de* cannot be used in a combination of Classifier + Thing.

4.2.2 Elements of the Experiential Structure: A Metafunctional Overview

I have discussed some general tendencies of the experiential structure of the nominal group, in terms of both the instantiation potential and the lexicogrammatical organisational potential. Before I move on to investigate each functional element in detail, it is necessary to give an overview of each of them in terms of their metafunctional potentials. It is important to note that not all the functional elements on the experiential structure are experiential in character, but all of them are able to be expressed in experiential terms through this structure. The situation is very similar when Halliday and Matthiessen describe English nominal groups. As they have explained, it is a general principle of linguistic structure that it is the experiential meaning that most clearly defines constituents (see further in Halliday and Matthiessen 2004: 328). Therefore, in this book, I will follow the practice by presenting all the functional elements in experiential terms.

The experiential structure of the nominal group has presented a picture different from the logical one: instead of being a univariate structure as interpreted logically, an experiential structure is a highly multivariate one, with each element playing different roles.

The **Thing** represents the most basic experiential class that can be construed as a participant. Semantically speaking, Thing is the core of the nominal group. It is the Thing that gives the group its basic nominal features, such as referentiality, generality and modifiability, etc. With its central status in the nominal group, Thing is significant in all the metafunctional contributions that a nominal group can make. Experientially, it represents the basic experiential class; interpersonally, it enacts attitude and provides person resources as interactant or non-interactant; textually, it presents a discourse referent as identifiable or unidentifiable. The Thing is typically realised by a noun or a pronoun.

The **Classifier** represents the sub-classes of the Thing and is typically realised by a noun. Therefore, experientially speaking, it is a very important resource in construing the specific classes of the Thing. In terms of its textual potential, the Classifier becomes significant when the Thing is elliptical and the Classifier works with some other elements, typically a Deictic and a Measure, to identify a referent. As discussed in the previous section, the Classifier works so closely with the Thing that they are often difficult to be differentiated from compound nouns in Chinese.

The **Epithet** represents the properties of the Thing: these properties can be either non-attitudinal, such as age, colour, size and so on, or attitudinal, such as the mental or emotional state of the Thing. The non-attitudinal properties are highly experiential, which reflect the material features of a thing, whereas the attitudinal ones are highly interpersonal, as they enact the speaker's attitude. Therefore, the Epithet is the important resource for making both experiential and interpersonal meanings, and it is typically realised by adjectives.

The **Qualifier** represents the qualifications of the Thing, which are highly instantial and transient in time and space. The Qualifier is significant in providing both experiential and textual resources. Experientially, the Qualifier helps to construe the participant by providing a specific and instantial experience in relation to the Thing. Textually, the Qualifier is important in managing the flow of information as the text unfolds. In terms of realisation, Qualifiers in Chinese, same as English, are rank-shifted grammatical units which function at the group rank, such as adverbial groups, prepositional phrases, embedded clauses and even nominal groups.

The **Measure**, similar to the Classifier, represents the subclasses of the Thing, which is typically realised by measure words. The major difference between the two lies in the motives behind these classifications. The Classifier helps to define the basic qualities of the Thing through classification, whereas the Measure uses classification to either identify or quantify the Thing (or both). Due to this difference, the qualities represented by the Classifier are generally more stable in time than the

Table 4.2 Functional elements across metafunctions

Metafunction	System	Functional element
Experiential	THING TYPE	Thing
	EPITHESIS	Epithet
	CLASSIFICATION	Classifier
	QUALIFICATION	Qualifier
	MEASURE	Measure
Interpersonal	ATTITUDE	Epithet, Thing
	NOMINAL MOOD	Thing
	PERSON	Thing, Deictic
Textual	DETERMINATION	Deictic, Thing
	NUMERATION	Numerative, Measure

When a word represents the name of a functional term, it is an SFL tradition to capitalise the first letter of the word

Measure. Functionally speaking, the Measure is important in terms of both experiential and textual functional potentials. It is also worth noting that the Measure, as a separate functional element in the Chinese nominal group, has no equivalent status in English, as the latter has rich grammar resources to distinguish the countable from the uncountable, and therefore makes the use of measure words optional.

The **Numerative** represents the quantitative property of the Thing. The nature of the qualities it represents has decided that it is not significant in its experiential functional potential. Rather, the Numerative is more concerned with instantial features of the Thing, and therefore has great textual functional potential. The Numerative can be realised by a numeral or an ordinal.

The **Deictic** represents the identifiability of the Thing in the referential space. As this is concerned with the instantial features of the Thing, the Deictic is textual in character. In terms of realisation, the Deictic is realised by a determiner.

Table 4.2 lists all the major metafunctional roles that a functional element plays based on the discussions above, and the table also presents the potential systems for which these elements provide metafunctional resources.

In the following sections, five functional elements with significant experiential functional potential (i.e. Thing, Classifier, Epithet, Qualifier and Measure), will be investigated and relevant systems will be presented.

4.3 Thing

This section focuses on the experiential resources of the Thing. I will first introduce Halliday and McDonald's TRANSITIVITY system of Chinese, based on which the System of THING TYPE will be presented in Sect. 4.3.1. Based on the System of THING TYPE, detailed discussion of each major selection on the system will be presented (see Sects. 4.3.2 and 4.3.3).

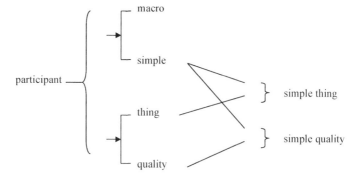

Fig. 4.3 Preliminary taxonomy of participants

4.3.1   System of THING TYPE

From an experiential perspective, a nominal group is significant in that it provides resources for construing participant, which is one of the central elements in modelling our experience of the world. When it comes to the interpretation of the lexicogrammatical system of THING TYPE, it is necessary to look at the potential of the Thing in construing participant roles from both the greater and the local environment: the semantic environment where participant functions as an element of a phenomenon, and the clause environment where the Thing construes different types of participant roles in lexicogrammar.

In semantics, Thing has been widely recognised as having two fundamental features: its persistence through time and its complexity in representing experience (Halliday and Matthiessen 1999). These two inherent features of the Thing bring grammatical implications. On the one hand, with its stability in time, Thing, which functions in a nominal group, construes participant roles. This also means that it can be established and identified in referential space. On the other hand, its experiential complexity means that Thing can be further elaborated into various categories and represent a participant carrying various qualities—in grammar this is achieved through a modification structure in a nominal group.

The examination of the semantic background of the Thing will be based on the work of Halliday and Matthiessen (1999), where they explore how different kinds of experiences are construed as meaning. At the level of semantics, the preliminary taxonomic cut is shown in Fig. 4.3 (Halliday and Matthiessen 1999: 182).[1] It is important to note that, although Halliday and Matthiessen's work is based on their observation of English, this basic taxonomy at semantics also applies to Chinese.

The preliminary groups of participants in Fig. 4.3 provide a general direction to the preliminary categories of the Thing type in lexicogrammar: **simple things** are congruently realised by the nominal in grammar, and **metaphorical things**, which are nominalised processes and qualities, are realised as the Thing through grammatical metaphor.

The examination of the lexicogrammatical environment will focus on the TRAN-SITIVITY system, where the nominal group provides resources to construe participant roles in a clause. There have been some descriptions of the system network of TRANSITIVITY in Chinese, such as McDonald (1998), Li (2003, 2007) and Halliday and McDonald (2004). The present study will adopt Halliday and McDonald's (2004) description as a basis to present the types of participant roles. Figure 4.4 shows a simplified system network of TRANSITIVITY with the presence of different types of participant (adapted from Halliday and McDonald 2004: 386).[2]

As shown in Fig. 4.4, the overall picture of the Chinese process types is very similar to English (cf. Halliday and Matthiessen 2014). Processes are categorised as doing, sensing, saying and being, with the different participant roles for each category. When nominal group is viewed experientially as the major resource for construing participant roles, it is essential, in the development of the system of THING TYPE, to look at the general potential of the Thing in construing different participant roles in relation to each type of process.

Figure 4.5 presents a basic system of THING TYPE, which draws upon and reflects the semantic and lexicogrammatical environment where the Thing functions.

The system of THING TYPE in Fig. 4.5 presents the selections in lexicogrammar to realise the functional potential of the Thing. Mainly five factors are taken into account in the development of the system: the metaphoric propensity of the noun, animacy, modifiability, generality and measurability.

The **metaphoric propensity** is reflected at the most basic level of categorisation of the Thing: a nominal is construed either congruently as the simple thing, or as metaphorically nominalised processes and qualities. In other words, Thing is first categorised in terms of its potential for construing nominalised processes and qualities through grammatical metaphor. This categorisation corresponds to the preliminary taxonomy of participants in semantics (cf. Fig. 4.3), with simple things being congruently realised by nouns and metaphorical things being realised through grammatical metaphor.

In terms of **animacy**, the congruent Thing can be further categorised as conscious and non-conscious. This distinction reflects the likelihood of anything being construed experientially as a senser or a sayer in a mental or a verbal process (cf. Fig. 4.4), as in reality only a conscious being can sense and/or say.

The **modifiability** of the Thing can be considered as a cline: on the one end, there are things that can be easily modified in terms of their objective qualities (such as colour, shape, make, size) as well as subjective qualities (such as moral judgement and so on); on the other end, there are things that can only be modified in the referential space through Measure, Deictic and so on, such as metaphorical things.

The **generality** of the Thing is reflected on the system in a linear manner: from the most general class on the left to the most specific on the right. Using lexical

---

[2] Copyright © 2004 from Halliday and McDonald (2004). Reproduced by permission of John Benjamin Publishing Company.

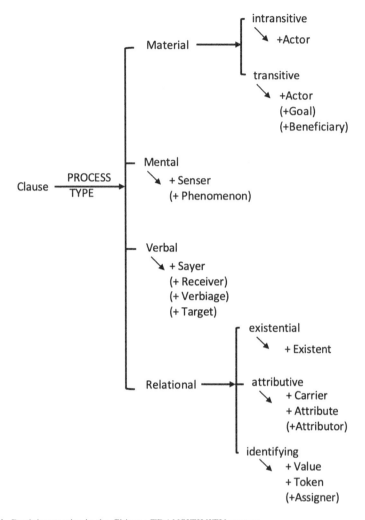

Fig. 4.4 Participant roles in the Chinese TRANSITIVITY system

resources, the system can be potentially developed further towards the right end as lexical taxonomy. So the system shown in Fig. 4.5 is mainly a grammatical one, which can be developed further towards the lexical end. For instance, 'human' can be further categorised in terms of gender, age, race and so on; 'object' can be further categorised in terms of function, origin, mobility and so on. With lexical resources, there are obviously many ways of grouping things into further categories. Halliday and Matthiessen (1999) have a very straightforward view of this:

> … lexically construed folk and scientific taxonomies do not start at the highest degree of generality in delicacy; they are ordered in delicacy after those systems that are construed grammatically. (p. 86)

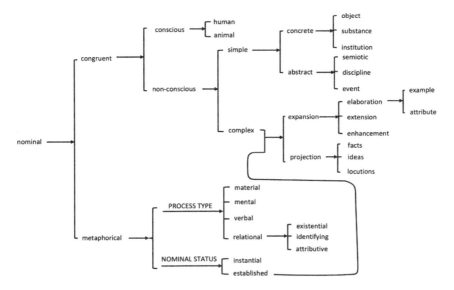

Fig. 4.5 System of THING TYPE

Figure 4.6 shows the cline of generality as the system of THING TYPE develops. As can be seen, the move from the 'general' end to the 'delicate' end also represents the move from the 'grammar' system to the 'lexis' system. When reflected on the system of THING TYPE, it means that the general classes on the left-hand side represent the grammatical categorisation, whereas the more specific classes on the right-hand side represent the lexical taxonomic categorisation. However, it is important to stress that, in the present study, the detailed exploration of this system focuses on the left end, that is, the categorisation in terms of grammatical features.

The **measurability** of the Thing is another important principle reflected in the categorisation. In Chinese, things generally get assigned to a measure type according to various criteria and the measurable potential depends on the properties embodied by each thing type. For example, simple concrete things can be measured according to their elaborating and extending potentials, in such terms as size, shape, state, repository manner (i.e. how they are packed into one) and so on. Nominalised processes, in comparison, can be measured according to their potential to be enhanced, in such terms as time, location, frequency and manner.

In the following sections, I will go through the special grammatical features of each major category on the system of THING TYPE, with examples presented where appropriate.

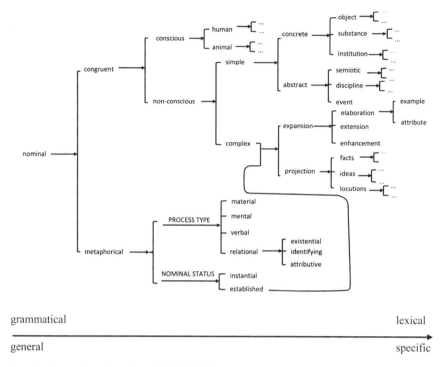

Fig. 4.6 Generality cline of the THING TYPE system

4.3.2 The Congruent Thing

Things are grouped as congruent in terms of their grammatical realisation. The congruent Thing bears the inherent characteristics that people recognise as things, such as the stability in time and space, the tendency to be elaborated into sub-categories according to its qualities and so on. In semantics, they represent what Halliday and Matthiessen term as 'simple things' (Halliday and Matthiessen 1999). Congruent Things are either conscious or non-conscious.

4.3.2.1 The Conscious Thing

Conscious Things are prototypically human, as in reality only human beings can sense and say through language. This feature is recognised as a category in grammar because it determines the roles of senser and sayer in mental and verbal processes. The other selection under this category is animal. Animals, higher animals in particular, are often treated as conscious beings which can construe physiological or psycho-logical behaviours like human. However, animals cannot construe the role of sayer in a verbal process unless they are personified. Human and animal are recognised as two distinct sub-categories of 'conscious Things' also because in lexicogrammar they are represented in different patterns. For example, to classify a conscious being in terms of gender in Chinese, one has to first make a selection between human and animal, as specific lexical items are used as classifiers to distinguish them (男 male or 女 female for human; 公/雄 male [animal]/male [insect] or 母/雌 female [animal]/female [insect] for non-human). Similarly, in the referential space, specific pronouns are used to refer to a human and a non-human (他/她 he/she for human; 它 it for non-human). It is interesting to note that, in terms of reference, a human Thing is more strictly distinguished from an animal Thing in Chinese than in English, as higher animals are often referred to as he/she in the latter, which is less common in Chinese.

The selections under 'human' and 'animal' can be further developed in lexical taxonomy. There are mainly two points worth noting on the potential of further distinctions under these two sub-categories.

Firstly, the domain of 'human' presents more potential for further categorisations than the domain of 'animal'. This is because 'human' takes on both natural and social roles, which gives human much more abundant qualities to define and distinguish himself in language. In contrast, an animal does not take any social roles, at least from the human's perspective, which limits its potential for further distinctions. For example, apart from age, gender and some other general physiological features, human beings can also be further distinguished by profession (such as 医生 doctor, 小偷 thief, 士兵 soldier), moral judgement (such as 好人 good man, 坏蛋 bastard, 分子 member of a particular group) and so on. These distinctions by social functions are recognisable in lexicogrammar as they provide distinct potentials for elaboration. Table 4.3 presents the examples of different measure words used to modify different 'humans' in terms of their professions.

Secondly, compared with English, the lexical resources to be used for further distinction of conscious beings in Chinese is rather limited. It is typical in Chinese to use a general noun to refer to a conscious being and rely heavily on the grammatical resources, rather than lexical resources, to further distinguish it. This is especially significant in presenting an animal. For example, English has separate lexical items to

Table 4.3 Further distinction of 'human' in configuration with Measure

		Human			
		Profession (examples)			
		医生 (doctor)	士兵 (soldier)	小偷 (thief)	学生 (student)
Measure	Singular	个 (neutral), 位 (honorific)	个	个	个
	Plural	群 (group, neutral)	群 (group, neutral), 列 (line, neutral), 队 (team, neutral), 组 (group, neutral)	群 (group, neutral), 伙 (group, negative), 窝 (den, negative), 帮 (gang, negative)	群 (group, neutral), 班 (class, neutral), 队 (team, neutral), 组 (group, neutral)

distinguish dogs in terms of gender, age, breeding and so on (such as bitch, puppy and poodle). In contrast, the equivalent distinctions are realised in Chinese by different classifiers modifying the general name of dog 狗 *dog* (such as 母狗 'female dog' *bitch*, 猎犬 'hunting dog' *hound*, 杂种狗 'cross-bred dog' *mongrel*). In fact, this difference has been found as applicable to the general picture of construing Things (Halliday and Matthiessen 1999):

> Likewise lexically, at least in construing participants, it is typical for Chinese to use a general term where the more specific one, even if relevant, is rendered unnecessary by the context. (p. 300)

4.3.2.2   The Non-conscious Thing

Non-conscious Things include all the other congruent Things that are neither human nor animal. It is important to emphasise that this is a category under 'congruent Things'. Although 'metaphorical Things' are also non-conscious in nature, they are recognised as a distinct category in terms of different lexicogrammatical realisations. In contrast, the non-conscious Things under this lexicogrammatical category are naturally (i.e. congruently) realised as nominals.

The non-conscious Thing can be further categorised into two groups: **simple Things** and **complex Things**. The latter refers to an entity embodying either an expansion or a projection, whereas the former includes all the other non-conscious Things. They are recognised as two distinct categories because the distinction brings different grammatical potentials. For example, with a thing of elaboration or extension, a nominal group can develop into a structure where Head and Thing are not conflated (see discussion in Section "Nominal Groups with Head and Thing Not Conflated"). With the Thing of enhancement, the nominal group is likely to be modified by a down-ranked embedded clause or an embedded phrase, but unlikely to be modified by an epithet. In comparison, the general modification potential by an epithet is much higher in the case of nominal groups with simple Things. Detailed exploration of the two categories under non-conscious things, namely simple things and complex things, will be presented in the following sub-sections.

The Simple Thing

Simple Things are categorised as either concrete or abstract. This categorisation is based on the modifiability of the Thing in terms of classification, epithesis, measure and deicticity. Table 4.4 lists the general modifying potential of each sub-category of the simple Thing based on the observation of the corpus. Generally speaking, concrete Things demonstrate a higher modifiability than abstract Things, which reflects the tendency that concrete Things tend to have more experiential qualities that expands the modification potential. In the following discussion, I will discuss the major grammatical characteristics of each sub-category based on the values listed in Table 4.4.

Table 4.4 Simple things and modification potential

| | | Measure | | Classifier | Epithet | | Deictic | | |
		个/种 Item/type	Other		Objective	Subjective	Post-deictic	Possessive	Demonstrative
Concrete	Object	H	H	H	H	L	H	H	H
	Substance	L	H	H	H	L	H	L	H
	Institution	H	H	H	L	L	H	H	H
Abstract	Semiotic	L	H	H	L	H	H	H	H
	Discipline	L	L	H	L	L	L	L	L
	Event	H	H	H	L	H	H	L	H

H: high potential; L: low potential

Concrete: object

A nominal group with an object Thing as the Head has the best modification potential, compared with any other type of Things. The Thing in this category can be measured according to various criteria in terms of quantity/type (个/种), shape, size, state, repository manner and so on, which reflect the semantic features embodied by an object thing: 一双鞋 *a pair of shoes*, 一本书 *a volume of book*, 一张桌子 *a spread of desk*, 一捆柴 *a bundle of firewood*. Things of this type also have good potential to be modified by an epithet, representing objective properties of the thing, as in: 一本新书 *a volume of new book*, 一张旧书桌 *a spread of old desk*, 一束美丽的鲜花 *a bunch of beautiful flowers*. It is important to point out that, although object things tend to bear objective quality in nature, sometimes these objective qualities may be used to enact attitude and therefore become significant in terms of interpersonal meanings. Examples: 一瓶廉价香水 *a bottle of cheap perfume*, 一双臭袜子 *a pair of stinky socks*. Here the epithets are used to modify the object things to represent their objective qualities: in terms of price and in terms of smell. However, both could be in effect very judgemental because these objective qualities have been generally considered as undesirable. Therefore, it is important to explore the motif of using these epithets: are they to represent the qualities of a thing or to enact an attitude, or both? 一双臭袜子 *a pair of stinky socks* in Chinese may not necessarily be stinky in reality, as the Chinese speakers could use such nominal group to express a negative judgement about the person wearing these socks. More discussion on the metaphorical use of objective epithet will be presented in Chap. 5.

In terms of classification, an object thing can be classified in various terms, such as make, function, time and so on: 木桌 *wood desk*, 课桌 *class desk*, 现代家具 *modern furniture*, 古典家具 *classic furniture*. In the referential space, an object thing can be modified by either type of deictic: 我的书桌 *my desk* (personal), 这张报纸 *this newspaper* (demonstrative). In general, a nominal group with an object Thing has a very good potential to be modified in various terms to present its experiential aspects.

Concrete: substance

The Thing of substance represents the material matter that a simple thing consists of. It is recognised as a category on the system of THING TYPE because this type of Things shows a different modification potential from an object Thing. For measure, the Thing of substance cannot be measured in terms of quantity (个, *item*), as a substance can hardly be individuated. They are similar to the set of Things being realised by nouns recognised as mass in English grammar. However, Things of substance type in Chinese can be measured in many other terms: time 一阵风 *a period of wind*, shape 一朵云 *a flower of cloud*, repository 一盆水 *a bowl of water*, which reflects the rich experiential potential of the substance Things. Same as the object Things, a substance Thing usually can be modified by an epithet representing its object quality: 一阵冷风

a period of cold wind, 一朵白云 *a flower of white cloud*, 一盆脏水 *a bowl of dirty water*. In classification, the substance Thing can be classified in terms of various scientific disciplines: 化学气体 *chemical gas*, 地下水 *underground water*. In the referential space, a nominal group with a substance Thing cannot be modified by a personal deictic, but can be generally referred with the use of a demonstrative. On the whole, the modification potential of a substance is not as good as an object.

Concrete: institution

Things of institution type are recognised as a category because, unlike other simple Things, the institution Thing can project in a mental or a verbal process, where they are construed as a collection of conscious members who can think and say collectively. Examples:

Example 1
Institution Thing construed as 'sayer' in a verbal process
该医院表示已暂停心脏病外科手术, 正在查找原因。
The hospital said that all the cardiological surgeries had been suspended and they were carrying out an investigation into the cause.

Example 2
Institution Thing construed as 'senser' in a mental process
多数学校认为 "早恋" 不光彩。
Many schools believe that 'puppy love' is disgraceful.

The institution Thing can be measured in terms of quantity as it is often considered as a unit. When construed as such, it is often modified by an Epithet representing an objective quality of the institution, such as size, outlook and so on. In comparison, when construed as a collection of human beings, it can be modified by an Epithet to enact attitude, and interestingly many of such subjective qualities represent the perception of human participants. Examples:

Example 3
记者卧底黑心医院曝光医疗器械利益链。
A journalist worked undercover in a black-hearted hospital to uncover the chain of interests in the medical equipment.

Example 4
南海实验小学是当地小有名气的贵族学校。
Nanhai Experiment Primary School is an elite school with some local fame.

In terms of classification and deictic, institution things have a good potential to be modified in various terms. Examples:

Example 5
一所希望工程小学
A Project-hope primary school

Example 6
三甲医院
Level A Grade III hospitals

Abstract

Abstract Things have no material extension in space, but share the general lexicogrammatical features with the concrete Things, as both are simple Things: they both are congruently realised by nouns. Abstract Things can be further categorised into semiotics, discipline and names of event. Generally speaking, abstract Things demonstrate less modification potential compared to concrete Things.

Abstract: semiotics

In semantics, semiotic Things refer to the signs and symbols used to create meanings and construe experiences. In lexicogrammar, they are recognised as either simple semiotic Things which cannot be modified by an embedded projection, or complex semiotic Things which can. A simple semiotic Thing typically functions as token in an identifying relational clause, which is easy to understand since semiotics in nature are used to identify meanings and content. For example:

Example 7
这首古诗向我们展示了一幅鲜活的牧童晚归休憩图。
This ancient poem depicts a vivid picture of a shepherd boy coming home late.

Example 8
这支舞蹈展现的是一群壮族姑娘在茶山上采茶, 劳作的情景, 表达丰收的喜悦。
This dance presents the scene of a group of Zhuang girls picking tea leaves on the mountain, which aims to express people's joy of harvest.

Sometimes a simple semiotic thing is personified as a conscious participant to construe a verbal process which often projects. Examples:

Example 9
这篇文章指出, 议论文写作有常见的三大问题。
This article points out that there are three common problems encountered in argumentative essay writing.

Example 10
诊断书说, 他膝关节有少量积水。
The diagnosis record says that there is a small amount of hydrops in his knee joint.

A simple semiotic Thing can be measured in terms of quantity as well as other aspects. The nature of semiotic Things has determined their unseparatable relations with human beings, as mainly human beings create and use semiotics to construe experience. Therefore, the Epithets modifying a semiotic Thing can represent both objective and subjective qualities: 一首长诗 *a long poem* (objective), 一部无聊的电影 *a boring movie* (subjective). In terms of classification and deictic, a simple semiotic Thing has a good potential to be modified. Examples:

Example 11
他为大家带来了一首忧伤的情歌。
He brought a sad love song to us.

Example 12
这部长篇历史小说将在两岸同步发行。
This long historical novel will be released at the same time on both sides of the Strait.

Abstract: discipline

Names of disciplines are recognised as a separate category because this type of Things has the least modification potential compared with all the other simple Things. Representing a general name of a range of learning or instruction, names of disciplines can hardly be modified in terms of Measure or Epithet. However, it can still be classified in terms of the sub-systematic features within the discipline: 高等数学 *higher mathematics*, 现代经济学 *modern economics*, 古代历史 *ancient history*. In the referential space, names of disciplines cannot be identified as a specific referent, as they often are referred to as something in general. Therefore, names of disciplines can hardly be modified by a deictic either.

Abstract: event

An event Thing represents a figure that is congruently realised by nouns. This figure may be prototypically configurational, containing participants, process and/or circumstance, but is construed as a Thing in grammar. They are different from metaphorical Things mainly because they are congruently realised by nouns representing happenings and natural phenomena, and they share the basic features with other simple Things in terms of grammatical potential. In terms of measure, nouns of this category have good potential to be measured in terms of circumstantial features, such as location and frequency. Examples:

Example 13
几十年前, 广东沿海发生了一次海啸。
A few decades ago, a (one occurrence of) tsunami took place along the coast of Canton.

Example 14
二战是人类有史以来参战国最多, 涉及地区最广, 人员财产损失最巨大的一场战争。
The WWII is a (a field of) war where most countries took part and most regions got involved and which caused the most devastating loss of lives and properties.

Example 15

汶川地震, 是一场灾难, 更是一次考验。

The Wenchuan Earthquake is both a disaster and test.

The collocation of circumstantial measure words with event nouns reflects the experiential nature of this type of Things, as semantically they are evolved from processes and figures.

Event Things also demonstrate a good modification potential in terms of epithesis, classification and deictic. In fact, many phenomenon Things are highly modifiable compared with the other sub-types of abstract Things. Examples:

Example 16

这是澳门自1968年以来所经历的最猛烈的台风

This is the strongest typhoon that Macau has experienced since 1968.

Example 17

这场罕见的天灾降临在山西。

This (occasion of) rare natural disaster happened in Shanxi.

The complex Thing

Complex Things represent features of either expansion or projection. It is important to note that these features are not construed through the relationship between a head noun and its modifiers. Rather, these features are embodied in the Thing itself: being realised by either a noun of expansion or projection (cf. Sect. 3.2.2.2). Complex Things are considered as a distinct category mainly because they have modification potentials that distinguish them from simple Things. For example, Things of projection generally can be modified by an embedded clause, whereas things of extension can be modified by a nominal group complex. In the following paragraphs, I will discuss each sub-category in detail.

Expansion: elaboration

Elaboration nouns being found in Chinese nominal groups generally fall into two types: nouns that are meant to be exemplified, such as 例子 *example*, 比方 *example*; or nouns that represent the name of general quality of a kind.

An elaboration noun of example is special in that it often signals a relationship of elaboration either between itself and its modifiers, or between a clause which contains it and a clause that comes before and/or after it in the discourse. Examples:

Example 18

可是在这种工房里面, [[生病躺着休养]]的例子是不能任你开的。

But in a workers house as such, an example of [[resting in bed due to illness]] cannot be set easily.

Example 19

‖‖过雪山的时候有过不少这样的例子，‖战士用惊人的毅力支持着自己的生命，‖但是一倒下去‖就再也起不来了。‖‖

‖‖In climbing over the snowy mountains, there were many such <u>examples</u>: ‖the soldiers tried to survive with extraordinary determinations, ‖but could never get up again ‖once they fell. ‖‖

In Example 18, 例子 *example*, a noun of exemplification representing a Thing of elaboration, is modified by a rank-shifted clause (being underlined), which elaborates the meaning of the head in its context by giving a specific example. In Example 19, the last three clauses (as indicated by clause boundaries) elaborate 例子 *example* by giving a general example of the kind. Nouns of exemplification can be modified by an adjective functioning as either a post-Deictic or an Epithet to express the speaker's comment on the Thing in general, such as 一个真实的例子 *a real example*; 一个简单的比方 *a simple example*; 活生生的例子 *a living example*; 打一个特殊的比方 *to give a special example*; etc.

Names of attributes are the other type of elaboration nouns. They represent the general quality of a kind, which is so general that it is treated as an entity. In semantics, qualities characterise things along various parameters (cf. Halliday and Matthiessen 1999). Correspondingly, they are congruently realised by adjectives to modify nouns in lexicogrammar. However, when different parameters of a quality need to be identified as a whole, nominal groups provide resources to name the quality. Things being represented by this type of names are highly abstract because they represent the value of a quality, away from any specific tokens—for instance, 尺寸 *size* is the name of an attribute representing the overall dimension of a thing, and 小 *small* is an elaborate representation of the attribute. From this perspective, names of attributes as a Thing type are very close to metaphorical Thing type. In fact, due to the indeterminacy of language, there are borderline cases which could fall into both categories. However, the two are different in terms of congruency in lexicogrammatical realisation: the former is recognised as a Thing and therefore is congruently realised by nouns, whereas the latter as quality and the congruent form would be adjectives and its nominal status may not be widely recognised.

Nouns of attribute name can be further categorised as 'human-only' and 'other'. The former sub-category refers to the general quality Things relevant to human beings only—the qualities that are used to define 'who you are' in the human society. It is distinguished from 'other' quality Things because it is more likely to be modified by subjective Epithets. Also, all human-related quality Things can be modified by personal determiners. Examples:

Example 20

Personal Deictic + de + Thing
<u>他们的职业</u>令人羡慕。
Their occupations are enviable.

Example 21

Post-Deictic + subjective Epithet + de + Thing

所谓高贵的血统其实是最蒙人的。
The so-called <u>noble lineage</u> is in fact most deceptive.

'Other' represents the more general, objective and material category of this type of Things. In terms of modification, they are mainly different from human-only quality Things in that the potential for them to be modified by a subjective Epithet is limited though possible. More often than not, they are modified by an objective Epithet: 飞快的速度 *fast speed*, 鲜艳的颜色 *bright colours*, 昂贵的价格 *high prices*. But both sub-types of nouns have a good potential to be sub-classified, as they inherently are at the most general end of classification.

In the referential space, both types of quality names can be modified by Deictics, either possessive and/or demonstrative. When being modified by a thing which bears these qualities, these quality kinds are highly elaborative and often come in a structure where Thing and Head are not conflated. Examples:

Example 22
布料的颜色, 品质及价格有很大差别。
The <u>colour, the quality and price</u> of **the clothes** vary widely.

Example 23
受访者的年龄, 婚姻状况, 性别和经济收入都纳入调查范围。
The <u>age, the marital status, gender and income</u> of the **interviewees** are all covered in the survey.

Expansion: extension

Nouns of extension generally can be categorised into three types in Chinese: being construed as parts of a thing, such as 部分 *part*, 成份 *ingredient*, 方面 *aspect*, or as a state of being in a logical relation of an extension between one thing and another, such as 集合 *collection*, 关系 *relation*, 对比 *comparison*, or as a position relative to Thing. Strictly speaking, nouns of extension do not represent a general Thing type unlike those being discussed above; rather, they represent an extension of Things. In grammar of nominal groups, this is reflected by a logical structure where Thing and Head are not conflated with an extension noun as the Head and another type of noun representing Thing (see Section "Nominal Groups with Head and Thing Not Conflated"). Examples:

Example 24
你所了解的只是真实情况的一部分。
What you have known is only **a part of the truth**.

真实	情况	的	一部分
true	situation	de	one part
	Thing		Head

Example 25

但是复杂一些的组合, 比如多项并列成分的组合, <u>多项修饰语与中心语的组合</u>, 有时可能会出现语序不合理的毛病。

However, some complicated combinations, such as the combination of multiple coordinate parts, or the combination <u>between multiple modifiers and the head word</u>, may cause inappropriate word orders.

多项修饰语	与	中心语	的	组合
multiple modifiers	and	the head word	de	combination
Thing 1	Conj	Thing 2	de	Head

When an extension noun construes a part of the Thing, sometimes the structural analysis of the nominal group can be ambiguous, which relies heavily on the context. Examples:

Example 26

一些品牌果汁饮料<u>果汁成分</u>少得可怜。

Fruit drinks of some brands contain very little <u>fruit ingredients</u>.

	果汁	成分
	fruit	ingredients
Interpretation 1	Thing	Head
Interpretation 2	Classifier	Thing/Head

Example 27

随着婴儿的一天天长大, <u>所需的营养成分</u>也日益增多。

As a baby grows, <u>the nutritional ingredients needed</u> also increase.

	所需	营养	成分
	that is needed	nutritional	ingredients
Interpretation 1	Qualifier	Classifier	Thing/Head
Interpretation 2	Qualifier	Thing/Classifier	Head

As Examples 26 and 27 show, sometimes it is difficult to decide if Thing and Head are conflated on the structure when a noun of extension realises the Head. Usually, additional contextual information is needed to help with the analysis.

When an extension noun represents a position relative to Thing, it is construed as a facet. Similar to English (cf. Matthiessen 1995; Halliday and Matthiessen 2014), facet in Chinese is typically realised by nouns, which function as Head in analogous constructions of nominal groups. Therefore, many facet nouns can be regarded as extension of Things and thus fall into this category. Halliday and McDonald name these facet words as 'post-nouns' or 'localiser' indicating relative position (see Halliday and McDonald 2004: 316). Their examples are presented below:

桌子	上
table	on
noun	post-noun
Thing	Head

桌子	的	上面
table	de	topside
noun	de	post-noun
Thing		Head

Compared with their English counterpart, nouns of extension in Chinese are limited both in terms of types and quantity. In English, many nouns used as measure words can be regarded as an extension of Things and therefore fall into this category on the THING TYPE system, as they can be 'transparent' to extend the Thing: 'a cup of strong tea' can be said as 'a strong cup of tea' (see further in Matthiessen 1995: 676). However, measure words in Chinese are more of a separate grammatical category, which are not used to realise Thing and are not as 'transparent' as in English: 一杯浓茶 *a cup of strong tea* cannot be transferred to 一浓杯茶 *a strong cup of tea**; similarly, 一大杯茶 *a large cup of tea* cannot be transferred to 一杯大茶 *a cup of large tea**, as Thing and Measure each play their own distinct roles in the nominal group structure.

Expansion: enhancement

Nouns of enhancement generally construe circumstantial Things of time, place, cause and manner. They are recognised as a category because enhancement nouns tend to be modified by a rank-shifted embedded clause and the logico-semantic relation between this embedded clause and the head noun is enhancement. Examples:

Example 28
他一直追到虞渊, 也就是[[太阳落下去]]的地方。
He had been chasing all the way to Yuyuan, the place where [[the sun sets]].

Example 29
这种[[反常情感产生]]的原因只能归结为食物的 缺乏, 雏鹰的父母在自己食物匮乏情况下, 尽量减少家庭成员数量。
The reason for [[having this abnormal emotion]] can only be attributed to the lack of food, as the parents of eyas try to reduce the number of family members when they don't have enough food.

Nominal groups with an enhancement noun as Head sometimes can function as circumstance in a clause, which is different from English where only prepositional phrases and adverbial groups can realise circumstance in a clause:

Example 30

[[湖水最深]]的地方立了三个石塔作为深水记号。

湖水最深	的	地方	立了	三个石塔	作为深水记号
it is deepest in the lake	de	**place**	stood	three stone towers	as marks of deep water

(In) the deepest **place** in the lake stand three stone towers to mark the deep water.

Example 31

[[我昨天给你打电话]]的时候看见他匆匆忙忙的出了门。

我昨天给你打电话	的	时候	看见	他匆匆忙忙出了门。
I yesterday called you	de	**time**	saw	he went out in a hurry.

I saw him go out in a hurry (at) the **time** when I called you yesterday.

It is worth noting that when a nominal group construes a circumstance in a clause, the circumstantial Thing is either about time or location. In terms of all the other sub-categories of this Thing type, such as cause or manner, the nominal group only functions within a prepositional phrase or an adverbial group, such as in 所有这些哲学都以这种或那种方式与政治思想联系着 *All these philosophies associate with political ideologies in either this or that way*.

There is an ambiguous case related to this type of Thing, which is about the boundary between an enhancement noun of location and an extension noun of relative position. In the local grammatical environment within a nominal group, the difference between the two does not seem to be a question, as an extension noun Head structurally does not conflate with Thing, whereas an enhancement noun does. However, from a logico-semantic perspective, a nominal group with a facet noun construing a relative position may also be treated as an enhancement of location and can function as a circumstance in a clause:

Example 32

屋顶的上面种着花。

Flowers are planted on the roof **top**.

屋顶	的	上面	种着	花。
roof	de	**top**	plant	flowers
Thing	de	Head		
Circumstance: location: place			process	participant

Table 4.5 Things of Expansion

			Examples
Expansion	Elaboration	Example	例子 example, 比方 example
		Quality name	年龄 age, 质量 quality, 速度 speed, 价格 price
	Extension	Part	部分 part, 方面 aspect
		Logical relation	集合 collection, 关系 relation, 对比 contrast, 排比 parallelism, 对等 parity
		Relative position	上面 side above, 下面 side below, 东部 east side, 西边 west side
	Enhancement	Time	时间 *time*, 时机 chance/timing, 时刻 *moment*
		Place	地方 place, 地点 location
		Cause/result	原因 reason, 起因 cause, 结果 result, 后果 consequence
		Manner	方式 way/manner, 方法 method/means/way, 办法 method

I have completed my discussion about different sub-categories of Things of Expansion, and Table 4.5 summarises all the major types within each sub-category as well as examples.

In general, nouns of elaboration, those representing quality names in particular, have very good potential to be modified by classifiers. In fact, these nouns of quality kind represent the most general names of classifications, which gives them a great potential to be elaborated in terms of sub-classification, such as 入学年龄 *school age*, 教学质量 *teaching quality*, 市场价格 *market price*, etc. In comparison, nouns of enhancement are less likely to be classified, but more likely to be qualified in terms of when, where, why and how, such as 作案时间 *time of the crime*, 会面的地点 *the location of the meeting*, 迟到的原因 *reason for being late*.

Projection

Things of projection are realised by projection nouns which are names of locutions, ideas and facts. In the experiential structure of a clause, Thing of this category often construes a participant in a mental or verbal process, being the phenomenon or the verbiage correspondingly. Examples:

Example 33
|||孙中山先生看到||周围的风景优美, ||地势也很开阔, ||就表示了<u>身后要埋葬在这里的愿望</u>。||| (as phenomenon in a mental clause)
After seeing the beautiful scenery and the broad and open view, Mr. Sun Yat-sen had expressed **his wish to be buried here when he died**.

Example 34
|||你可以先说出<u>自己的意见</u>, ||然后把是非交付公论。||| (as verbiage in a verbal clause)

You can express **your own opinion** first, and leave it for public discussion.

The projection Thing are recognised as a category because when a projection noun realises the Thing, it tends to be qualified by a rank-shifted embedded clause construing the content of the projection. As detailed discussions about different types of nouns of projection, as well as their potentials to be modified by an embedded clause, have been presented in Chap. 3 (see Section "Projection"), they won't be repeated here. In this section, the discussion will mainly focus on the modification of projection nouns by experiential elements other than Qualifiers.

Nouns of projection can be modified by a measure word, but the measurability is quite limited compared with nouns realising simple Things. 个 (*itemised quantity*) and 种 (*kind*) are the commonly used measure words to modify this category, as many names of locutions, ideas and facts can be counted either through elaboration (种 *kind*) or extension 个 (*itemised quantity*). They can hardly be measured by other terms due to their inherent experiential feature of being related to the inner experience of human.

Projection nouns are often modified by possessive Deictic, which is typically realised by possessive pronouns referring to a person, which is easy to understand as only human can generate ideas and locutions in reality. Examples:

Example 35

老舍先生的意见表现了他对人的理解, 对一个人生活习惯的尊重, 同时也表现了对白石老人真正的关怀。

Mr. Laoshe's opinion reflects his understanding of others, his respect of one's life habits, which also shows his genuine consideration to Senior Baishi.

Example 36

他也将从"狮子舞", "划龙船", "放风筝"这三种民族形式的民间娱乐, 来描写祖国人民的生活, 理想和要求。

Through three forms of folk entertainment, the 'lion dancing', the 'dragon boat', and 'flying kites', he will describe **people's lives, dreams and demands in his homeland**.

Nouns of projection are often modified by a subjective Epithet and/or a post-Deictic to express the speaker's attitude, such as 真实想法 *real thoughts*, 愚蠢的主意 *stupid ideas*, 崇高的理想 *lofty ideals*, 伟大的口号 *grand slogan*. Again, this is associated with the close connection between projection Things and human's inner experience, as what one thinks and says are generally subject to others' judgement.

It is important to point out that, although they have high propensity to project, the projection Thing does not necessarily project—it is just that it has the grammatical ability to project through modification. Examples:

Example 37

|||孙中山先生看到||周围的风景优美, ||地势也很开阔, ||就表示了[[身后要埋葬在这里]]的愿望。|||

After seeing the beautiful scenery and the broad and open view, Mr. Sun Yat-sen had expressed **his wish [[to be buried here when he died]]**.

Example 38

女孩在纸上写下了<u>自己的愿望</u>。

The girl wrote **her wishes** on the paper.

Till now I have finished the discussion of 'congruent Thing' by exploring the categories and sub-categories of this major Thing type. Despite their differences in terms of modification potential (when viewed from around) as well as grammatical contributions to the clause (when viewed from above along the rank-scale), all the sub-types of congruent Thing share one basic grammatical feature: they represent things that are congruently realised by nouns when viewed from below. Semantically, this means that things of this category inherently are construed as being experientially ordinary 'simple things' in semantics (see further in Halliday and Matthiessen 1999), which is distinguished from the other major selection on the system of THING TYPE, the metaphorical Thing.

4.3.3 The Metaphorical Thing

A metaphorical Thing is a nominalisation of either a process or a quality, which would have been congruently realised by a verbal group or an adjectival verb, rather than a noun. It is termed as 'metaphorical' because the process of nominalisation is in fact a grammatical metaphor (see further in Halliday and Matthiessen 1999). Compared with congruent Things, metaphorical Things have much less modification potential than congruent Things in terms of expansion, as they are generally less stable in time (when realised as a nominalised process) and experientially less complex (when realised as nominalised quality). However, there is no such a clear-cut boundary line between 'metaphorical' and 'congruent': very often it is simply a matter of tendency when Thing type is discussed. I would like to quote Halliday and Matthiessen's (1999) point in viewing the two:

> … we have to acknowledge that the metaphorical relationship is not a symmetrical one: there is a definite directionality to it, such that one end of the continuum is metaphorical and the other is what we shall call congruent. Thus given the pair, we shall locate the two respects to each other on a metaphor scale …. (p. 221)

Based on the point above, which is supported by semihistorical evidence (cf. Halliday and Martin 1993; Halliday 2003), it is possible to interpret any type of Thing as metaphorical, and the congruent thing simply represents the least metaphorical type on the metaphor scale (see Fig. 4.7).

Due to the indeterminate nature of language (see further in Halliday and Matthiessen 1999), there is no fixed boundary between congruent and metaphorical Thing types as language itself is so dynamic that the grammatical feature of

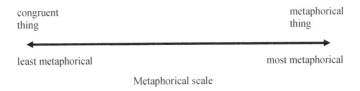

congruent thing — metaphorical thing

least metaphorical — most metaphorical

Metaphorical scale

Fig. 4.7 Thing type on the Metaphorical scale

one category may evolve and eventually overlap with another category. Therefore, to reflect this reality, there are two simultaneous selections in the system of metaphorical Thing Type: Things can be categorised in terms of the process types that are nominalised, and meanwhile they can be differentiated in terms of the degree of nominalisation (nominal status).

4.3.3.1 Nominal Status of Metaphorical Things

The selections in terms of **nominal status** are concerned about the lexicogrammatical nature of the Thing: although being a process or quality in semantics, the process or quality has been nominalised as a 'metaphorical thing', and in some cases, this nominal status is so established that it is treated as if this is a congruent Thing type in lexicogrammar. For example, 行动 *action* is concerned about a material experience of doing, so semantically it corresponds to material process. However, nowadays, 行动 *action* has been so widely accepted as a nominal entity in Chinese that it bears similar grammatical features to a congruent nominal item in lexicogrammar. In other words, its nominal status has been well established. Therefore, although it is a metaphorical Thing, the lexical item realising the Thing is a congruent noun due to its established nominal status. Generally speaking, metaphorical Things with established nominal status have better modification potential than metaphorical Things resulting from an instantial nominalisation, whose nominal status is not stable. Table 4.6 gives examples of metaphorical things for each category.

As Table 4.6 illustrates, Things with instantial nominal status, which are closer to the 'metaphorical' end on the metaphorical scale (see Fig. 4.7), are less modifiable than those Things with an established nominal status, which are moving in the 'congruent' direction on the metaphorical scale. In particular, it is not very likely for a metaphorical Thing with an instantial nominal status to be classified or measured in quantity, as they are semantically transient in space and time, which makes the classification and measure difficult. In terms of deicticity, the limited nominal nature of a metaphorical Thing means that it is less likely to be identified by a demonstrative determiner such as 这 *this* and 那 *that* (see further discussion in Chap. 6). Instead, Things with instantial nominal status usually can only be identified by a possessive determiner such as 我的 *my* or 你们的 *your*. This is because, when the process or quality is nominalised, the participant carrying out the process or the carrier of the

Table 4.6 Example metaphorical things and modifiers

		Example thing with modifiers				
		Measure	Qualifier	Epithet	Classifier	Deictic
Metaphorical thing	Instantial	–	长时间的注意 (long-time **noticing**)	密切的注意 (close **noticing**)	–	人们的注意 (people's **noticing**)
		一场等待 (one MEA **waiting**)	对结果的等待 (the **waiting** for the result)	漫长的等待 (long **waiting**)	–	我们的等待 (our **waiting**)
	Established	一次评估 (one MEA **assessment**)	根据情况做出的评估 (**assessment** based on the circumstance)	客观的评估 (objective **assessment**)	教学评估 (teaching **assessment**)	这次评估 (this MEA **assessment**)
		一份情感 (one MEA **feeling**)	对国家的情感 (**feeling** about the country)	强烈的情感 (strong **feelings**)	正向情感 (positive **feeling/emotion**)	这份情感 (this MEA **feeling**)

attribute becomes a significant item in identifying the nominalised Thing in the refer-ential space, as no other deictic items, that are congruently used in identifying Things, are available to modify the metaphorical Thing. In comparison, those metaphorical Things with an established nominal status tend to have better modification potential, similar to a congruent Thing type.

In the following discussion, I will investigate those nominalised processes which are presented as things, and their common collocations with other experiential elements within a nominal group. Discussion of nominalised quality will also be included in this part, as metaphorical things of quality can be interpreted as the result of the nominalisation of an attributive relational process.

4.3.3.2 Nominalised Processes

In general, nominalised processes fall into four categories on the system of THING TYPE: they are nominalised material process, nominalised mental process, nomi-nalised verbal process and nominalised relational process—the distinction corre-sponds to the four process types at the level of clause (cf. Halliday and McDonald 2004). Among them, one sub-category of nominalised relational process, namely attributive relational process, provides resources to construe quality as Thing.

Before the detailed discussion begins, it is important to distinguish a metaphorical thing resulting from a nominalised process from an act clause (see Sect. 1.1.3). In fact, they share something in common in terms of lexicogrammar: both are nominalisations of process and both can take on participant roles. The major difference lies in that they represent two different kinds of grammatical realisation of nominalisation. When a process is nominalised, the speaker can choose to realise it as a Thing, which is the concern of the current section, or to realise it as an act clause (see Sect. 1.1.3). In terms of realisation, the former is a nominal group with a metaphorical noun as Head, whereas the latter is a rank-shifted embedded clause without Head. It is also common to see an act clause functioning as Qualifier in a nominal group. Examples below illustrate the different grammatical environments for an act clause and a nominalised process as Thing:

Example 39
Act clause as participant
[[选择学校]]比[[选择专业]]更重要。
[[Selecting a school]] is more important than [[selecting a profession]].

Example 40
Act clause as Qualifier in a nominal group
在[[选择专业]]的问题上，家长们应该尊重孩子的意愿。
On the matter of **[[selecting a profession]]**, parents should respect their children's wish.

Example 41

Nominalised process as Thing in a nominal group
应该根据自己的实际情况来做出专业的选择。
One should make a profession **choice** based on his actual situation.

Material Process Construed as Thing

When a material process is construed as Thing, the nominal group can be expanded
by various modifiers which correspond to the functional roles in a material clause.
Examples:

Congruent clause structure	Actor + Circumstance (manner) + process	Example: 火山突然爆发了。 The volcano suddenly erupted.
Metaphorical nominal group structure	Deictic + Epithet + Thing	Example: 火山的突然爆发吓呆了所有人。 **The volcano's sudden eruption** shocked everyone.

Congruent clause structure	Process + goal	Example: 他养殖水产。 He breeds aquatic products.
Metaphorical nominal group structure	Deictic + Thing	Example: 水产的养殖需要科学的指引。 **The breeding of aquatic products** needs scientific guidance.

As the above two examples show, when a material process is nominalised, the
participant roles in the congruent structure can function as Deictic in the nominal
group, and this transformation may happen to either Actor or Goal.

Apart from participant, circumstance in a clause may also be transformed to a
modifier when the nominalisation happens. Examples:

Congruent clause structure	Circumstance (manner: quality) + process	Example: 他们热情的款待了我们。 They treated us with hospitality.
Metaphorical nominal group structure	Epithet + Thing	Example: 他们给予了我们**热情的款待**。 They gave us **a hospitable treatment.**

Congruent clause structure	Actor + Circumstance (location: place) +process + Circumstance (extent: frequency)	Example: 我们在异乡遭遇了许多。 We experienced a lot of things in the foreign place.
Metaphorical nominal group structure	Deictic + Qualifier + Epithet + Thing	Example: 我们在异乡的很多遭遇都无法诉说。 Many of our experiences in the foreign place cannot be told.

Congruent clause structure	Process + Circumstance (extent: duration)	Example: 我们等了很长时间，‖ 车终于来了。 We were waiting for a long time, ‖ and the bus finally came.
Metaphorical nominal group structure	Epithet + Thing	Example: 在**漫长的等待**之后，车终于来了。 After **a long waiting**, the bus finally came.

As the above examples illustrate, the circumstance elements can be transformed into different types of modifiers when the process is nominalised: the 'extent' and 'manner' types of circumstance tend to become Epithet in the corresponding nominal groups, whereas the 'location' type of time and place tends to become Qualifier.

Nominalised Mental and Verbal Processes as Thing

When a mental or a verbal process is nominalised, a mental process noun or a verbal process noun function as Thing in the agnate nominal group. Before the detailed examination of this type of metaphorical things, it is necessary to identify the boundary between a mental/verbal process noun and a noun of projection (see Sect. 4.3.2.2), as the two represent two separate categories in the system of THING TYPE. The main difference still lies in the degree of congruency: a projection noun is more congruent whereas a verbal/mental process noun is more metaphorical. Due to this difference, a projection noun has greater modification potential than a mental/verbal process noun. The other difference between the two is that, unlike a projection noun, which has the potential to project, a mental/verbal process noun may not be able to project, as it represents a wider category where being able to project is only a sub-categorical feature. For example, among the four sub-types of mental clauses in Chinese (see further in Halliday and McDonald 2004), affective mental process rarely projects. As a result, when this sub-type of mental process is nominalised as Thing, it can hardly be modified by a rank-shifted projection clause.

Despite the above-mentioned differences, the boundary line between these two types of nouns is in fact rather blurry, with some borderline cases falling in between. This is mainly because, when we judge the projection nouns from a semogenetic point of view, they are all metaphorical in nature—they are all derived from nominalised mental and verbal processes, and semantically they still represent process. It is just that they are now generally treated as Thing in grammar, and the congruent lexical realisation of them are by nouns, rather than verbs. In comparison, a mental/verbal process noun represents a nominalisation that is not yet common enough to become a congruent form of nouns—the categorical shift from verb to noun is still instantial, and the more congruent realisation is still by verb instead of noun. However, as said before, there are always ambiguous cases which lie somewhere in between: words such as 回答 (*answer*), 保证 (*promise*), 渴望 (*desire*) may be treated as either type, as the congruency of these words may well be argued in different contexts.

In the following paragraphs, I will discuss mental and verbal process nouns separately.

Mental process nouns

Mental process nouns can be further categorised into cognitive, affective, desirative and perceptive nouns, corresponding to the four sub-categories of mental processes at the clause level. When construed as Thing, these nouns have limited modification potential due to their metaphorical nature—after all, they are the results of grammatical metaphor through which a mental process is nominalised as if it is a Thing. Due to this reason, these metaphorical nouns do not bear the typical grammatical features that real nouns generally have. In terms of classification, they can hardly be modified by a classifier. However, many of these metaphorical nouns can still be modified by Qualifier, Epithet and Measure. Table 4.7 presents the types of mental process nouns and their modifiability in terms of the above three aspects.

Table 4.7 Mental process nouns and modification potential

Mental process nouns		Measure Item/type	Epithet Other	Objective	Subjective	Qualifier Expanding	Projecting
	Cognitive	H 一个猜测 a guess 一种理解 an understanding	L	L	H 片面的理解 one-sided understanding 主观臆断 subjective assumption	H 完全不同的理解 the understanding which is completely different	M 关于'他就是凶手'的猜测 the speculation that he is the killer
	Affective	L	H 一丝烦恼 a trace of misery 一腔热情 a vessel of passion	H 强烈的愤怒 strong anger 浓淡的忧伤 slight sadness	L	H 挥之不去的烦恼 the worry that is haunting me	L
	Desirative	H 一个决定 a decision 一种愿望 a wish	L	H 强烈的欲望 strong desire 极度的渴望 desperate craving	L	H 爱的欲望 crave for love 婚姻里的欲望 desires in marriage	H 被溺爱的渴望 the crave for being indulged 早日成才的愿望 the wish to become successful one day

(continued)

Table 4.7 (continued)

	Measure	Other	Epithet		Qualifier	
	个/种 Item/type		Objective	Subjective	Expanding	Projecting
Perceptive	L	L	H 强烈的感觉 strong feeling	L	H 沿途的见闻 the sights and hearings* (what one sees and hears) in the journey	L

H: high potential; L: low potential

As Table 4.7 shows, cognitive and perceptive mental process nouns can be modified by projecting Qualifier, whereas affective and perceptive nouns cannot, which corresponds to the situation at the clause level. And mental process nouns show a very low level of measurability, which is also due to its semantic feature of being a process rather than a thing.

In terms of Epithet, most of the mental process nouns can be modified by adjectives representing manner (degree), which corresponds to the circumstance of degree in the agnate mental clause structure. For example,

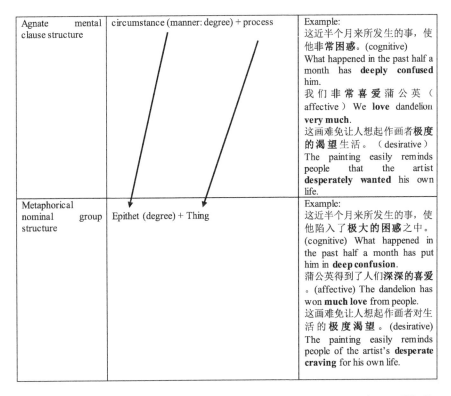

| Agnate mental clause structure | circumstance (manner: degree) + process | Example: 这近半个月来所发生的事，使他非常**困惑**。(cognitive) What happened in the past half a month has **deeply confused** him. 我们非常**喜爱**蒲公英（affective）We **love** dandelion **very much**. 这画难免让人想起作画者**极度的渴望**生活。（desirative）The painting easily reminds people that the artist **desperately wanted** his own life. |
| Metaphorical nominal group structure | Epithet (degree) + Thing | Example: 这近半个月来所发生的事，使他陷入了**极大的困惑**之中。(cognitive) What happened in the past half a month has put him in **deep confusion**. 蒲公英得到了人们**深深的喜爱**。(affective) The dandelion has won **much love** from people. 这画难免让人想起作画者对生活的**极度渴望**。(desirative) The painting easily reminds people of the artist's **desperate craving** for his own life. |

In terms of Deicticity, all the four types of mental process nouns can be modified by a possessive pronoun functioning as Deictic, and this possessive pronoun typically represent a conscious being, which reflects the nature of the senser in the agnate mental clause. Examples:

	Nominal group (possessive Deictic + Thing)	Agnate mental clause (senser + process)
Perceptive	鸟的叫声，引起了有心人的注意。 The bird's song attracted the attention from someone.	有心人注意到了鸟的叫声。 **Someone noticed** the song of the bird.

(continued)

(continued)

	Nominal group (possessive Deictic + Thing)	Agnate mental clause (senser + process)
Cognitive	感谢领导的信任。 I thank my supervisor for **his trust**.	领导信任我, 我很感谢。 **My supervisor trusts** me, for which I am thankful.
Desirative	你以为创造了一个用新的方式操琴的演奏家, 可是你的打算完全落空了。 You thought you have brought about a performer who plays the instrument in a new way, but **your intention** came to nothing.	你打算创造一个用新的方式操琴的演奏家, 可是却落了空。 **You intended** to bring about a performer who plays the instrument in a new way, but this came to nothing.
Emotive	他的烦恼又有谁知道呢? Who would know about **his worries**?	又有谁知道他为什么烦恼呢? Who would know what **he worries about?**

Verbal process nouns

Verbal process nouns, in general, have the similar modification potential to mental process nouns: some of the verbal process nouns can be modified by a qualifier functioning as projection, which reflects the ambiguous boundary between verbal process nouns and projection nouns of locution, similar to the situation of mental process nouns and projection nouns of idea. Apart from the verbal process nouns which can project, there is another sub-type, which represents targeted verbal activities, and can hardly project. Table 4.8 presents some examples of verbal process nouns being categorised in terms of their propensity to project.

In terms of Epithet, verbal process nouns are typically modified by an adjective representing manner (quality), which corresponds to the circumstance of manner (quality) in the agnate verbal clause structure. Examples:

Table 4.8 Examples of verbal process nouns and their projectability

	Examples of verbal process nouns
Projectable	号召 call, 感叹 exclamation, 解释 explanation, 保证 promise, 要求 requirement, 回应 response, 回答 answer, 指示 instruction, 威胁 threat, 质问 query, 预告 prediction, 抱怨 complaint
Non-projectable	批评 criticism, 表扬 compliment, 解说 comment, 讲话 talks, 发言 talk, 提问 raising questions, 辱骂 verbal abuse, 指责 blame, 谴责 denouncing, 演讲 speaking, 争执 argument, 讨论 discussion, 问答 question and answer, 辩论 debate, 反对 objection, 责怪 blame, 埋怨 whinge

| Agnate verbal clause structure | circumstance (manner: quality) + process | Example: 他把想法告诉了教练，可是教练却没有**明确**回答他。He told his coach what he thought, but the coach didn't **reply** him **clearly**. 家长们**严厉的批评**了我们的行为。Parents **severely criticised** us for our behaviour. |
| Metaphorical nominal group structure | Epithet (quality) + Thing | Example: 他把想法告诉了教练，却没有得到**明确的回答**。He told his coach what he thought, but didn't get **a clear reply**. 我们的行为遭到了家长们的**严厉批评**。Our behaviour received **severe criticism** from the parents. |

In terms of Deicticity, a verbal process noun is typically modified by a possessive pronoun functioning as Deictic, which corresponds to the sayer in the agnate verbal clause. Examples:

Nominal group (possessive Deictic + Thing)	Agnate verbal clause (sayer + process)
我们不能盲目地接受过去认为的真理, 也不能等待'学术权威'的指示。We cannot blindly accept what we used to believe, neither can we wait for **the 'academic authority's' instructions**.	'学术权威'指示我们接受所谓的真理。**The 'academic authority' instruct** us to accept the so-called truth.
我的回应和我的证据已经在前几篇文章里说的很清楚。**My response** and my evidence have been clearly presented in the previous articles.	我已经在前几篇文章里回应得很清楚。I have clearly **responded** in my previous articles.
对于媒体的质疑, 我无话可说。Facing the questioning from the media, I have nothing to say.	媒体质疑我的表现, 我无话可说。The media questioned my behaviour, about which I have nothing to say.
面对不明真相者的辱骂, 他选择了沉默。Facing **the verbal abuse** from the people who know nothing about the truth, he chose to remain silent.	不明真相者辱骂他, 他却选择了沉默。The people who know nothing about the truth **verbally abused him**, but he chose to remain silent.

Nominalised Relational Process as Thing

Compared with the other three types of process discussed above, the nominalisation of a relational process is more complicated. On the system of TRANSITIVITY in Chinese, the relational process type can be further divided into three sub-types:

existential, identifying and attributive (Halliday and McDonald 2004). When nominalisation occurs to a relational clause, the three sub-types go through different transformations: existential and identifying process can be transformed into a limited number of metaphorical Things, representing the existence of a participant and the abstract relationship of identity, whereas attributive process is nominalised with the attribute being construed as Thing. In the following discussion, I will first investigate the nominalisation of the first two sub-categories, existential and identifying processes, and then examine the attributive process separately.

In Chinese, the examples of nominalisation of existential and identifying relational processes are quite limited, which is due to the same limited number of verbal groups in Chinese being available to construe such a process at the clause level.

In the case of existential process, there is mainly one verb being typically used to construe the existence: 有 (yǒu, *there is/are*). However, 有 *there is/are* cannot be nominalised. The only case of nominalisation of an existential relational clause being found in the present corpus is the nominalisation of the verb 存在 (cúnzài, *existence*), which presents the existence of things as a being. Example:

Example 42
如何证明*神的存在*?
How to prove the existence of God?

Example 43
金属检出机就能检测到*金属的存在*。
A metal detector is able to detect the existence of a metal.

As Examples 42 and 43 illustrate, through nominalisation, the existential relation is construed as Thing, and the existent becomes a Deictic realised by a possessive determiner. Sometimes, this metaphorical Thing can be modified by Epithet, which corresponds to circumstance in an agnate existential clause:

Example 44
这些问题*的严重存在*, 直接影响今后 "2131工程" 的实施。
The serious existence of these problems will directly impact the implementation of the '2131 Project' in the future.

Example 45
*校车的大面积存在*恰恰证明, 小孩子在这里的"*就近入学*"首先是不科学的。
The wide existence of school buses has just proven that it is not sensible for kids to 'go to a nearly school' in this place.

In the case of an identifying relational clause, the general sense of the Value-Token relation, which is typically realised by the verb 是 (shì, *is/are*), can hardly be nominalised. However, some other sub-types of this category, such as the relations of 'symbolisation', 'equivalence', 'demonstration' and 'constitution', can be construed as Thing, which are often found in some prestigious registers, such as political and academic discourses. Examples:

Example 46

这繁茂的"季荷", 不正是<u>绵绵生命的象征</u>吗? (symbolisation)

Isn't this luxuriant 'seasonal lotus' a **symbol** of continuous life?

Example 47

再次, "同等条件"还应包括<u>其他交易条件的等同</u>。(equivalence)

Once again, an 'equal condition' should also involve the **equivalence** of other trading conditions.

Example 48

他的面相完全没有特征, 完全属于普通的俄罗斯人, 因此, 我们得把他称为普通人, 而且此刻会产生这么一种感 觉, 即天才没有任何特殊的长相, 而是<u>一般人的总体现</u>。(demonstration)

There are completely no characters in his facial appearance, as he is just an ordinary Russian. So we have to call him an ordinary person, and then we will come up with such a feeling, that is, that a genius does not have an extraordinary look, rather he is a **general representation** of ordinary people.

Example 49

了解<u>新一届中共政治局委员的构成</u>有什么意义? (constitution)

What is the point of interpreting **the constitution the newly elected CPPCC**?

It is interesting to note that, when a Value-Token relation is construed as Thing, it is often the Value that remains in the nominal group to modify the relation. Sometimes, it is also possible to interpret the Value as Thing, and the nominalised relation as Facet which elaborates the Thing:

绵绵生命	的	象征
Continuous life	*de*	*Symbol*
Value		Identifying relation (symbolisation)
Modifier	de	Head
Thing		Facet

I have discussed the nominalisation of the first two sub-types of relational process, existential and identifying relational process, where the process is construed as a metaphorical Thing through nominalisation. Next, I will investigate the third sub-type, attributive relational process, the transformation of which is very different from the other two sub-types when nominalisation occurs.

The attributive relational processes can be divided into four further sub-types: circumstantial, possessive, categorising and ascriptive (see further in Halliday and McDonald 2004). The first three sub-types of attributive processes are typically realised by verbs of 在 (zài, *is/are*, circumstantial), 有 (yǒu, *have/has*, possessive) and 是 (shì, *is/are*, categorising) respectively, all of which can hardly be nominalised.

The present discussion will thus focus on the fourth type, the ascriptive attributive relational process, which provides resources to construe quality things.

Unlike the other three types of attributive processes where the process is construed by a verb and the two participants stand to each other as Carrier and Attribute, an ascriptive attributive process is conflated with Attribute and is congruently realised by an adjective, which is a subclass of verb, and therefore is also termed as 'adjectival verb'. Examples:

Example 50
Adjectival verb
a. 这本书很有趣。
This book (is) very interesting.
b. 空气很潮湿。
The air (is) very humid.
c. 经过精心挑选和编排的轻音乐，格调高雅。
The style of the carefully selected and arranged music (sounds) very elegant.

As Examples 50a–c illustrate, in an ascriptive clause, the attribute and process are fused into one lexical item, an adjectival verb, and therefore quality functions as Process (see further in Halliday and McDonald 2004). This is different from English, where adjectives are generally considered as a subclass of noun, and therefore as nominals, and the corresponding relational process is still realised by a verb.

When nominalisation happens to an ascriptive attributive relational process, quality, which is congruently construed as Process, becomes the Thing. In Sect. 4.3.2.2, I have discussed 'names of quality', which is a sub-type of elaboration Thing. It is important to distinguish the metaphorical quality Thing from the Thing of quality kind. In general, there are two major differences between the two types of the Thing. The first difference is again in the degree of congruence. 'Names of quality' is more congruent than metaphorical 'quality thing', as the former is typically realised by nouns whereas the latter by nominalised adjectives. Secondly, as 'names of quality' represents the general name of a quality kind, it has great potential to be modified through elaboration. In comparison, 'quality thing' has very limited modification potential, as it represents a highly specific quality. Below are some examples of 'Names of quality' being modified by adjectives, and the more specific qualities being construed as metaphorical Thing through nominalisation of these adjectives (see Table 4.9).

Figure 4.8 illustrates the relationship between Names of quality realised by nouns and specific qualities realised by adjectives on the cline of generality. As 'Names of quality' stands at the general end, it has great potential to be further elaborated, whereas 'Quality thing' stands at the specific end, which determines its limited modification potential.

Despite the limited modification potential through elaboration, nominalised attributes can be extended by possessive deictic, which corresponds to the agnated clause structure of 'Carrier + Attribute'. Examples:

Table 4.9 Names of quality and metaphorical quality things

Names of quality	Metaphorical quality thing
美丽的外表 *beautiful* **appearance**	人们感叹大自然的美丽 People are touched by the **beauty** of the nature
优雅的举止 *elegant* **manner**	在一个 宽松的社会里，人们可以收获到优雅 In a comfortable society, people can be endowed with **elegance**
无耻的人格 a *shameless* **personality**	人格上的无耻导致学术上的堕落 The **shamelessness** in personality leads to the fall in academic values

Fig. 4.8 Names of quality and Quality on the cline of generality

Agnate attributive relational clause structure	Carrier + Attribute/Process	Example: 大自然既美丽又神奇。 The nature is both **beautiful and mysterious.** 他勇敢诚实，让对手肃然起敬。 He is **brave and honest**, for which his opponent respects him.
Metaphorical nominal group structure	Deictic + **Thing**	Example: 人们感叹大自然的美丽与神奇。 People are touched by the **beauty and the mystery** of the mother nature. 他的勇敢诚实让对手肃然起敬。 His **bravery and honesty** wins respect from his opponent.

Sometimes, nominalised attributes can be modified by adjectives functioning as post-Deictic, which identify the attribute in terms of authenticity, commonality, or similarity. Examples:

Example 51

每个人都有自己最独特的美, 最独特的自己, 才是最真实的美。

Everyone has got his own unique beauty, for the most unique self represents the most real beauty.

Example 52

他总是用同样的诚恳和热情对待每一个来访者。

He always accepts every visitor with the same sincerity and passion.

Chinese Idioms as Quality Thing

Apart from adjectives which can be nominalised to construe quality Thing, there is also a very special category in Chinese, 成语 (chéngyǔ, *Chinese idioms*), which provides resources in construing metaphorical quality Thing.

Chinese idioms are a type of traditional idiomatic expressions in Chinese which are typically realised by four characters. Most of the idioms were originally derived from a story or a myth in ancient Chinese literature, or from a historical event and reflect the essence or the moral of the stories and events. Semantically it is possible to view them as a highly condensed event or quality, so condensed that it is represented by only four characters.[3] Idioms are very flexible in use with a potential to play different roles on a grammatical structure. Compare the following examples:

Example 53
As a subject
他的自以为是让人看了就生气。
His self-righteousness is very annoying.

Example 54
As a predictor
他很自以为是。
He is self-righteous.

Example 55
As a premodifier in a nominal group
他的脸上一副 [[自以为是]]的表情。
On his face is an expression of [[being self-righteous]].

Example 56
As Token in a relational clause
他最大的毛病就是[[自以为是]]。
His biggest problem is [[being self-righteous]].

An idiom like 自以为是 *being self-righteous* may function in the same way as a nominalised act clause (see Example 56). However, a nominalised act expressed by an idiom may not necessarily mean the act—it often has a deeper meaning, a connotation which carries the moral of the original act or event. It is because of this connotation that a Chinese idiom can often be descriptive with adjectival features.

In her investigation on the grammatical functions of Chinese idioms, Tao finds that Chinese idioms are predominantly verbal and adjectival, with a small number of them adverbial and nominal (Tao 2002). Here are some examples:

---

[3] There are a small number of idioms which consist of more than 4 characters, and they bear the same linguistic features as the 4-character idioms.

Example 57a
Verbal idiom
他的一席话让我茅塞顿开 (the blocking thatch suddenly being removed)。
His words <u>enlightened</u> me all of a sudden.

Example 57b
Adjectival idiom
这消息千真万确 (thousand truth and ten thousand correctness)。
The news is <u>a 100% true</u>.

Example 57c
Adverbial idiom
听到叫他名, 他<u>大步流星</u> (*with big stride*) 的迈过去。
Hearing his name called, he came up <u>with vigorous strides</u>.

Example 57d
Nominal idiom
花虽然多, 但是没有奇花异草 (strange flowers and rare herbs)。
Although there are lots of flowers, one cannot find <u>an exotic and rare one</u>.

Although the grammatical versatility of idioms makes most of them being able to function as a nominal group in a clause, not all of them can be recognised as nominal groups. Strictly speaking, only nominal idioms, which have a nominal head in its structure, can be considered as a special type of nominal groups. Below are some examples of nominal idioms that have a nominal head:

Example 58
残花败<u>柳</u> withered ***flowers*** *and faded **willows***, referring to women who lost their chastity

Example 59
阴谋诡<u>计</u> **schemes** and **intrigues**

Example 60
肺腑之<u>言</u> ***words*** *out of lung and stomach*, referring to words from the bottom of heart.

Many nominal idioms have a coordinated structure with two heads (see Examples 58 and 60), and these two head nouns are from the same taxonomic category to create a rhetorical effect of being symmetrical. Another interesting feature shared by all types of idioms is that they can hardly be further modified. In the case of nominal idioms, this means that they cannot be further qualified, classified or given another epithet. A possible reason for this is that idioms, as discussed before, can be viewed as highly condensed event or quality. A nominal idiom is usually a compact form of 'quality + head', thus no further modifications are needed since the potential qualities a modifier can give to the Head is already an integral part of the meaning of that idiom. Experientially speaking, these nominal idioms provide resources in construing congruent Things, as congruently they are nominal in nature.

In comparison, there are some other types of idioms, which construe nominalised fact or quality, but cannot be considered as nominal groups—the main reason is that they do not have a nominal head and are not nominal in nature. However, thanks to the grammatical versatility and the adjectival features carried by these Chinese idioms, non-nominal idioms become an important source in construing metaphorical things. The situation corresponds to the nominalisation of process and quality: the verbal idioms can be used to construe a nominalised process, and adjectival idioms to construe a nominalised quality. Compared with their lexical counterparts, these idioms are playing the same role in the nominalisation, and they are only different in terms of lexical realisation. Some examples of idioms construing a process or a quality thing are presented here:

Example 61
他的自以为是最终害了他自己。(Quality as thing)
His self-righteousness finally got himself punished.

Example 62
他的急流勇退是明智的。(Process as thing)
His retirement at the height of his career was very wise.

In this section, I have discussed the nominalisation of the four major process types in Chinese, material, mental, verbal and relational processes, which provides resources in construing metaphorical Thing. Based on the investigation, it is clear that nominalisation is a powerful grammatical device that makes these transformations possible. As a highly inflexive language, Chinese nominalisation happens less explicitly than English, as in the latter case the transformation is directly reflected through the change of lexical form. However, despite this difference, the nominalisation in both languages is driven by the incongruent realisation of an element in a clause, viewed through grammatical lens.

Till now I have completed the discussion of each major categories and subcategories in the system of THING TYPE. In the following sections, I will move onto the other functional elements on the experiential structure of a nominal group, which represent different experiential aspects of the Thing. The discussion will mainly focus on four elements which play significant experiential roles in construing a participant: Classifier, Epithet, Qualifier and Measure.

4.4 Classifier

The experiential complexity of the Thing provides great potential for it to be further specified through classification, which is particularly true in the case of congruent Things as they can be highly elaborated in terms of taxonomy.

Classifiers are structurally the closest element to the Thing in the experiential structure and semantically it represents the most basic features that people may use to classify a type of things. In the case of Chinese nominal groups, the subordinating particle 的 *de* can be used as an effective marker to indicate the difference between Classifier and the other modifying elements in relation to the Thing: 的 *de* typically exists between the other functional elements and Thing but not between Classifier and Thing. Sometimes, Classifier and Thing are so closely bound that they develop into a new compound noun—in fact, the close relationship between Classifier and Thing is often a driving force for generating new nouns. In Chinese, a typical example of this type of lexical expansion usually results from the wide use of abbreviations of Classifier + Thing, such as 川菜 (*Sichuan cuisine*), 国企 (*state-owned enterprise*), 快件 (*express mail*).

4.4.1 Classifiability and Thing Type

Things are not always classified, and the Thing Type plays an important role in deciding the Thing's potential for classification. Figure 4.9 illustrates the relationship between classifiability and different Thing Types.

As Fig. 4.9 illustrates, the more congruent a Thing is, the more potential it has to be classified, and due to this tendency, metaphorical things can hardly be classified. In fact, this tendency is a further elaboration of the relationship between congruency and modifiability of the Thing in general, as classification itself can be interpreted as a kind of modification from a logical perspective.

In the following section, I will present the system of CLASSIFICATION, which mainly reflects the selections of classifiers to modify conscious beings and simple things.

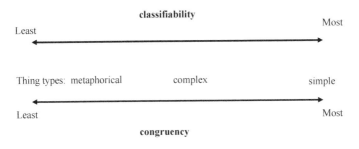

Fig. 4.9 Classifiability and Thing Type

4.4.2 System of CLASSIFICATION

Figure 4.10 presents the system of CLASSIFICATION. In general, this system reflects three concerns: 1. the type of Things being classified; 2. the semantic quality being represented to classify a Thing; 3. the logico-semantic relations between Thing and Classifier. In the following paragraphs, discussions will focus on each major selection on the system.

First of all, it is important to stress that this system is relevant to congruent Things only, conscious beings and simple Things in particular, as metaphorical Things can hardly be classified (see discussion in Sect. 4.3.3). And in the case of congruent Things, the complexity of the Thing type plays an important role in making a selection on the system. For example, most simple Things can be classified in terms of both ascriptive features and non-ascriptive acquired features, whereas complex Things tend to be classified in terms of activity-based situational features only.

Secondly, I will discuss the two major selections in terms of 'classifying quality': ascriptive and acquired qualities. This categorisation reflects the semantic nature of classifiers: they are thing-like qualities semantically (see further in Halliday and Matthiessen 1999). **Ascriptive** qualities represent those simple and specific characteristics that are assigned to a thing, such as colour, shape, size, age and so on. It is clear that conscious beings, as well as concrete objects and substances, have a great potential to be classified in terms of their ascriptive qualities. Examples: 棉袜

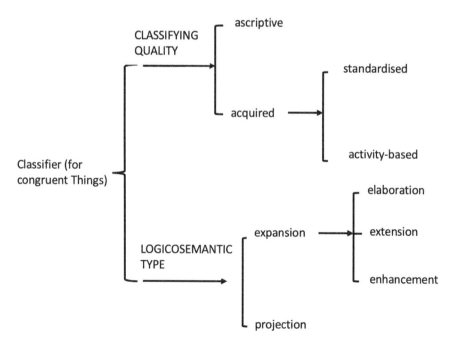

Fig. 4.10 System of CLASSIFICATION

cotton socks, 木椅 *wooden chair*, 方桌 *square table*, 红细胞 *red cell*. However, less concrete Things, such as semiotics and complex Things, cannot be classified along these values, as they represent more complex experiences which cannot be specified by a quality of a single dimension as such. Rather, these abstract and complex Things tend to be classified in terms of **acquired** features, which are qualities that derive from context (both sociocultural and situational) and represent experientially more complex values that can be defined only in a specific context, such as social class and status (特级教师 *a special-grade teacher*, 重点中学 *key school*, 已婚妇女 *married women*), domain (外科医生 *surgical doctor*, 古典音乐 *classic music*), function (出口商品 *export commodity*, 比赛项目 *competing events*) and so on. It is important to note that acquired features can be used to classify all types of congruent Things, unlike ascriptive features, which are only used to classify conscious beings and concrete Things. This again reflects the relationship between congruency of Thing type and modifiability of the Thing.

The categorisation between 'ascriptive' and 'acquired' is based on the stability of the qualities being construed through time and space. To put it in a simple way, ascriptive features represent qualities on the stable end, whereas acquired features represent qualities on the transient end, which is less stable in time and space and usually defined by language users in a given context. Another concern being reflected by this categorisation is about the objectivity of the quality being represented by these classifiers: acquired classification is often subject to personal interpretation based on the context, whereas ascriptive classifiers represent a more objective classification (see Fig. 4.11). In the referential space, ascriptive classifiers helps to build a natural identity of the Thing, whereas acquired classifiers contribute to the social identity of the Thing.

Both ascriptive and acquired classifiers can be further categorised along various dimensions. The sub-categorisation is full of taxonomic features, which forms a cline from ascriptive to acquired as the elaboration moves further. Figure 4.12 illustrates the cline with an example of cloth taxonomy.

Under the category of 'acquired', the classifiers can be further classed into 'standardised' and 'activity-based'. Standardised classifiers are used in identifying things sharing some similar qualities and formally recognised as an established discipline or category. Classifiers of this kind often modify Things of institution, discipline, semiotics and human of a specific profession. Examples: 古代历史 *ancient history*, 古典音乐 *classic music*, 重点中学 *key school*, 甲等医院 *A-level hospitals*, 本科院校 *undergraduate institutions*, 电影学院 *film academies*, 陆军士兵 *army soldiers*, 外

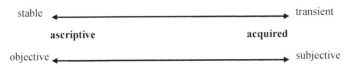

Fig. 4.11 Ascriptive and acquired classifiers

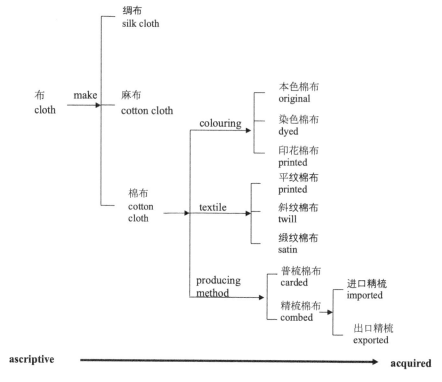

Fig. 4.12 Taxonomy of cloth on the 'ascriptive-achieved' cline

科医生 *surgical doctor*. The other sub-category under 'acquired', namely 'activity-based', refers to those classifiers that are used to classify things based on the activities they are involved. This type of classifications is less stable compared with the other type and is not well established as standards in recognising a discipline or a profession. The activities that these classifiers represent are not instantial activities. Rather, they are those activities where the Thing being modified will typically involve as participant. Examples: 原装机 *machines made in the original country*, 组装机 *machines assembled in another place*, 失业人口 *unemployed population*, 已婚人口 *married population*, 批发商 *wholesale company*, 经销商 *distributing company*. As the examples show, the classifications of this kind are not permanent, but only make sense in a given context.

Next, I will discuss the other major selection on the system of CLASSIFICATION, the 'logico-semantic type'. This category reflects the logico-semantic relations between the classifier and the Thing being classified. Again, it can be categorised into **projection** and **expansion**, which are prevalent in the organisation of the ideation base. Table 4.10 lists some examples of each logico-semantic type and sub-types of Classifiers.

Table 4.10 Examples of logico-semantic types of classifiers

Type	Sub-type		Examples	
			Ascriptive	Acquired
Elaboration	Intensive		蓝鲸 blue whale 幼鲸 baby whale 圆桌 round table 干粮 dry food	高级职称 senior titles 清洁能源 clean energy 可回收垃圾 recyclable waste
	Role			已婚妇女 married women 被告人 the accused person 继承人 the inheriting person, i.e. *heir*
Extension (possessive)			短毛猫 shorthair cat 多音节词 multisyllable words	核武大国 nuclear big country, i.e. *nuclear power* 癌症患者 cancer patient 双门跑车 two-door sport car, i.e. *coupe* 酒精饮料 alcoholic drinks
Enhancement	Time		春笋 spring bamboo shoots 早餐 morning meal, i.e. *breakfast*	夏令时 summer time 古代史 ancient history 现代文学 modern literature 课间餐 school recess meal
	Place		法国人 French man 蓝山咖啡 Blue mountain coffee 波斯猫 Persian cat	户外活动 outdoor activities 农村劳动力 country labour 沙滩排球 beach volleyball 外来人口 non-native population
	Manner	Means		超声波检查 ultrasound check 水路运输 water transport 油炸食品 deep-fried food 线装书 thread-bound books

(continued)

Table 4.10 (continued)

Type	Sub-type		Examples	
			Ascriptive	Acquired
		Materials	棉被 cotton-padded quilt 红木家具 redwood furniture 真皮沙发 genuine leather sofa	蛋筒冰淇淋 ice-cream cone 纸杯蛋糕 cup cakes
	Conditional	Purpose		儿童设施 children facilities 消防设备 fire-fighting equipment 感冒药 cold medicine 圣诞树 Christmas tree
		Result/effect		迷幻药 hallucinogenic drug 致癌物 carcinogenic substances 节能灯 energy-saving lights
	Matter			航天史 aerospace history 教育产业 education industry
Projection	Topic			战争片 war film 家庭伦理小说 novels about family 山水画 landscape painting
	Angle (source)			马克思理论 Marxist theory 莎士比亚戏剧 Shakespeare plays

I will make comments on two issues being reflected in the examples presented in Table 4.10. First, the two major selections on the system of CLASSIFICATION, 'classifying quality' and 'logico-semantic type', are not independent from each other. Rather, these are two simultaneous selections reflecting semantic concerns, and the two major selections can influence each other. For example, in terms of material manner of enhancement, only ascriptive classifying qualities can be selected at the same time, as only material things and substances carry the ascriptive quality of a material making. Second, in terms of projection, only semiotic things have the potential to project and this quality is regarded as acquired. In the previous section about Thing Type (see Sect. 4.3.1), I have discussed the projection potential of Things of ideas and locutions. Although these complex Thing Types have a good potential to develop a projection through modification, it is commonly realised by qualification, not classification. More discussion will be given in Sect. 4.6 when I investigate Qualifiers.

I have explored the major two selections on the system of CLASSIFICATION. In the following section, I will present some sample text analysis to further demonstrate how things can be classified in texts.

4.4.3 Case Study: Analysing Classifiers

In this section, I will present the analysis of three sample texts, all of which are expounding texts with taxonomic features. The focus of the analysis is on how the key subjects being explored in these texts are further classified in nominal groups. First, I will compare the classification selections in texts 1 and 2, and then will discuss the case of Text 3 separately. Table 4.11 presents the context information of the three texts.

I will focus on the three key things being expounded by these texts: glass, whales and animal languages. Figure 4.13 presents how 玻璃 (glass) is taxonomised in Text 1, and the analysis of the classifiers in terms of CLASSIFICATION.

Figure 4.14 presents how 鲸 (whales) is taxonomised in Text 2, and the analysis of the classifiers in terms of CLASSIFICATION.

A comparison of the classification analysis between Figs. 4.13 and 4.14 illustrates that Thing Type tends to play a decisive role in how the Thing can be further classified: objects like 'glass' have good potential to be classified in terms of its acquired qualities such as purpose (as function), or manner (as how they are made); in comparison, a conscious Thing like 'whale' has a great potential to be classified in terms of their ascriptive qualities through elaboration (in terms of size, age, gender) or extension (in terms of physical features that they have).

Figure 4.15 presents the analysis of Text 3. In terms of logico-semantic relations, the subject of the text, animal languages, is classified through enhancement of means: different varieties are recognised in terms of how they are realised. In terms of classifying quality, these classifiers represent an acquired quality in that it is through the interpretation of the author that the qualities are defined to classify the Thing 语言 language. This is a special case, as the common-sense understanding of 语言 language is that this is a Thing exclusive to human beings, and the qualities that are expounded in this text are not recognised as usual qualities to classify the Thing 语言 language. This text, however, defines the Thing 语言 language in a broader sense to include semiotics produced by conscious beings other than human, and therefore the 语言 language in this particular context can be classified in terms of a wider range of qualities, such as 超声波 ultrasound, 运动 movement, 色彩 colour and 气味 smell, which are not the default qualities being recognised in the common-sense understanding of 语言 language. As the text unfolds, the relationship

Table 4.11 Context of sample texts

	Text 1: 新型玻璃 *New types of glass*	Text 2: 鲸 *Whales*	Text 3: 千奇百怪的动物语言 *All kinds of animal languages*
Field	The socio-semiotic function of this text is expounding and the situation type is that of taxonomy. The domain is concrete and concerned with four new types of glass and their functions	The socio-semiotic function of this text is expounding. The domain is concrete and concerned with all kinds of features of whales of different species	The socio-semiotic function of this text is expounding. The domain is concrete and concerned with all sorts of animal languages. In demonstrating how the languages are used, animals are personified
Tenor	The institutional roles are a glass expert to the primary school students; an adult to children readers. The evaluation of the experiential domain is neutral	The institutional roles are an expert of whales to the primary school students; an adult to children. The evaluation of the experiential domain is neutral	The institutional roles are an expert to the junior high school students; an adult to young readers. The evaluation of the experiential domain is neutral to positive, with the writer making some positive appraisal to the use of animal languages
Mode	The text is monologic, written and constitutive of its contextual situation. No technical language is used in the text, and concrete scenarios are presented to demonstrate the functions of glass	The text is monologic, written and constitutive of its contextual situation. Some simple terminologies are used	The text is monologic, written and constitutive of its contextual situation. Some simple terminologies are used

新型玻璃
new glasses
Thing type: object

夹丝玻璃 *wired glass* - enhancement: manner + acquired

变色玻璃 *colour-changing glass* - enhancement: manner + acquired

吸热玻璃 *heat-absorbing glass* - enhancement: purpose + acquired

吃音玻璃 *sound-absorbing glass* - enhancement: purpose + acquired

Fig. 4.13 Classification in Text 1

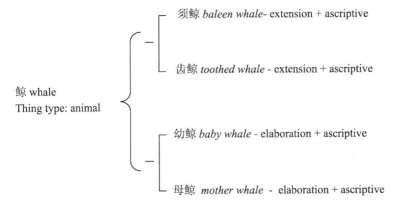

Fig. 4.14 Classification in Text 2

between these qualities and 语言 *language* is built up, which is set as the context, and in turn gives these qualities a classifying function. As Matthiessen points out, this kind of logogenetic build-up can ensure that the Classifier + Thing combination is interpretable in its discourse environment (Matthiessen 1995: 667). Again, this sample analysis illustrates that Classifiers have to rely on context to classify Things.

I have now completed my discussion about classifiers. In the next section, I will move onto another important experiential element in the nominal group structure: Epithet.

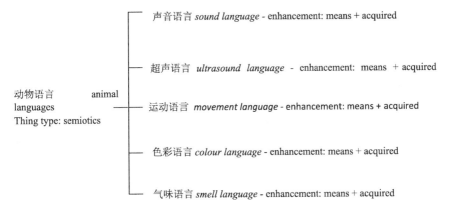

Fig. 4.15 Classification in Text 3

4.5 Epithet

Like the Classifier, the Epithet also represents properties of the Thing, but it is typically realised by adjectives. Being experientially complex, the Thing has a great potential to be further described by Epithets. In the following discussion, I will first explore the differences between Epithet and Classifier; and then the system of EPITHESIS will be presented; finally, a sample text analysis is presented to illustrate how the properties of Things are represented.

4.5.1 Epithet Versus Classifier

Compared with Classifiers, Epithets represent the less basic and less defining characteristics of the Thing, and therefore have the potential to modify a wider range of Things, both simple and complex. However, in terms of lexical realisation, there are some overlaps between the two functional categories: the same adjectives may be realised as Epithet in one text, but as Classifier in another. For example, adjectives representing such qualities as colour, weight, size and so on, can be used either to classify things or to further describe things by assigning an epithet to them. Examples:

Adjectives: 红 *red* 白 *white*
Example 63
As Classifier
葡萄酒以成品颜色来说, 可以分为红葡萄酒和白葡萄酒两大类。
According to the colour of the products, wine generally falls into two categories: **red** wine and **white** wine.

Example 64
As Epithet
那个姑娘身着白衣红裙, 在人群中显得十分醒目。
Wearing a **white** top and a **red** skirt, that girl was highly noticeable in the crowd.

As can be seen in Examples 63 and 64, the qualities represented by Classifiers are the more stable ones which serve to classify things into subsets (see Example 63), whereas Epithets represent properties that are more transient in time and space and less defining but more descriptive than those of classifiers (see Example 64). And the overlapping area covers those objective qualities which can either classify or further describe the Thing.

Also, there is a structural difference between the two functional elements: the Classifier is closer to the Thing than the Epithet on the experiential structure of the nominal group, and the difference is often marked by '的 *de*', which unmarkedly appears after an Epithet, but always before a Classifier. Figure 4.16 illustrates the relations between the two elements. As illustrated by the example in Fig. 4.16, 的 *de* is an important marker indicating the closeness of the relationship between a modifier and the Thing. In this example, there are two Epithets modifying the Thing, 漂亮 *nice* representing a subjective quality and 蓝色 *blue* representing an objective quality which is more defining in nature. The subordinating particle 的 *de* appears before Epithet 2 蓝色 *blue* and the Classifier 轿 *sedan*, as they construe the basic defining qualities of the Thing 车 *car*.

一辆 yī liàng	漂亮 piāoliàng	的 de	蓝色 lán sè	轿 jiào	车 chē
one Measure	nice	de	blue	sedan	car
Numerative +Measure	Epithet 1	SUB	Epithet 2	Classifier	Thing

A nice blue sedan

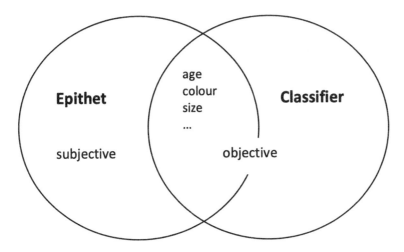

Fig. 4.16 Relations between Classifier and Epithet

4.5.2   System of EPITHESIS

Figure 4.17 presents the system of EPITHESIS, which lists the selections of epithet one can make to further describe the Thing.

In general, this system reflects both the **ideational** and **interpersonal** metafunctional aspects of Epithets. As the system shows, the selections on both ideational and interpersonal categories are simultaneous, as the Epithet is significant in terms of both at the same time. Apart from representing certain properties of the Thing ideationally, Epithets also enact attitudes towards the participant being construed. In the following discussion, however, I will focus on the ideational categories only, which is the concern of the current chapter, and will reserve the 'interpersonal' category for the following chapter (see Chap. 5).

Ideationally speaking, an Epithet represents two simultaneous selections: in terms of experiential meaning and of logico-semantic relations with the Thing.

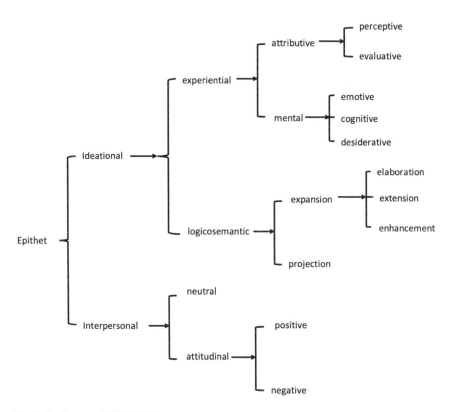

Fig. 4.17 System of EPITHESIS

4.5.2.1 Experiential Meaning of Epithet

Experientially, an Epithet characterises the Thing by assigning a quality to it, and this can be achieved from one of two perspectives: it may either characterise the Thing by assigning an attribute, which represents a quality that relates an inner experience of perception and evaluation with the material world, thus an **attributive Epithet**; alternatively, Epithet also characterises the Thing by construing a quality based on our inner experience of emotions, cognitions and desires about the Thing, thus a **mental Epithet**. This categorisation is related to the Thing Type: attributive Epithets modify most types of Things including conscious, non-conscious, simple and complex Things, as most Things can be distinguished or characterised in some way by certain qualities they have; mental Epithets tend to modify conscious Things, especially human Things, as well as the manifestations of human mental activities such as behaviour and semiotics. Only conscious beings are able to construe experience of emotions, cognitions and desires, which makes it possible for Epithets to further characterise these inner experiences realised as the Thing.

Attributive Epithets

Attributive Epithets can be further categorised into two types: **perceptive** Epithets, which represent the properties that the Thing is understood to have in the material world, such as colour, size, shape, which is based on the human perception of seeing, hearing, smelling, touching, tasting of the Thing; and **evaluative** epithets, which represent the properties being mentally assessed by human in terms of various standards, such as human social status, attitude, importance, evidentiality, authenticity, possibility, obligation, complexity, usuality and so on. Based on the definitions, it is clear that both types of attributive Epithets represent qualities that relate the inner experience of human (sensing or evaluating) with the outer experience of the material world. As Epithets are realised by adjectives, which also function as adjectival verbs in Chinese, the same adjectives realising attributive Epithets in nominal groups can also construe attributive relational processes in clauses. Examples:

Example 65
Attributive Epithet in nominal group: perceptive
漂亮的房子
A **nice** house

Example 66
Attributive relational clause: intensive
房子很漂亮。
The house is **nice**.

Example 67
Attributive Epithet in nominal group: evaluative

重要的会议
An **important** meeting

Example 68
Attributive relational clause: intensive
会议很重要。
The meeting is **important**.

The distinction between perceptive and evaluative Epithets is closely related to the type of Thing that they modify. Generally speaking, a perceptive Epithet characterises conscious Things and simple Things, those that can be easily perceived by human. In comparison, an evaluative Epithet characterises not only conscious and simple Things, but also complex Things and even nominalised metaphorical Things, as basically any Thing (congruent or metaphorical) is subject to human judgement.

Many evaluative Epithets reflect complex qualities with values on multiple dimensions and can be perceived in the outer world experience, but at the same time also represent some inner world reflections. For example, adjectives such as 孤零零 *alone and lonely*, 正经 *serious and decent*, which represent the state of the Thing from different angles, reflecting an evaluation of the Thing by the speaker according to his outer world experience. In other words, the attributes being realised by these adjectives are fused with both objective quality and subjective attitude. Under experiential lens, they are treated as evaluative attribute; and at the same time, they enact attitudes and are important interpersonal metafunctional elements.

Table 4.12 gives some examples demonstrating the categories of perceived and evaluative Epithets. Note that the categorisations in Table 4.12 are not conclusive, as the analysis must be context-based. For example, 忙碌 *busy* can be an evaluative Epithet characterising a human Thing, such as 忙碌的上班族 *the busy office workers*, but it can also be an evaluative Epithet characterising a complex Thing, such as 忙碌的时段 *the busy hours*.

Mental Epithets

In terms of the experiential metafunction, apart from the attributive Epithet, the other major selection is the mental Epithet, representing qualities that result from the inner experience of emotional feeling, thinking and desire about the Thing. Correspondingly, mental Epithet can be further categorised as emotive, cognitive and desirative. Note that at the clause level, a mental process generally falls into four types, namely perceptive, cognitive, desiderative and emotive (Halliday and Matthiessen 2014; Halliday and McDonald 2004). All of the four types of sensing can result in the assigning of a property to the Thing when it is being 'sensed' in the mental process. However, only three types are concerned with 'mental Epithets' in the system of EPITHESIS, because the other type, perceptive sensing, is more closely related to the qualities that are usually 'noticeable' in the outer experience, such as taste (酸 *sour*, 甜 *sweet*, 苦 *bitter*, 辣 *spicy*), colour (红 *red*, 黑 *black*, 白 *white*), touch feelings

Table 4.12 Examples of attributive epithets

			Examples	
			Neutral	Attitudinal
Attributive epithet	Perceptive		酸 sour, 甜 sweet, 苦 bitter, 辣 spicy, 红 red, 白 white, 蓝 blue, 软 soft, 硬 hard, 冷 cold, 热 hot, 大 large, 小 small, 光滑 smooth, 粗糙 rough, 高 tall, 低 low	香喷喷 appetising, 脏兮兮 dirty, 臭哄哄 stinky, 毛茸茸 fluffy
	Evaluative	Human	胖 fat, 瘦 thin, 左 left (political), 右 right (political)	高贵 noble, 漂亮 beautiful, 孤零零 all alone, 文雅 elegant, 粗鲁 rude, 亲密 intimate, 轻盈 light and graceful, 魁梧 tall and strong, 优秀 outstanding, 平凡 ordinary, 丑陋 ugly, 伟大 great, 生硬 stiff, 死板 rigid, 亲切 amiable, 贫穷 poor, 富有 rich, 正经 serious and decent
		Simple	新 new, 旧 old, 生 raw, 熟 ripe, 昂贵 expensive, 低廉 cheap, 奇怪 strange, 普通 ordinary, 柔和的 gentle, 强烈的 strong, 剧烈的 violent	繁盛 prosperous, 贫瘠 barren, 舒适 comfortable, 豪华 luxurious, 高档 superior, 精密 accurate, 丰富的 plentiful, 充足的 abundant, 稀有的 rare
		Complex	复杂 complex, 简单 simple, 困难 difficult, 容易 easy, 明显 explicit, 隐晦 implicit, 一般 general, 特殊 special, 重要 important, 频繁 frequent, 罕见 rare, 飞快的 rapid, 缓慢的 slowly, 完整 complete, 遥远 remote	热闹 boisterous, 冷清 desolate, 震撼 spectacular, 精彩 wonderful, 合理 reasonable, 正当 justified, 虚假 fake, 正确 accurate, 错误 wrong

(软 *soft*, 硬 *hard*, 冷 *cold*, 热 *hot*). In comparison, the qualities being construed by the mental Epithets tend to be less 'noticeable' in the material world, and are more concerned with the inner world experience, concerning the human interpretation of the Thing through cognition, emotion and desire. Table 4.13 presents some examples of the mental Epithets.

Mental Epithets modify conscious beings (as senser) and any projected ideas and locutions, as well as anything that arouse and/or reflect emotions, cognition, desire

Table 4.13 Examples of mental Epithets

		Examples
Mental Epithet	Emotion	深情 affectionate, 羞涩 shy, 可怕 frightening, 愤怒 furious, 可怜 poor, 伤心 sad, 愉快 pleasant, 自信 confident, 善良 kind, 真诚 honest, 孤独 lonely, 豪爽 generous
	Cognition	狡猾 crafty, 笨 stupid, 聪明 clever, 愚蠢 foolish, 犹豫 hesitant, 虚伪 hypocritical, 困惑 confused, 可疑 suspicious
	Desire	可爱 lovely, 厌恶 disgusting, 期盼 expecting, 渴望 desirable, 讨厌 annoying

and hatred (as phenomena). They are highly attitudinal, as they reflect the speaker's judgement and subjective interpretation of things.

4.5.2.2   Logico-Semantic Types of Epithet

Same as other functioning elements in the nominal group, the Epithet enters into different logico-semantic relations with the Thing, and the selections reflect the same major types as those being found between clauses: expansion (including elaboration, extension and enhancement) and projection. Table 4.14 gives some examples in each category.

As demonstrated by the examples in Table 4.14, the Epithet may construe a mental quality that represents the emotion, desire and thoughts that a Thing projects. In terms of projection, this means that an Epithet of this type plays dual roles: on the one hand, the Epithet construes a quality representing the emotion, thoughts and intention that the Thing projects; on the other hand, the Epithet characterised the Thing by ascribing the mental quality to it. For example, in the nominal group 悲伤的表情 *the sad look*, the Epithet 悲伤 *sad* characterises the Thing 表情 *look* by ascribing an emotional quality to it. Meanwhile, the Thing 表情 *look* also projects its semiotic meaning through Epithet: the Thing 表情 *look* is interpreted as a token of the senser's sensing and the Epithet 悲伤 sad is the projected emotive message by 表情 *look*. In fact, many Things construe human behaviours, such as facial expression, look, tone, and voice, which can function as tokens of a senser's feelings, emotions and thoughts, may form a projecting relation with a mental Epithet.

Till now, I have finished the investigation of the experiential resources of Epithet. In the next section, I will focus on another functional element on the experiential structure, the Qualifier.

4.6   Qualifier

From an experiential perspective, Qualifier represents the qualification of a certain thing type, the circumstance where the Thing is construed. On the one hand, the

Table 4.14 Logico-semantic types of Epithets

				Examples of Epithets in nominal groups	
				Attributive	Mental
Expansion	Elaboration	Attributive		丑陋的面孔 an ugly face, 粗糙的表面 the rough surface, 平凡的外表 plain appearance, 蓝色的海洋 the blue ocean	饥饿的老虎 the hungry tiger, 有趣的话题 an interesting topic, 虚伪的个性 a hypocritical personality, 孤独的生活 a lonely life, 欢快的曲调 a happy tune, 愚蠢的问题 a stupid question
		Identity		相似的经历 similar experience, 疑似的症状 suspiciously similar symptom	
	Extension	Additive		额外的费用 additional cost	
		Contrastive		相反的例子 an opposite example	
	Enhancement	Extent	Distance	悠久的历史 long history, 遥远的乡村 a remote village	
			Duration	漫长的旅程 a long journey, 短暂的相聚 a brief reunion	
			Frequency	普遍的现象 a common phenomenon; 常见的症状 the common symptom	
		Manner	Degree	巨大的变化 huge change, 细微的改善 tiny improvement	深情的表白 an affectionate confession, 吓人的数字 shocking numbers

(continued)

Table 4.14 (continued)

				Examples of Epithets in nominal groups	
				Attributive	Mental
			Means	舒缓的音乐 soothing music, 缓慢的节奏 a slow rhythm, 匆忙的脚步 hurried footsteps	温柔的抚摸 the gentle touch, 滑稽的表演 a funny performance, 伤心的话语 heart-breaking words
	Cause-condition	Purpose		有用的东西 useful things	鼓励的话 encouraging words
		Result			感人的话 touching words
Projection					厌学的情绪 the school-hating feeling (*the feeling of hating school*)
					怀疑的口吻 a doubtful tone (*a tone of doubt*), 欢乐的笑声 the happy laughter (*the laughter of happiness*)
					悲伤的表情 the sad look, 渴望的眼神 eager eyes, 期盼的语气 a longing tone (*a tone of longing*)

experiential aspects the Qualifier represents are less basic and less defining compared with some other functional elements such as Classifier or Epithet. On the other hand, the experiential aspects represented by the Qualifier are also more transient and instantial than Classifier or Epithet (refer to Figs. 4.1 and 4.2).

In the following discussion, I will first take a look at the realisation of Qualifier in lexicogrammar. Then I will move on to the system of QUALIFICATION, with a focus on those Qualifiers being realised by an embedded clause.

4.6.1 The Realisation of Qualifier

In terms of realisation, a Qualifier can be realised by a rank-shifted clause (i.e. an embedded clause), or an adverbial group, or a nominal group. Unlike English where a Qualifier comes after the Head, a Qualifier in Chinese precedes the nominal Head as a premodifier. A hypotactic conjunctive particle 的 *de* is typically used to connect the Qualifier and the Thing.

There are mainly three types of nominal groups that can function as a Qualifier. The first type is typically a locative one, indicating relative position of the Thing, and the typical structure of the nominal group that functions as the Qualifier is like this: head noun + locative post-noun (see further in Halliday and McDonald 2004), such as 房子里 *house inside* (*inside the house*), 桌子上 *desk top* (*on the desk*). Logico-semantically, a Qualifier realised by such a nominal group forms a relationship of enhancement with the Thing, where the Thing is qualified in terms of location.

The second type of nominal group functioning as Qualifier is typically realised by nouns of events such as 地震 *earthquake*, 事故 *accident*, 会议 *meeting*, which qualify a special type of Things—Things of enhancement, or circumstantial Things, repre-senting names of location, time, result and reason, such as 时间 *time*, 地点 *location*, 结果 *consequence*, 原因 *reason* (see discussion in Section "The Complex Thing"). Logico-semantically, a Qualifier realised by event nouns forms a relationship of enhancement with the type of Thing that represents a general name of enhancement. However, this type of enhancement is special in that, when the Thing represents the name of an enhancement, the circumstantial sense is located in the Thing itself and the Qualifier further specifies or elaborates this enhancement, such as 地震的原因 *the cause of the earthquake*, 会议的地点 *the venue of the meeting*.

The third type of nominal group functioning as Qualifier also forms a relationship of enhancement with the Thing, but this time the sense of enhancement remains in the Qualifier: the Qualifier qualifies the Thing by reference to the circumstantial qualities such as extent of distance, duration or frequency—as most of these nominal groups in Chinese are often made up of a word of quantity and a measure word of distance, time, or frequency. Below are some examples of Qualifiers being realised by nominal groups of these three types:

Nominal group as Qualifier
Example 69
Qualifier realised by locative nominal groups
a. 屋子里的笑声
The laughter in the house
b. 书架上的书
The books on the shelf

Example 70
Qualifier realised by event nouns
a. 火灾的原因
The reason of the fire

b. 地震的后果
The consequence of the earthquake
c. 会议的时间
The time of the meeting

Example 71
Qualifier realised by nominal groups of enhancement
a. 两万五千里长征
The twenty five-thousand miles march
b. 上下五千年的悠久历史
five thousand years long history
c. 无数次的失败
Numerous failures

A Qualifier can also be realised by an adverbial group, which typically indicates location or time, such as 这里 *here*, 今年 *this year* and so on. Examples:

Example 72
Qualifier realised by adverbial group
a. 这里的人们
People here
b. 今年的收成
The harvest this year
c. 明天的火车
The train tomorrow
d. 很久以前的事情
The event a long time ago

Other types of adverbial groups in Chinese, which functions as verbal adjuncts (see further in Halliday and McDonald 2004), cannot function in a nominal group directly, and therefore are out of the scope of this discussion.

Apart from nominal groups and adverbial groups, a rank-shifted clause, namely an embedded clause, is commonly used as a Qualifier in a nominal group. In the following section, I will mainly focus on this type of realisation of the Qualifier and their experiential contribution to the nominal groups on the system of QUALIFICATION.

4.6.2 System of QUALIFICATION

In Chap. 3 where the logical resources are explored, I have presented a system of MODIFICATION (see Sect. 3.3). In this section, I will represent this system, but in the version of QUALIFICATION instead. Generally speaking, the categorisation of expansion and projection can be seen in nearly all the systems being introduced in this book, which supports Halliday and Matthiessen's view that 'the categories of projection and expansion are very prevalent in the organisation of the ideation base' (Halliday and Matthiessen 1999: 62). I need to make it clear that, although an experiential system, the system of Qualification is based on its logico-semantic categorisation. Figure 4.18 presents the system of QUALIFICATION.

As the system shows, theoretically the qualification can go on again and again. However, in reality, few the nominal group structures have more than one Qualifier, as more qualifiers may easily cause awkwardness, especially in the Chinese case where all the modifiers precede the nominal Head. More commonly, a speaker would express the meaning at the clause level. When a Qualifier is selected to modify the Thing, it forms a relationship of either 'expansion' or 'projection' with the Thing. And among the sub-categories of these two logico-semantic types, a Qualifier realised by a nominal group or an adverbial group is typically selected to further clarify the Thing (thus 'elaborating' logico-semantically), or to enhance the meaning of the Thing by reference to its extent, time, or place. The unmarked realisation of a Qualifier is by rank-shifted embedded clauses. Let me quote Halliday and Matthiessen's description of 'embedding' here (Halliday and Matthiessen 2014):

> Embedding is a semogenic mechanism whereby a clause or phrase comes to function as a constituent within the structure of a group, which itself is a constituent of a clause. (p. 491)

When focusing on the embedded clause as a Qualifier of a nominal group, one may view embedding from another angle: this time not only the embedded clause is viewed as a constituent within the structure of a nominal group, the Head/Thing can also be viewed as playing a potential participant role within the structure of the

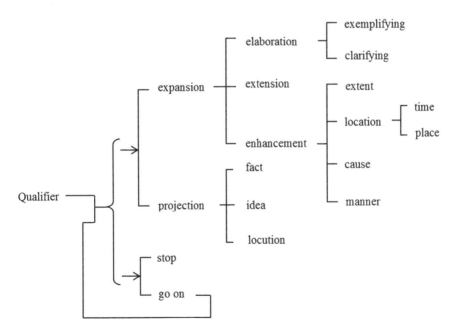

Fig. 4.18 System of QUALIFICATION

embedded clause when we suppose the embedded clause were up-ranked to clause level. By viewing the relationship in this way, I tend to seek answers to the following two questions: (a) What types of clause can be potentially down-ranked to function as a Qualifier modifying a particular type of Thing; (b) Does the process type of such an embedded clause have an impact on the logico-semantic relations it forms with the Thing? To explore answers to these questions, I present below some examples of embedded clause in different types of expansion with the Thing: together with these nominal groups are the agnate/related ranking clauses where the Thing takes a participant role (see Tables 4.15, 4.16 and 4.17).

Note that, for some of the examples in Table 4.17, no agnate ranking clauses are available as the Things in these examples represent some general circumstance names, such as result, reason, degree and manner, which are inherently circumstantial, and their corresponding role in a ranking clause would be a circumstance, not a participant.

I would like to present three points based on the examples listed in Tables 4.15, 4.16 and 4.17. First, in the case of elaboration, the prototypical process type of the

Table 4.15 Embedded clause elaborating the Thing

Embedded clause elaborating the Thing	Agnate/related ranking clause	Role of Thing/process type	Thing Type
[[他昨天刚买]]的一本书 A book [[he bought yesterday]]	他昨天刚买了一本书 He just bought a book yesterday	As Goal/material	Object
[[我们爬]]的那座山 The mountain [[we climbed]]	我们爬那座山 We climbed that mountain	As Range/material	Object
[[从监狱里逃走]]的罪犯 The criminals [[that were on the run from the jail]]	罪犯从监狱里逃走了 The criminals were on the run from jail	As Actor/material	Human
[[孩子们喜爱]]的儿歌 The nursery rhymes [[loved by children]]	孩子们喜爱(这些)儿歌 Children love these nursery rhymes	As Phenomenon/mental	Simple semiotics
[[认识我]]的人 People [[who know me]]	(这些)人认识我 (These) people know me	As Senser/mental	Human
[[他撒的]]谎 The lies [[told by him]]	他撒了谎 He lied	As Verbiage/verbal	Locution
[[和我谈话]]的警官 The police officer [[who talked to me]]	警官和我谈了话 The police officer talked to me	As Sayer/verbal	Human

Table 4.16 Embedded clause/phrase extending the Thing

Embedded clause/phrase extending the Thing	Agnate ranking clause	Role of Thing/process type	Thing Type
[[头发少]]的人 People [[whose hair is thin]]	(有些人)头发少 Some people have thin hair	As absolute Carrier/relational	Human
[[叶子少]]的树 The trees [with few leaves]	(有些树)叶子少 Some trees have few leaves	As absolute Carrier/relational	Object
[[分子密度大]]的物质 The substance [with high molecular density]	(有些)物质分子密度大 Some substances have high molecular density	As absolute Carrier/relational	Substance
[[亲朋好友多]]的家庭 The families [with a large number of relatives and friends]	(有些)家庭亲朋好友多 Some families have a large number of relatives and friends	As absolute Carrier/relational	Institution

Table 4.17 Embedded clause enhancing the Thing

Embedded clause/phrase enhancing the Thing	Agnate ranking clause	Role of Thing/process type	Thing Type
[[事故发生]]的地点 The place [[where the accident happened]]	事故发生在(这个)地点 The accident happened in this place	As Circumstance/material	Location
[[开学]]的日期 The date [[when school starts]]	在(这个)日期开学 School starts on this date	As Circumstance/material	Time
[[发表演说]]的广场 The square where speeches are given	在广场发0078表演说 Speeches are given in the square	As Circumstance/verbal	Location
[[绝食]]的后果 The consequence [of hunger strike]	–	As Circumstance/material	Result
[[吵架]]的原因 The reason [for the argument]	–	As Circumstance/verbal	Reason
[[喜爱]]的程度 The degree [of fondness]	–	As Circumstance/mental	Degree
[[奋斗]]的目的 The goal [[of working hard]]	–	As Circumstance/material	Purpose
[[谈话]]的方式 The way [[of talking]]	–	As Circumstance/verbal	Manner

embedded clause includes all the major process types except relational, and the transitivity roles taken by the Thing in the corresponding ranking clauses vary, ranging from actor in a material clause to verbiage in a verbal clause. These transitivity roles are related to the Thing types being selected: for example, only a conscious being like human can be a senser in a mental clause; a complex thing of locution can construe verbiage in a verbal clause. When these ranking clauses become down-ranked to modify the Thing, it is the Thing type that decides the experiential potential of the embedded clause when it realises a Qualifier.

Second, in the case of extension, the typical process type of an embedded clause is attributive relational, and the Thing is the absolute Carrier of the attribute in this construction. There is an interesting difference between Chinese and English in this case: in English there is only one 'Carrier' in an attributive relational clause, whereas in Chinese there could be two, one as 'absolute', and the other as the 'direct' Carrier of the attribute. The relationship between these two Carriers is typically possessive: the absolute Carrier as the possessor, and the direct Carrier as the possessed. I borrow the term 'absolute' from Fang et al. in their description of the textual resources of Chinese clause (Fang et al. 1995), where the first group or phrase in the clause taking the Theme position is termed as 'absolute theme'. When a relational clause of this type becomes down-ranked, it has the potential to form a relationship of extension with the absolute Theme/Carrier taking the Thing position. It is also interesting to note that the Thing type of this kind of nominal groups tends to be either conscious or simple concrete. In other words, it is less likely for the complex thing types to be selected, as normally these complex Things can hardly develop a possessive relationship with something else, and rarely do they carry attributes. So again, one can say that it is the Thing type that plays a role in selecting an extending embedded clause as Qualifier. Furthermore, another feature of this type of embedded clause is that they function similarly to a Classifier: this kind of embedded clause tends to classify a group of things by assigning a common attribute, though this attribute represented by the embedded clause is more transient and less defining than the one that a real Classifier represents. Examples:

Example 73
Classifying Qualifier realised by embedded clause (extension type)
a. 这个政策主要针对那些[[父母双方都已再婚]]的子女。
This policy mainly targets *those people [[whose parents married others later]]*.
b. [[头发多]]的人是劳碌命。
People [with thick hair] are predestined to have a lot of things to look after in their lives.

Thirdly, in terms of enhancement, there seems to be no limitations on the process type choices of an embedded clause: any of the four major process types can be selected. It is worth noting that the enhancement is not realised by the embedded clause, but by the Thing, as the Thing belongs to a particular type on the THING TYPE system—they are all complex Things of enhancement, representing the names of various types of enhancing relations. This is different from the case of enhancement where an adverbial group functions as a Qualifier, as in that case it is the adverbial group that is circumstantial, not the thing. Compare the examples below:

Example 74
Enhancement: time
a. [几年前]的事情 (circumstantial adverbial group as Qualifier)
The incident [a few years ago]
b. [[他到达]]的时间 (circumstantial Thing as Head)
The time [[when he arrives]]

Example 75
Enhancement: location
a. [北京]的婚礼 (circumstantial adverbial group as Qualifier)
The wedding [in Beijing]
b. [[上次见面]]的地方 (circumstantial Thing as Head)
The place [[where we met last time]]

Apart from the embedded clause, such circumstantial Thing can also develop a relationship of enhancement with another nominal group—some examples have been provided in Sect. 4.6.1.

There are some ambiguous cases, where the logico-semantic relations cannot be decided easily. For example, 生孩子的痛苦 *the pain of giving birth* can be interpreted as either elaborating or different types of enhancing: 生孩子的痛苦 *the pain of giving birth* = 生孩子所带来的痛苦 (elaborating) *the pain brought by birth-giving*; 生孩子的痛苦 *the pain of giving birth* = 生孩子时的痛苦 (enhancement: time) *the pain when giving birth*; 生孩子的痛苦 *the pain of giving birth* = 生孩子导致的痛苦 *the pain that results from birth-giving* (enhancement: result). Similarly, in the case of complex Things of enhancement like 时间 *time*, 地点 *location*, 结果 *consequence*, 原因 *reason,* when they are modified by a Qualifier, sometimes their logico-semantic relations are ambiguous. Compare:

Example 76
这是[[我们第一次相遇]]的地方。
a. Interpretation 1 (enhancement: location):
This is the place [[where we met for the first time]].
b. Interpretation 2 (elaboration):
This is the place [[in which we met for the for the first time]].

In English, conjunctions such as *which* and *where*, which are valid indicators of the logico-semantic relations, are used to connect a qualifying embedded clause with the Head. In comparison, no structural conjunctions are required to connect the modifying elements with the Head noun in a Chinese nominal group. 的 de, the subordinating particle, is often used to connect a Qualifier with the Head, but 的 de cannot indicate their logico-semantic relations. The examples presented above

demonstrate that the logico-semantic analysis of a Chinese nominal group structure could be uncertain as the language is so implicit in terms of the grammatical
realisation of these relationships.

So far, my discussion has not covered the other major category of the logico-
semantic relations, namely the Projection. This is because a detailed exploration with
examples has been presented in Chap. 2 when I investigated the logical resources (see
Section "Projection" for details), and therefore won't be repeated here. It is important
to emphasise though that Thing type, again, is a determining factor in developing the
relationship of projection, as only complex things of facts, ideas and locutions have
the potential to project. And this sense of projection can be realised not only by an
embedded clause, but also by a nominal group or a prepositional phrase in the form
of 'matter'. Examples:

Example 77
Projection: matter
a. 人们展开了[关于战争]的思考。
People started the **contemplation** [on the topic of war].
b. 这个[现代办公系统]概念让人耳目一新。
This **concept** of [modern office system] is eye-opening.

Up to now, I have discussed all types of logico-semantic relations being realised
by different types of Qualifier and the related Thing type choices. Table 4.18 presents
the general picture of different Qualifiers and their realisations in lexicogrammar.

4.7 Measure

Measure words provide resources to help construe participants and circumstances
by reference to different ways that they are measured in quantity. In the case of
nominal groups, Measure is recognised as a functional element in the experiential
structure of the Chinese nominal group because it is a prevalent element representing
the membership of a certain kind that the Thing belongs to. As its function is similar
to that of a Classifier, measure words are often termed as 'classifier' by linguists (e.g.
Chao 1965). However, in the present study, Measure and Classifier are considered as
two distinct functional elements, as they represent different aspects of the Thing. The
Classifier represents the most basic subclass of the Thing, and is significant in terms
of experiential function. Measure, on the other hand, represents certain experiential
features that a group of things share, based on which this kind of things can be further
measured in terms of quantity and identified in the referential space. For example,
both 绳子 *rope* and 鱼 *fish* have the experiential feature of being long and thin,
and therefore both can be measured in terms of 条 (tiáo, *slip*), which represents the
common property that these two things share. And clearly these two things belong
to different Thing types and are classified differently in terms of classification.

Table 4.18 Examples of Qualifiers

Type	Sub-type	Examples (with Qualifier in bold)	
		Embedded clause	Adverbial/nominal group
Elaboration	Exemplifying	[[唐太宗纳谏]] 的例子 The example [[of Emperor Tang Taizong adopting advices]]	[交通事故]的例子 Examples of [traffic accidents]
	Clarifying	[[漂浮在北冰洋上]] 的 冰山 The icebergs [[floating on the Arctic Ocean]]	[桌子上]的书 The book [on the desk]
Extension	Possessive	[[父母双亡]] 的子女 Those children [[whose parents are both dead]]	
Enhancement	Extent: distance		[两万五千里]的征程 A march of [25,000 miles]
	Extent: duration		[两个小时]的会议 A meeting of [two hours]
	Location: time	[[洋槐开花]] 的季节 The season [[when the locust tree is in blossom]]	[白天]的时间 The time of [daylight]
	Location: place	[[我们初次相遇]] 的地方 The place [[where we first met]]	
	Cause: purpose	[[用来酿酒]] 的好材料 The nice materials [[for making wine]]	[北京奥运会]的圣火 The holy flame of [Beijing Olympic Games]
	Cause: result	[[我们共同努力]] 的结果 The result from [[we working together]]	
	Cause: reason	[[我支持他]] 的原因 The reason why [[I support him]]	[事故]原因 The reason for [the accident]
	Manner: means	[[当地人酿酒]]的方法 The way [[for the local people to make wine]]	
Projection	Locution	[[要求延期审理此案]]的提议 The request that [[this case be adjourned]]	[关于民主] 的争论 The argument [about democracy]
	Idea	[[毕业后出国留学]]的想法 The thoughts of [[studying overseas after graduation]]	
	Fact	[[全球气候变暖]]的事实 The fact that [[the global climate is changing]]	

The following discussion will be divided into two parts: first, I will investigate the relations between Thing Type and measurability (Sect. 4.7.1); then I will present the system of MEASURE (Sect. 4.7.2).

4.7.1 Measurability and Thing Type

Compared with English, Chinese is a highly 'measurable' language: measure words provide rich resources for things to be measured in one way or another. The measurability is closely related to the type of the Thing being measured (see Fig. 4.19). The general tendency is that the more concrete the Thing is, the more measurable it seems, and complex Things and metaphorical Things have very limited potential to be measured, and when they do, they are typically measured in terms of 种 (zhòng, *type*) or 个 (gè, *instance*). Examples:

Example 78
Complex things
a. 这个时间我来不了。
This (MEA) time I cannot come.
b. 出于某种原因, 他未能出席。
Out of certain (MEA) reasons, he couldn't come.
c. 这个结果我早预见到了。
This (MEA) result I have long foreseen.

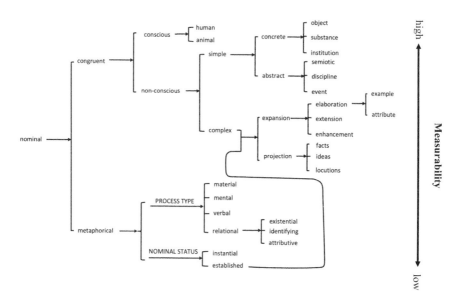

Fig. 4.19 Thing Type and measurability

Example 79
Metaphorical things
a. 善于放弃是一种智慧。
Being able to give up is a (MEA) wisdom.
b. 孤独也是一种美。
Being alone is also a (MEA) beauty.

Unlike English, there is no clear boundary between countable and uncountable nouns in the lexicogrammar of Chinese. However, through the relations between measurability and Thing Type, it can be seen that the distinction exists implicitly. It is just that the distinction is not reflected through the change of word forms, but through the use of measure words.

4.7.2 System of MEASURE

Figure 4.20 presents the system of MEASURE. The most fundamental categories on the system represent the experiential and logico-semantic potentials of Measure. There are three selections under the experiential category, representing the quantity, quality and both quantity and quality aspects of the Thing.

A measure of quantity presents either a singular or a plural quantity—apart from quantity, it does not provide any other features of the Thing. A typical measure word representing singular quantity is 个 *ge*, which can be used to measure any entity that is construed as countable—it can be regarded as a grammatical marker for those

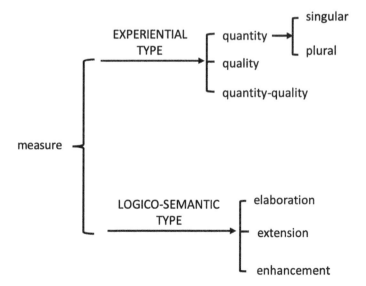

Fig. 4.20 System of MEASURE

things that are construed as count in English (cf. Halliday and Matthiessen 1999: 286). There are a few other measure words that are used to construe a plural quantity, such as pair 对 *couple*, 双 *pair*, 打 *dozen*. Same as 个, these words, often working together with numeratives, solely construe the quantity feature of the Thing, and only modify countable things.

A measure of quality is realised by type words, typically two in Chinese: zhǒng 种 variety and lèi 类 type. This kind of measure words differentiates the Thing from the other things of the same Thing type, as if it assigns a quality to the Thing—a highly general quality of being 'a kind'. It represents a 'variety' or a 'kind' of a particular Thing type. Textually, they are significant in identifying a participant with a certain quality. Measure of quality has the best potential to modify things, including both congruent and metaphorical things. Examples:

Example 80
Congruent: conscious
a. 这种人到处都是。
This **kind** of people are everywhere.
b. 你认识这种鸟吗?
Do you know this **kind** of birds?

Example 81
Congruent: non-conscious: concrete
a. 从那时起, 蒲公英成了我们最喜爱的一种花。
Since then, dandelion has become our favourite **kind** of flower.
b. 经常饮用这种水, 会使人的新陈代谢减缓。
If you often drink this **type** of water, your metabolism will slow down.

Example 82
Congruent: non-conscious: complex
a. "有德者得天下", "无德者失天下"这类说法的问题在哪里?
What's wrong with this **type** of arguments such as 'People with morals will win support from others' and 'those without morals will lose support'?
b. 这种情况是什么原因导致的呢?
What caused this **type** of circumstances?

Example 83
Metaphorical
a. 好的文艺作品中总含有一种人生见解和社会观察。
Good literary works always involve a **kind** of contemplation on life and social observation.
b. 所有他们的作品都给我一种神圣, 一种清明, 一种灵魂沐浴的通畅爽洁, 一种对于人生价值包括人生的一切困扰和痛苦的代价的理解和肯定。
All of their works bring me a **kind** of sacredness, a **kind** of enlightening, a **kind** of thorough satisfaction to soul, a **kind** of understanding and affirmation of the value of life, including the cost of all the worries and pains in life.

The third sub-type of the experiential category are those measure words that represent both quantity and quality features of the Thing. In other words, the Thing is measured in terms of its quantity and quality all at the same time. Therefore, measure words of this type play dual roles: on the one hand, they construe the quantity of the Thing, and at the same time, they indicate the qualities through which the Thing is measured. Unlike the Measure of quality, this type of Measure construes a much more specific property of the Thing. For example, 张 *spread* is used to measure things that can spread or open or set out in space, such as 一张纸 *a piece of paper*, 一张嘴 *a (open) of mouth*, 三张床 *three (sets) of bed*; 台 *stand/desk* is used to measure things that can stand on a flat surface, such as 一台电脑 *a (desk) of computer*; 这台缝纫机 *a (stand) of sewing machine*; 杯 *cup/glass* is used to measure things can be contained in a cup, such as 一杯水 *a cup of water*; 两杯酒 *two glasses of wine*; 三杯米 *three cups of rice*.

The other major selection on the system of MEASURE reflects the logico-semantic relations between the Measure and the Thing, and all the potential relations fall into the three expansion types: elaboration, extension and enhancement. Table 4.19 presents each type and sub-type with examples.

Up to now, my discussion has covered five functional elements on the experiential structure of the nominal group: Thing, Classifier, Epithet, Qualifier and Measure. These five elements are experientially significant in that they provide resources to construe participant roles by representing different aspects of the general experience of a participant. When relevant, some of these five elements will be brought forth again in the following chapters, as many of these functional elements simultaneously play roles in more than one metafunctions (see further in Sect. 4.2.2).

4.8 Case Study

In this final section, I will present a case study where the focus will be given to the analysis of the modification environment for Things of different types. The case study aims to serve as an illustration of how Thing Type plays a decisive role in determining the modification potential of the Head noun.

Altogether 4 nouns are selected in this case study, representing 4 distinguished types of Things on the system of THING TYPE. Table 4.20 presents the information about these 4 nouns.

Note that among these four nouns, three of them, 人 *person*, 树 *tree* and 话 *words*, are one-character words, meaning that a single character functions as a word. These four nouns realise Things of different types, ranging from the congruent conscious type to the metaphorical Thing type. Drawn on the reference corpus, *Chinese Web 2017*, the corpus-based analysis will present observations of different functional elements that serve as modifiers of the four Things. In particular, the analysis will focus on the modification potential of the Things in terms of Classification, Epithesis and Measure. Qualifiers are not included in this case study due to the fact that it is

Table 4.19 Types of Measure

Type of Measure	Sub-types		Examples
Elaboration	Expository	State	滴 drop, 座 block/mount, 股 ply/strand, 坨 lump, 页 page/leaf, 汪 pool
		Shape (with state)	扇 flap, 片 slice, 叶 leaf, 条 strip/bar, 行 line, 张 spread, 束 bunch/bundle, 页 sheet, 块 block
		Size	粒 particle/grain, 颗 grain
		Animacy	位 (for human), 只 (for animals and insects), 匹 (for horses), 头 head (for donkeys, cows, cattle), 口 mouth (for human)
	Exemplification	Instance	个 item, 件 item, 项 instance
		Type	类 type, 种 kind
Extension	Aggregate		群 group, 堆 pile, 批 batch, 套 set
	Measure (repository)		杯 cup/glass, 箱 box, 盒 box, 盘 plate, 包 bag, 瓶 bottle
	Partitive		头 head, 尾 tail, 边 side, 面 face
Enhancement	Space	Time	阵 spell/period, 段 period, 天 day, 代 generation
		Location	场 field, 台 stage, 间 room, 屋 room
		Dimension (area, length, width, height, etc.)	亩 mu, 尺 chi, 里 li, 米 metre, 升 litre
	Manner	Means	把 handful, 摞 stack, 撮 pinch, 串 skewer/string, 口 mouthful, 出 presentation
	Extent	Quantity (specified and unspecified)	双 pair, 对 pair, 打 dozen, 点 bit, 些 some
		Frequency	顿 time (meal), 次 time, 番 time

Table 4.20 Four types of Things

Noun	Thing type
人 rén *human, person*	Congruent: conscious: human
树 shù *tree*	Congruent: non-conscious: simple
话 huà *words, locution*	Congruent: non-conscious: complex
管理 guǎnlǐ management	Metaphorical: material

not possible to conduct collocation frequency search of Qualifiers, many of which are realised by down-ranked embedded clauses.

To analyse the use of different types of modifiers, a word sketch was first conducted to get a summary of the grammatical behaviour of each of the four nouns—this will profile the word in terms of classification, epithesis and measure. Then a collocation search in terms of each category was conducted and the top 20 most typical collocations of classifiers and epithets with the head noun were listed for analysis. For some nouns, there were no more than 20 instances found in the search, and then all the instances found in the category will be included in the analysis (see details in the analysis below). In terms of Measure, all the measure words resulting from the search were included in the analysis, as I will investigate the measurability of the four types of Things, and a full count would be necessary.

Classification

Table 4.21 presents the use of different classifiers in modifying the four types of Things.

In terms of classifying quality, 人 *person* and 树 *tree* can be classified in terms of their ascriptive qualities such as origin or type, like 男人 *male person* and 桂花树 *persimmon tree*, which represent the most basic and inherent qualities that a conscious or a simple Thing have as a being. Meanwhile, these two types of Things which are closer to the congruent nominal end, can also be classified in terms of acquired qualities such as time and function, the properties that are acquired through time, such as 变性人 *transgender person* and 发财树 *fortune tree*. In comparison, 话 *words* can only be classified in terms of a quality that is acquired. The metaphorical Thing, 管理 *management*, is not subject to classification, though it can collocate with some nouns to distinguish certain types of 管理 *management* in terms of the domains to be managed, such as 资源管理 *resources management*, 项目管理 *project management*, 企业管理 *corporate management*. Note that, although these collocations have a similar function to the 'Classifier + Thing' construction in distinguishing one type of 管理 *management* from another type, the modifying elements in these examples are not real Classifiers: this can be tested by inserting 的 *de* between these modifiers and the Head noun, and the use of 的 de does not impact the grammaticality of the structure. This indicates that the properties realised by these modifiers are not the

Table 4.21 Analysis of Classifiers

			人 *person*	树 *tree*	话 *words*	管理 *management*
Classifying quality	Ascriptive		13	16	0	–
	Acquired		7	4	20	–
Logico-semantic type	Expansion	Elaboration	9	16	10	–
		Extension	1	0	0	–
		Enhancement	10	4	6	–
	Projection		0	0	4	–

most defining characters of the Thing, as 的 *de* is typically used to connect the Thing with a less defining quality. Also worth commenting is the classifiers of 话 *words*, which is a complex Thing of projection. Several classifiers on the list for 话 *words* are borderline cases: they can be regarded either as a Classifier or an Epithet, such as 真话 *honest words*, 假话 *lie words*, 疯话 *mad words*. Again, the judgement needs to be based on each specific context, as the quality of 'being honest' could be highly defining to the Thing 话 *words* in one context, but less so in another.

In terms of logico-semantic type, 话 *words* is the only type of Thing that can be classified through projection: in this case, the Thing 话 *word* represents the token of a verbal process whereas the Classifier represents the verbiage resulting from the verbal process. For example, 谎话 *lie words* corresponds to the verbal process of 'telling a lie', and 玩笑话 *joke words* corresponds to the verbal process of 'telling a joke'. The other two types of Things, 人 *person* and 树 *tree*, can be classified through expansion. More specifically, all of these expansions are either elaboration or enhancement.

Generally speaking, in terms of classification, it is clear that the type of the Thing is critical in determining whether the Thing can be classified and how it is classified. The more congruent Thing types in these examples, 人 *person* and 树 *tree*, have the best potential to be classified in terms of their qualities. Only the Thing type with projection potential, such as 话 *words*, can be classified through a projecting relation. Metaphorical Thing type, such as 管理 *manage*, has little potential to be classified.

Epithesis

Table 4.22 presents the use of Epithets in modifying the four types of Things.

In terms of the experiential aspects of the Epithets, 人 *person* and 树 *tree*, the more congruent Thing types, can be modified by Epithets construing perceptive qualities, such as like 活生生的人 *living person* and 绿树 *green tree*. 话 *words* and 管理 *management* do not have Epithets of this category on their lists, which is probably due to the fact that these two Things themselves cannot be perceived, and therefore they do not carry perceivable qualities. Another interesting observation is that only 人 person and 话 *words* can be modified by a mental Epithet. Again, it seems to be closely related to their closeness to the mental experience, as 人 *person* typically

Table 4.22 Analysis of Epithets

			人 person	树 tree	话 words	管理 management
Experiential	Attributive	Perceptive	2	16	0	0
		Evaluative	12	4	12	20
	Mental		6	0	8	0
Logico-semantic type	Expansion	Elaboration	16	20	12	10
		Extension	1	0	0	0
		Enhancement	3	0	8	10
	Projection		0	0	0	0

construes the participant role of senser in a mental process and 话 *words* typically construes the participant role of Verbiage in a verbal process, both of which are related to the inner world experience of mental consciousness. Naturally, neither 树 *tree* nor 管理 *management* can be modified by a mental Epithet.

In terms of Logico-semantic relations, no projection is found among the Epithets listed and this applies to all the four Things. Note that, in terms of Epithesis, those Things with a potential to enter a relationship of projection with its Epithet are typically names of human behaviours, such as 表情 *face expression*, which can serve as a token of human emotions and therefore can be modified by an epithet through projecting the content of the emotion (see discussion in Section "Mental Epithets"). As none of the four Things in this case study represents human behaviour, it is not surprising that no instances of projection are found in the analysis. Another interesting point is that, similar to the analysis of Classifiers, elaboration and enhancement are the two major types of expansion in the logico-semantic relations between Epithet and Thing.

Measure

The examination of Measure will be carried out in two perspectives: on the one hand, I will compare the measurability of the four Things; on the other, I will investigate the ways in which they are measured. Table 4.23 presents the total number of measure words being found in the corpus in measuring the four Things and counts in each category on the system of MEASURE.

In terms of Measurability, it is clear that 人 *person*, the most congruent type on the Thing Type system, is most measurable with a total of 30 measure words found. In contrast, 管理 *management*, the most metaphorical type of Thing, is least measurable with only 3 measure words being found in the corpus: 次 (*times*), 种 (*kind*) and 项 (*item*). The simple type of Thing, 树 *tree*, and the complex type of Thing, 话 *words*, are found to have a moderate potential to be measured, with 16 and 14 measure words found respectively. The findings are consistent with the general cline of Measurability reflected in Fig. 4.19 (see Sect. 4.7.1).

In terms of how these Things are measured, Table 4.23 shows that all the types can be measured in terms of quantity such as 一个人 *one MEA (individual) person*, 一

Table 4.23 Analysis of Measure

		人 person	树 tree	话 words	管理 management
Total number of instances		30	16	14	3
Experiential	Quantity	4	3	2	1
	Quality	6	2	2	1
	Quantity-quality	20	11	10	1
Logico-semantic type	Elaboration	11	5	3	2
	Extension	10	4	2	0
	Enhancement	9	7	9	1

些树 *one MEA (some) trees*, 一项管理 *one MEA (item) management*, also in terms of quality such as 一类人 *one MEA (type) person*, 一种话 *one MEA (kind) words*, and in terms of quantity-quality such as 一伙人 *one MEA (gang) people*, 一行树 *one MEA (row) tree*, 一席话 *one MEA (seat) words*, and 一次管理 *one MEA (once) management*. In particular, the quality Measure 种 kind are found in the list for all the four types of Things. This indicates that, in terms of measure, nominal and nominalised entities can be widely measured in terms of kind/type, which represents possibly the most general way of measuring the quantity of a Thing.

In terms of the logico-semantic relations between the Measure and the Thing, Table 4.23 shows that 人 *person* and 树 *tree* can be measured in all the three expansion types, and the distribution of instances in each category looks balanced, indicating that these Things have rich potential to be measured in terms of various ways. In comparison, the predominant type of Measure to measure the complex Thing 话 *words* is enhancement (9 measure words), especially those concerning manner and frequency, such as 一席话 *one MEA (seat) words*, 一番话 *one MEA (occurrence) words*. Due to the low number of Measure words found to modify 管理 *management*, it is hard to comment on the selections of logico-semantic types. However, it is reasonable to assume that enhancement would be a common selection of Measure type in modifying a nominalised process or quality, as this type of Measure is concerned about the circumstantial features such as place, time and manner.

To sum up, this case study can demonstrate that, among the functional elements in the experiential structure of the nominal group, Thing plays a decisive role in determining the potential of the nominal group in expanding its experiential structure and how it can be expanded. In other words, Thing type is clearly the core in construing the experiential meaning of the nominal group and in determining how and to what extent the Head noun can be modified.

4.9 Summary

In this chapter, I have investigated the experiential resources of the nominal group and introduced the systems of five major elements that are important in terms of the experiential metafunction: the systems of THING TYPE, CLASSIFICATION, EPITHESIS, QUALIFICATION and MEASURE. Throughout the discussion in this chapter, we can see that logico-semantic types of expansion and projection are a common principle reflected in the experiential systems of all the major functional elements. This corresponds to the same general principle in semantics when semantic things are categorised (cf. Halliday and Matthiessen 1999: 202).

Many of these elements are multimetafunctional, such as Thing and Epithet, which are also important interpersonally, and they will be discussed again in the coming chapters where relevant.

References

Chao YR (1965) A grammar of spoken Chinese. University of California Press, Berkeley and Los Angeles

Fang Y, McDonald E, Cheng M (1995) On theme in Chinese: from clause to discourse. In Hasan R, Fries, PH (eds) On subject and theme: a discourse functional perspective. John Benjamins, Philadelphia, pp 235–273

Halliday MAK (2003) On language and linguistics. Continuum, New York

Halliday MAK, Martin J (1993) Writing science: literacy and discursive power. Falmer Press, London

Halliday MAK, Matthiessen C (1999) Construing experience through meaning. Cassell, New York

Halliday MAK, Matthiessen CMIM (2004) An introduction to functional grammar, 3rd edn. Arnold, London

Halliday MAK, Matthiessen CMIM (2014) Halliday's introduction to functional grammar. Routledge, London

Halliday MAK, McDonald E (2004) Metafunctional profile of the grammar of Chinese. In: Caffarel A, Martin J, Matthiessen C (eds) Language typology: a functional perspective. John Benjamins, Amsterdam, pp 305–396

Li ES (2003) A text-based study of the grammar of Chinese from a systemic functional approach. PhD thesis, Macquarie University, Sydney

Li ES (2007) Systemic functional grammar of Chinese: a text-based analysis. Continuum, London, New York

Matthiessen CMIM (1995) Lexicogrammtical cartography: English systems. International Language Sciences, Tokyo

McDonald E (1998) Clause and verbal group systems in Chinese: a text-based functional approach. PhD thesis, Macquarie University, Sydney

Tao Y (2002) Shixi hanyu sizige chengyu de leixing jiqi shiyi fangshi. 试析汉语的四字格成语的类型及其释义方式 [Exploring the types of Chinese four-character idioms and their interpretations]. Xueshu yanjiu. 学术研究 [Acad Res] 9:130–137

Chapter 5
Interpersonal Resources of Chinese Nominal Groups

5.1 Introduction

In this chapter, I will investigate the interpersonal resources of the nominal group. From an interpersonal perspective, nominal groups are significant in the following aspects: firstly, in terms of speech function, especially in realising the fundamental types of speech role, a nominal group provides choices to either give or demand further information about a referent; secondly, in terms of Person, nominal groups provide resources to realise a Person choice as an interactant or a non-interactant; thirdly, in terms of modality, the system of THING TYPE provides resources to metaphorically realise probability and usuality, and post-Deictic provides resources to elaborate the degree of modality; fourthly, nominal groups are very significant in the prosodic realisation of attitude. The following discussion will be unfolded along these aspects: in Sect. 5.2, I will introduce an interpersonally oriented nominal group system, which presents an overview of the major interpersonal selections in terms of 'nominal mood', 'person', 'attitude' and 'modality'; in Sects.5.3, 5.4, 5.5 and 5.6, I will present detailed discussions about these major selections, with Sect. 5.3 focusing on nominal mood, Sect. 5.4 on subject person, 5.5 on attitude and 5.6 on modality. In the final section of this chapter, Sect.5.7, a case study will be presented to illustrate how the interpersonal analysis of the nominal group can reflect the overall interpersonal colour of the texts.

5.2 An Interpersonal Nominal Group System

Figure 5.1 presents a nominal group system with interpersonal orientation:

The system presented in Fig. 5.1 is a very general one, which gives only an overview of the major interpersonal selections that nominal groups can provide. As can be seen, nominal groups provide resources to make four interpersonal selections:

© Springer Nature Singapore Pte Ltd. 2022
J. Fang, *A Systemic Functional Grammar of Chinese Nominal Groups*,
The M.A.K. Halliday Library Functional Linguistics Series,
https://doi.org/10.1007/978-981-19-4009-5_5

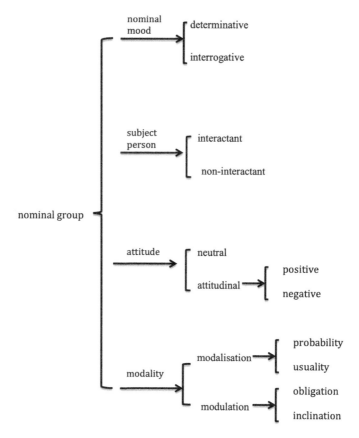

Fig. 5.1 Interpersonal nominal group system

nominal mood, subject personal, attitude and modality. This system reflects the real-isational relations between semantics and lexicogrammar. For example, attitude can be enacted through the choice of lexical words with certain connotations, or through a grammatical metaphor. For another example, the selection on Person can reflect the social distance between the speaker and the listener. In terms of realisation, these interpersonal selections can be realised by different functional elements of a nominal group, such as Deictic, Epithet, Numerative or Thing. In the following three sections, I will explore these major selections in detail.

5.3 Nominal Mood

The term 'nominal mood' is borrowed from Matthiessen's *Lexicogrammatical Cartography* (see Matthiessen 1995: 687), where he uses the term to refer to the distinction between determinative and interrogative. Determinative represents the choice where the nominal group gives information about a referent, whereas interrogative represents the choice where the nominal group is used to demand information about a referent. Interpersonally, this distinction is important in two aspects. On the one hand, it corresponds to the two fundamental choices in terms of speech role at the semantic level: giving and demanding. On the other hand, the choice of interrogative is also significant in realising the mood type at the clause level. The following discussion will focus on these two options.

5.3.1 Determinative

A determinative nominal group gives information about the Thing. It may appear in any types of clauses, and in the case of declarative clauses, it takes the positions of subject and/or complement. In terms of realisation, nouns, pronouns and determiners can all realise a determinative nominal mood. Examples:

Determinative nominal mood realised by a noun:
Example 1
As proper noun (names)
埃菲尔铁塔是世界著名建筑, 法国的象征之一。
The Eiffel Tower is a worldly famous building, a symbol of France.
你认识小王吗?
Do you know Xiao Wang?
北京是中国的首都和政治文化中心。
Beijing is China's capital and the country's centre of politics and culture.

Example 2
As a general noun (i.e., non-specific):
花园里种满了玫瑰花。
In the garden, roses were planted everywhere.
埃菲尔铁塔对面的广场上聚集了数千名示威人员。
On the square opposite the Eiffel Tower, thousands of demonstrators gathered.

Determinative nominal mood realised by a pronoun:
Example 3
As personal pronoun
咱们看月食去。
Let's go to watch the eclipse of the moon.
你叫什么名字?
What name are you called?

Example 4

As demonstrative pronoun
这是什么?
What is this?
光讲这些没有用。
It's useless to talk about these.

Determinative nominal mood realised by a determiner:
Example 5

As possessive determiner
两只孔雀咬住她的筒裙, 不让她走。
Two peacocks gripped her tube skirt, not letting her go.
小鹿的玫瑰花开了。
Little Deer's roses flowered.

Example 6

As demonstrative determiner
那个人很可疑。
That man looks very suspicious.
这个问题非常棘手。
This problem is very touch.

As shown in the examples above, when a noun is used to realise the determinative mood, it gives the information about a referent by giving it a name, either a specific one or a general one. In particular, when a determinative pronoun is used, it takes the position of Head/Thing in a nominal group and gives the information about a referent either by referring to it from the standpoint of speaker (such as in Example 3, 咱们 inclusive *we*, 你 *you*), or by referring to it according to the proximity to the speaker (such as in Example 4,这 *this*, 那 *that*). In either case, the speaker assumes that the Thing being referred to is identifiable to the addressee. When a determiner is used to realise the determinative mood, it comes either as a possessive or demonstrative determiner, and functions as Deictic in the nominal group. Further discussion about Deictic will be provided in Chapter 6.

5.3.2 Interrogative

An interrogative nominal group demands information about the referent. The sense of demanding is realised when it is used in an interrogative clause. In Chinese, there are two types of interrogatives: the elemental interrogative (similar to Wh-interrogative in English) and the polar interrogative (similar to yes/no interrogative in English) (see further in Halliday and McDonald 2004: 333). Interrogative nominal groups provide important resources in realising an elemental interrogative clause, which is characterised by the presence of an interrogative word. In terms of realisation, an interrogative nominal mood can be realised by a pronoun, a determiner or a numeral, functioning as Thing, Deictic or Numerative, respectively, in a nominal group. All of these words are interrogative in nature, demanding certain information about the referent in some way. Table 5.1 presents some examples of the main words used in the Chinese nominal groups in realising the interrogative mood at the clause level:

The interrogative items listed in Table 5.1 are very similar to the wh-items in English in realising an interrogative clause. However, unlike English where the wh-elements typically come at the beginning of an interrogative, the interrogative items in Chinese remain in the same place in an interrogative as in a declarative. Therefore, it is possible to say that these interrogative items are crucial in realising an elemental interrogative in Chinese.

The functional position of the interrogative item within a nominal group determines which part of the information is demanded about the referent. For example, as Table 5.1 shows, when the interrogative item functions as Thing like 谁 who or 什么 what, the information demanded is about the most fundamental experiential information about the referent. Also, the use of different types of interrogative pronouns may indicate the consciousness of the referent: as human such as 谁 who or non-human 什么 what. When the interrogative item functions as Numerative, then the information requested is about either the quantity or order of the referent. Sometimes, two interrogative items may appear in the same nominal group, thus demand two types of information about the referent at the same time:

Table 5.1 Interrogative words in Chinese nominal groups

		Lexical items	Example interrogative clauses
Pronoun as Thing/Head	Personal	谁 who	谁动了我的奶酪? Who touched my cheese?
	Demonstrative	什么 what, 啥 what (colloquial)	这是什么? What's this? 你的什么丢了? What did you lose?
Determiner as deictic	Possessive	谁的 whose	谁的书忘在这儿了? Whose book is left here?
	Demonstrative	哪 which, 什么what, 啥 what (colloquial)	这是什么地方? What's this place? 到底是哪扇门没关呢? Which door on earth is left open?
Numeral as numerative	Ordinative	几 which/what	你在看第几页? What page are you reading?
	Quantitative	多少 how many, 几 how many	一共有多少只小羊? Altogether how many little lambs?

Example 7

谁的什么丢了？

Whose what was lost?

Apart from an elemental interrogative clause, the above interrogative words may also appear in a declarative clause in Chinese, which is typically a mental clause in terms of experiential metafunction, and the information in question is the projection of the mental process. Examples:

Example 8

我不知道你在想什么。

I don't know what you are thinking about.

Example 9

我记得你叫什么名字。

I remember what name you are called.

Sometimes, these interrogative items may also appear in an imperative clause, which is also typically a mental clause experientially:

Example 10

猜猜我是谁。

Guess who I am.

Example 11

让我想想这到底是什么原因。

Let me think what reasons this is for.

In Examples 7–11, whether in a declarative, interrogative or an imperative clause, the presence of the interrogative words gives no information about the referent. Therefore, the local mood, that is the nominal mood, of the nominal groups where these items are functioning, remains interrogative, though the mood at the clause level may be of a different type.

5.4 Person

The system of PERSON provides choices between speech roles as interactant or as non-interactant in a speech exchange. Figure 5.2 presents the Chinese PERSON system. In the following discussion, I will explore each major selection on the system with examples. In Sect. 4.1, I will discuss the three sub-categories under 'interactant' in detail, focusing on how these selections will bring impact on the interpersonal meanings being conveyed. In Sect. 4.2, I will mainly examine the two types of realisation of 'non-interactant' in lexicogrammar: as pronominal and as nominal.

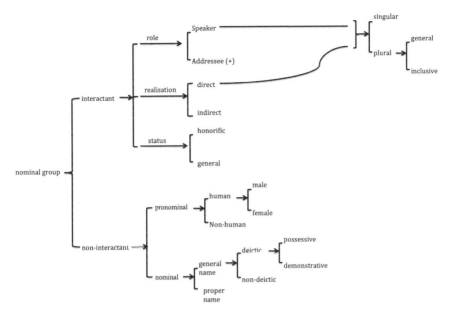

Fig. 5.2 System of person

5.4.1 Interactant

The role of an 'interactant' is either presented as speaker or addressee in a speech exchange. A typical realisation of speaker is through the use of a first-person pronoun, such as 我 *I* or 我们 *we*, and correspondingly, the typical realisation of addressee is through the second-person pronouns, such as 你 *you* (singular), or 你们 *you* (plural). In Chinese, however, there is another option in terms of realisation of an interactant role, where a word other than a first-person or second-person pronoun is selected to represent the role of a speaker or an addressee. As this mode of realisation is not as direct as the use of a personal pronoun, which often relies on the context to gain the interactiveness of the speech role, I present it as an 'indirect' option of realisation on the system of PERSON. Correspondingly, the direct realisation of an interactant, that is by means of a first- or a second-person pronoun, is presented as the other option in terms realisation. Table 5.2 presents some examples under each sub-category of realisation.

In the following subsections, I will examine each selection in detail.

5.4.1.1 Direct Speaker

When the role of Speaker is realised directly in Chinese, it opens for more options: the speaker is presented either as **singular** (i.e. the speaker himself) or as **plural** (i.e. the group that the speaker represents). As for the latter, there are further two options:

Table 5.2 Examples of direct and indirect interactants

		Direct	Indirect
Interactant	Speaker	我 *I*, 我们 *we*, 咱们 *we* (colloquial)	我商场 *this/our shopping centre*, 本公司 this/our company, 我校 this/our school, 本人 *I* (formal, written), 笔者 *this author = I*, 记者 *the reporter = we/I* (in news texts)
	Addressee	你们 *you* (plural), 你 *you* (singular), 您 *you* (honorific)	贵公司 *your company* (formal), 你们学校 *your school*, 大家 *everyone*, 各位 *everyone*

as **general**, where the inclusion of the addressee as a part of the group represented by the speaker is not certain and shall depend on the context, or as **inclusive**, where the addressee is particularly included as part of the group. Examples:

Example 12
Speaker: singular
<u>我</u>每天都去上学 。
<u>I</u> go to school everyday.

Example 13
Speaker: plural: general
我们都喜欢小动物。
We all like little animals.

Example 14
Speaker: plural: inclusive
快下雨了, <u>我们</u>快点回家吧。
It is going to rain, so **<u>let's</u>** rush home.
咱们把林奶奶扶到楼上去吧。
<u>Let's</u> help Granny Lin go upstairs.

As illustrated by Examples *12–14*, the pronoun 我们 *we*, which represents a plural form of speaker in Chinese, may be used as either a Speaker + in general (Example 13), or as a Speaker + that particularly includes the addressee (Example 14a). As both general and inclusive pronoun 我们 *we* is realised in exactly the same lexical form, one has to rely on the specific context for judgement. In comparison, another plural pronoun, 咱们 *we* (Example 14b), is always inclusive, which is equivalent to 'let's' in English when used in an imperative clause. The pronoun 咱们 *we* is commonly used in informal spoken texts and often comes with an indication of a close interpersonal distance between the speaker and the addressee.

5.4.1.2 Indirect Speaker

When the role of Speaker is realised indirectly, a noun, other than a personal pronoun, is selected. These nouns, when taking the role of Speaker, in general fall into two groups on the system of THING TYPE: they either represent institutions, or a conscious human (i.e., the speaker). When an institution is presented as the Speaker, the nominal group that construes it has a typical structure of Deictic + Thing. There are two deictic items that are commonly used in this situation: 我 (wǒ, *I/we*), and 本(běn, *one's own*), both referring to the speaker. And the Thing in this structure is a general type, representing the name of a kind of institution. This type of nominal groups often appears in a formal discourse. Examples:

Indirect Speaker (Deictic + Thing)

Example 15
<u>我公司</u>是一家集设计、生产、销售为一体的大型服装生产企业。
<u>We company</u> are a large apparel company, which is a designer, manufacturer, and seller at the same time.
= **We** are a large apparel company, which is a designer, manufacturer, and seller at the same time.

Example 16
<u>本</u>商场对本次促销活动中商品的价格拥有最终解释权。
<u>This store</u> have the right of final explanations about the prices of the goods involved in this sale.
= **We** have the right of final explanations about the prices of the goods involved in this sale.

Where a speaker uses a noun, rather than a first-person pronoun, to refer to himself, it tends to be formal, especially in written discourse. For example, a commonly used noun referring to the speaker himself, 本人 *(this person),* typically appears in formal statements (see Example 17):

Example 17
<u>本人</u>谨此声明, 有关收购交易系正常商业行为, 交易过程均遵循内地法律法规和香港上市公司规则进行。<u>本人</u>对有关造谣中伤、蓄意捏造事实的言行保留采取法律行动之权利。

<u>**This person**</u> (= **I**) hereby declare that the relevant acquisitions are normal business practices, and the process of the acquisitions all comply with the law and regulations of Mainland China and the rules of the listed companies in Hong Kong. <u>**This person**</u> (= **I**) reserve the right to take any legal actions against the behaviour of defamation, and intentional fabrication of facts.

Sometimes in a written text, a speaker will use 笔者 *the person holding the pen (=this author)* or 作者*this writer/author* to refer to himself, which is considered as a common feature in academic discourse—a similar example in English academic writing is 'the current author'.

As demonstrated by the discussion above, the use of a non-interactant item to realise an interactant choice can be interpreted as a grammatical metaphor, which is significant interpersonally. When a noun, instead of a first-person pronoun, is selected to take the role of 'Speaker', the actual sayer is distancing himself from the role of 'Speaker' and thus increases the objectivity of the saying. This seems to be a common motive behind the selection of an indirect Speaker role. The category of 'indirect Speaker' represents a common selection in the formal Chinese discourse, which is highly different from the situation in English. It is believed that further studies within a multilingual framework of language comparison are needed to cast a new light on the realisations of speaker roles.

5.4.1.3   Direct Addressee

When a second-person pronoun is used as an Addressee in an exchange of speech, it is defined as a 'direct addressee'. In Chinese, there are three second-person pronouns that can be used to refer to the Addressee: 你 *you* (general singular), 您 *you* (honorific singular) and 你们 *you* (general plural). The first pronoun, 你 *you*, is the most generally used one in addressing the listener, and it has a plural form, 你们 *you*, which is used to refer to a group of listeners. The other singular pronoun for addressee, 您 *you*, is an honorific one, the use of which means to show the speaker's respect towards the addressee. Therefore, it is often used to refer to an addressee with a higher social status than the speaker, or between two people of considerable social distance. In Beijing and its surrounding areas of North China, 您 *you* is also commonly used in dialogues between two people of a long social distance, such as between strangers, and the purpose of using an honorific pronoun is to show politeness. There have been some ongoing debates about the use of 您们 *you* (plural and honorific), the honorific plural form of 您 *you*. As it is not widely accepted in major Chinese lexicographic works, the discussion here will not cover the term. A good example to demonstrate the difference between 你 (general singular *you*) and 您 (honorific singular *you*) is the Chinese translation of a Russian poem by Alexander Pushkin. The translation was done by a well-known translator, Feng Chun, whose translation of the poem serves a good purpose for illustration:

> 她无意中失言，把空泛的您
> With a slip of tongue, she didn't use the feelingless '***you***' (honorific)
> 说成了亲热而随便的你
> Instead it became a sweet and casual '***you***' (general)

5.4.1.4   Indirect Addressee

When the role of 'Addressee' is not realised by a second-person pronoun, it is defined as an 'indirect Addressee'. The nominal groups that realise an indirect Addressee can be further categorised according to the specifiability and the deicticity of the referent. Table 5.3 presents a general picture of the choices in Chinese with examples.

There are a few points that need to be further discussed based on the examples in Table 5.3. Firstly, there is one pronoun, 大家*everyone*, which is not an explicit second-person pronoun like 你们*you* that identifies the addressee directly. Instead, it is used to address everyone in an audience group and is commonly used in spoken texts such as public speeches.

Secondly, when a nominal is selected to take the role of Addressee, it can be further categorised in terms of its specifiability (the choices between specific and non-specific) and deicticity (the choices between using a Deictic or not). In referring to a specific addressee, the speaker may select a nominal group with a Deictic, which typically happens when the addressee is an institution rather a human. And there are two commonly used possessive determiners functioning as Deictic in this situation: 贵 (honorific 'your') and 你 (general 'your'), which are similar to 您 (honorific) *you* and 你 (general) *you*, respectively, in the pronouns realising the direct addressee. However, when the honorific determiner 贵 (honorific 'your') is selected, it can only modify a non-conscious Thing such as an institution or organisation like 贵公司 *your (honorific) company* or 贵国 *your* (honorific) *country*, though the actual audience are conscious human beings who are the spokesperson on behalf of these institutions and organisations. The purpose of using such an honorific term is to show respect or politeness and at the same time also indicates a certain distance between the speaker and the addressee. Therefore, 贵 (honorific *your*) is usually used in a formal discourse, written texts in particular. More examples:

Example 18

我们对贵公司目前的运营情况深表担忧。

We are deeply concerned about the current operation of **your** company.

Example 19

贵校的外语专业一直名列全国前列。

The foreign language programme at **your** university has remained at the top of the national list.

Table 5.3 Different types of indirect addressee

		Nominal		Pronominal
		Deictic	Non-deictic	
Indirect addressee	Specific	贵公司 **your** (honorific) company 你校 your school	领导 leader = you	
	Non-specific	各位同学 **every** student = everyone		大家 everyone

Compared with the honorific 贵 (honorific *your*), its equivalent in the general context, 你 *you*, is used to indicate a different tenor relationship between the speaker and the addressee with less respect being indicated.

Thirdly, when a non-deictic nominal group is selected to refer to the addressee indirectly, it implies a huge gap between the speaker and the addressee both in terms of social status and social distance. It is generally perceived by Chinese speakers that it is neither respectful nor polite enough to use a second-person pronoun to directly address a listener/reader whose social status or rank in a given context is obviously higher than the speaker himself. This common perception gives a speaker an understandable reason to avoid using a direct Addressee, even in the case of a face-to-face exchange. Instead, a general nominal group is selected to take the role as an indirect Addressee (see Examples 20–22). And this nominal group may include a title attached to the addressee from the speaker's perspective, which functions as an acknowledgement by the speaker of the unequal relations with the addressee (see Example 21). Therefore, this kind of realisations typically occurs in a context where a speaker with lower social status addressing to a listener/reader with higher status. Examples:

Example 20
以下是昨天的会议纪录, 请领导审阅。
Below is the minutes of the meeting yesterday for leader (= you) to check and approve.

Example 21
请刘部长在这里签个名行吗?
Can Minister Liu (= you) please leave (your) signature here?

Example 22
请首长放心, 我们坚决完成任务。
Director (= you) may rest assured that we will definitely complete the tasks.

Fourthly, when addressing to a group of audience, apart from the pronouns, there is a non-specific Deictic item in Chinese which can be used: 各位 *every* (for human only). This determiner has good potential to modify all types of nouns representing human, irrespective of social values being connotated and is non-specific to anyone of the group being addressed. Examples:

Example 23
请允许我向各位来宾表示热烈的欢迎!
Please allow me to extend our warm welcome to every guest (every one of you) here!

Example 24
我希望各位同学能利用假期多参加社会实践。
I hope every student (= every one of you) will involve in some social activities during the holiday.

5.4.2 Non-Interactant

The role of a 'non-Interactant' represents the person outside a speech exchange, which is neither a speaker nor an addressee. In traditional grammar, it corresponds to role of the 'third person'. In terms of realisation, a non-Interactant may be realised by either a pronoun or a nominal group. Table 5.4 presents the third-person pronouns in Chinese that can function as non-Interactant.

As can be seen, the situation here is very similar to English, except that the plural forms of Chinese third-person pronouns are further distinguished by gender and humanity. When a third-person pronoun is used, the speaker assumes that his listener/reader is able to identify whom the referent is, as this type of pronouns is typically anaphoric in the text. For example,

Example 25
你找谁?
Whom are you after?
我找小王。他回来了吗?
*I'm looking for Xiao Wang. Is **he** back?*

When a non-Interactant is realised by nominal group other than a pronoun, there are two further choices: the speaker may use a proper name to refer to the non-Interactant if the referent bears one, or a nominal representing a name of a general kind. It is worth noting that, the use of a proper name in referring to a non-Interactant typically happens with an assumption that the name of the referent is the given information to both parties in an interaction. Example:

Example 26:
你刚才在和谁讲话?
Whom were you talking to?
小王。
Xiao Wang.
小王是谁?
Who's Xiao Wang ?
住在隔壁的那个小伙子, 我以为你们认识呢。
The man living next door. I thought you knew each other.

Alternatively, a general name may also be selected to represent a non-Interactant, in which case further selections become available in terms of deicticity. For those general names modified by a deictic, the distinctions can be further specified: (a)

Table 5.4 Third-person pronouns in Chinese

		Human		Non-human
		Male	Female	
Singular		他	她	它
Plural		他们	她们	它们

in terms of demonstrative proximity to the speaker, which comes with options of demonstrative determiners such as 这 *this* and 那 *that*; (b) in terms of the possessive relation from the perspective of the speaker, which comes with options of possessive determiners such as 我的 *my*, 你的 *your* and 他的 *his*.

5.5   Attitude

The term 'attitude' is very semantic, which can be interpreted as a kind of appraisal meaning, and which is related to the speaker/writer's judgements about people's behaviour, and the quality of things in terms of social value and social standard. Nominal groups are an important resource for enacting attitude. The attitude-enacting process is somewhat like colouring: the effect is cumulated as the text unfolds, and attitudinal items are scattered across the text without a regulated position. Many scholars refer to this feature as 'prosodic'—I will quote Halliday's comment as further explanation (Halliday 1979):

> Interpersonal meanings cannot easily be expressed as configurations of discrete elements...this interpersonal meaning...is strung throughout the clause as a continuous motif or colouring...the effect is cumulative...we shall refer to this type of realisation as 'prosodic', since the meaning is distributed like a prosody throughout a continuous stretch of discourse (66-67).

When it comes to nominal groups, this prosodic effect is achieved by a number of resources: attitudinal Epithets, attitudinal Things, some other attitudinal elements such as Deictic and Measure, and delicate lexicogrammatical metaphors. Some resources manifest attitude explicitly, such as attitudinal Epithet and attitudinal Thing, by which the speaker/writer's attitude is expressed through connotation of the lexical items realising the Thing and Epithet. Other resources, such as lexicogrammatical metaphors, manifest attitude more implicitly, where attitude is indirectly enacted through delicate lexical and grammatical resources. In the following discussions, I will explore these resources in detail. Section 5.1 will focus on attitudinal Epithet, and Sect. 2 on attitudinal Thing, Sect. 3 on some other attitudinal elements functioning in the nominal group, and Sect. 4 on lexicogrammatical metaphor.

5.5.1   Attitudinal Epithet

An attitudinal Epithet is the epithet that manifests the speaker/writer's attitude. I presented the system of EPITHESIS in Chapter 4, where one of the two simultaneous major selections, the 'experiential' selection, has been discussed in detail. In this section, I will review this system with a focus on the other major selection, the 'interpersonal' selection.

When viewed through the interpersonal lens, Epithets, which represent various properties of the Thing, generally fall into two categories in terms of the assessment and opinion of a speaker/writer: they are either 'neutral', representing the objective physical properties of the Thing, such as size, make, thickness and so on; or 'attitudinal', representing the subjective qualities that are subject to the speaker/writer's assessment. The predominant use of a certain type of Epithet makes an important contribution to the overall interpersonal profile of a text type and thus should be considered as a discourse feature. For example, neutral Epithets are typically used in some expounding taxonomic texts, which are supposed to be objective about the subject matter. In comparison, attitudinal Epithets often appear in casual conversations between people in a close social relationship, where one's attitude or opinion about the subject matter is the key commodity for exchange. Attitudinal Epithets can be further categorised into two types: positive Epithets, which are realised by purr words, and negative Epithets, which are realised by snarl words.

It is usually very explicit and straightforward for the speaker/writer to enact his attitude through the use of an attitudinal Epithet, as the connotation of an adjective realising an appreciative (i.e. a purr word) or a derogative (i.e. a snarl word) sense could be manifest enough. Many languages, including Chinese, have rich lexical resources in manifesting a speaker/writer's attitude through the use of certain Epithets. Below are examples of different adjectives in Chinese that are used to describe the characteristics of Cao Cao, a highly controversial figure in Chinese history, a statesman and warlord in ancient China, who was described in literature and history books as being both 'good' and 'bad' at the same time. In modern times, there are a good number of reviews about Cao Cao, which reflect the controversy of his characters. As can be seen in Table 5.5, the adjectives used to reflect different attitudes towards him (examples extracted from (Luo 2011):

The adjectives in Table 5.5 are all about human-related characters, which are highly attitudinal as they are subject to the judgement against accepted social values. And most of the Epithets construing the human-related characters can be assessed according to the mainstream social values, so the attitude they enact, either positive or negative, is generally stable in all contexts.

In comparison, some other Epithets, which are not human-specific, may be more reliant on the context to be assessed. When discussing the experiential selections of Epithet, I make a distinction between 'attributive' and 'mental' Epithets (see further in Sect. 4.5.2). It is important to note that the attributive Epithets, which represent qualities that can be perceived or evaluated based on the experience of the material

Table 5.5 Adjectives used in describing Cao Cao

Positive	Negative
豪迈 heroic, 勇敢 brave, 坚韧 tenacious, 果断 resolute, 乐观 optimistic, 幽默 humorous, 简朴 simple, 实干 practical, 坦诚 frank, 威严 commanding, 悲天悯人 compassionate, 叛逆 rebellious, 大度 generous	自私 selfish, 奸诈 fraudulent, 狡猾 cunning, 虚伪 hypocritical, 残忍 cruel, 自卑 self-abased, 自大 arrogant, 多疑 distrustful, 好色 lewd, 急躁 impatient

world, are not equivalent to 'neutral' interpersonally, as a speaker may assess a perceived attribute, such as weight, smell or size, according to a certain standard in order to enact attitude. In other words, the neutrality of an attribute is subject to the view of the speaker in each specific context. For example, the property of being fat could be interpreted as either 'positive' or 'negative' depending on the context. In Chinese culture, being fat is generally assumed as a desirable feature when used in describing children, which bears the implication that the child is healthy, strong and cute. However, the same feature may be interpreted as just the opposite when used in describing a woman, which may come with the indication that the woman is overweight.

The other type of Epithets, namely mental Epithets, are inherently attitudinal as they represent the qualities that are concerned with emotive, cognitive and desirative sensing, which is subjective in nature, such as 讨厌 *annoying*, 可恨 *hateful* and 迷人 *charming*.

As a modifier which precedes the Thing, the attitudinal Epithet is significant in setting the tone of the whole group. When explaining the prosodic effect realised by the Epithet, Poynton makes the following comment (Poynton 1996):

> It may be that the first realisation of attitude as initial Epithet has particular significance, functioning rather like a key signature announcing the tonality of the music it precedes. An initial attitudinal 'key' whose scope is, initially, the whole nominal group, spreading it over the rest of the group (and ultimately the utterance), having the effect of foregrounding the attitudinally salient information and backgrounding experiential content (p.217).

Although Poynton's comment is related to the Epithet in English, it can also be used to describe the situation of the Chinese nominal groups, where the attitudinal Epithet plays a significant role in signalling the interpersonal tonality of the whole utterance.

5.5.2   Attitudinal Thing

Apart from attitudinal Epithets, attitudinal Things are also an important resource in manifesting the speaker's attitude. Viewed on the system of thing type, attitudinal Things tend to fall into the category of 'human' and other human-related categories, such as locutions, ideas and nominalised attributes, which is not surprising because attitude has much to do with all kinds of human behaviour, material or mental. In comparison, some other thing types, such as animal, objects, substance and so on, tend to fall into the 'neutral' category. However, this does not mean that these types of Things cannot enact attitude—the attitude is enacted through resources other than the Thing, such as Epithet. Table 5.6 presents some commonly used attitudinal Epithets modifying a neutral Thing, 狗*dog:*

As presented by the example Epithets in Table 5.6, the different properties of a dog represented here are interpreted from the human perspective as desirable or

Table 5.6 Different attitudes towards 狗 (dog)

Attitudinal epithet		de	Neutral thing
Positive	Negative		
活泼 active, 忠诚 loyal, 可爱 cute, 聪明 clever	凶恶 ferocious, 脏兮兮 dirty, 凶狠 fierce	的 de	狗 dog

Fig. 5.3 Value cline of 'object'

undesirable, and these properties do not represent the inherent characteristics of a dog Rather, they represent an attitude, like or dislike, towards a dog from the speaker's perspective.

When it comes to the Thing type of 'objects', there are quite some nominal resources to enact attitude according to the value of the object, which again is interpreted from the speaker's perspective (see Fig. 5.3):

As Fig. 5.3 shows, the attitude towards an object is enacted through nouns carrying different 'values' assessed by the speaker.

Metafunctionally speaking, an attitudinal Thing plays dual roles: on the one hand, it construes the general experiential Thing type; on the other, it enacts the speaker's attitude.

When construing a human thing, there are even more nominal selections in Chinese which can play dual roles. This can again be demonstrated by the example of Cao Cao, a controversial figure in the Chinese literature and ancient history—Table 5.7 presents different nouns functioning as attitudinal Thing that are used in describing Cao Cao (examples from Luo 2011):

The examples in Table 5.7 indicate that the interpersonal attitude towards a human Thing heavily depends on the cultural values based on which the Thing is assessed. For example, '家' (jiā, an equivalent morpheme in English would be '-ist') in Chinese represents a group of people who are masters in a certain socially recognised profession or domain, which is often valued high in the Chinese culture. So when Cao Cao is referred to as a 军事家 *military strategist*, he is assigned to a group different from a simple group of war masters, as the latter does not bear the same high social value in the Chinese culture.

Table 5.7 Nouns describing Cao Cao

Positive	Negative
政治家 statesman, 军事家 military strategist, 大文豪 great writer, 英雄 hero	奸雄 bad hero, 统治者 ruler, 奸臣 traitor, 小人 vile character

When an attitudinal Thing and an attitudinal Epithet are selected simultaneously, the prosodic effect is harmonious—the Thing sets the attitudinal tone, which is then strengthened by the attitudinal Epithet. Therefore, collocations such as 'positive Epithet + neutral/positive Thing' and 'negative Epithet + neutral/negative Thing' are very common. Examples:

Example 27
Positive Epithet + **Positive Thing**
曹操是一位 了不起的政治家、军事家, 也是一个 了不起的诗人。

Cao Cao was a remarkable **statesman, military strategist**, as well as an outstanding **poet**.

Example 28
Positive Epithet + **Neutral Thing**
他是个很聪明的人。
He was a very clever **man**.

Example 29
Negative Epithet + **Negative Thing**
他同时也是一个自私冷酷、奸诈虚伪的统治者。
At the same time he was also a selfish and cruel **ruler** who was both fraudulent and hypocritical.

Example 30
Negative Epithet + **Neutral Thing**
曹操同时也是一个极端自私的人。
Meanwhile, Cao Cao was also an extremely selfish **person**.

When the attitudinal tone of an Epithet does not match that of the Thing, it is highly marked and usually brings some rhetorical effects, such as irony or humour, and the attitude becomes ambiguous and heavily context-based, as both positive and negative tones are combined in the nominal group. Examples:

Example 31
Positive Epithet + **Negative Thing**
遗忘是可爱的小偷, 把幼小心灵的记忆都偷走了。
Forgetting is a lovely **thief**, who has taken away all the memories of the little heart.

Example 32
Negative Epithet + **Positive Thing**
我是个聪明的傻瓜, 更是一个愚蠢的天才。

I am such a clever **idiot**, and a stupid **genius**.

5.5.3 Other Attitudinal Elements

Apart from Epithet and Thing, there are some other functional elements on the experiential structure which can enact attitude, which again contribute to the prosodic nature of interpersonal meanings. For example, it is easy to enact attitude with qualifiers realised by embedded clauses that contain attitudinal lexical items. Examples:

Example 33
他是个[[妒忌心很强]]的人。
He is a person [[who easily gets **jealous**]].

Example 34
曹操还是个[[充满才气]]的诗人。
Cao Cao was also a poet [full of **talent**].

Example 35
这是一个既现代而又[[充满诗情画意]]的城市。
This is a city [[which is both modern and **poetic**]].

Sometimes, even measure words could be attitudinal, provided that the Thing being measured is an attitudinal human Thing. In fact, in the construction of 'Measure + Thing', Thing plays a decisive role in setting the tone of the attitude: when the Thing is attitudinally neutral, the nominal group is neutralised even when the Thing is modified by a measure word that is generally used negatively (see Examples 36a, 37a and 38a). When a measure, which usually modifies a negative thing, collocates with a positive Thing, the attitudinal colour of the whole nominal group can become positive (see Examples 37b and 38b).

Example 36
Negative:
一小撮敌人正在刚来的路上。
A small bunch (= group) of **enemies** are on the way here.

Neutral:
只有一小撮人是清醒的。
Only a small bunch of **people** are clear-headed.

Example 37
Negative:
警察抓住了一伙罪犯。
Police arrested a gang of **criminals.**
Positive:
我们一伙朋友经常约着一起吃饭。
Our bunch of friends often eat out together.

Example 38
Negative:
门口有一帮<u>无赖</u>。
A <u>gang/bunch</u> of **scoundrels** were in the doorway.
Neutral:
我跟一帮同学去看电影。
I went to the cinema with a <u>bunch</u> of **classmates**.

In terms of Deictic, there is one item realised by a determiner, 某 *certain*, which can be attitudinal when used to modify a human Thing. For example,

Example 39
这是某集团的无耻,恰是李先生的光荣!
This reflects the shamelessness of a **certain** group, and also the glory of Mr. Li.

Example 40
中方谈斯诺登事件,奉劝某些人先照照镜子。
China talks about the incident of Edward Snowden and asks **certain** people to look at themselves first.

In Examples 39–40, 某 *certain* is used as a non-specific Deictic. It indicates that the speaker intentionally chooses not to identify the referent, though the speaker clearly knows whom he is talking about. Such use bears a strong connotation of contempt and disapproval of the referent.

Another common attitudinal Deictic item in Chinese is 人家 (rénjiā, *used to refer to either a third person or the speaker herself*), which may function either as a determiner or a pronoun. When used as a determiner, it modifies a non-Interactant, a third party, with an indication that the referent is in an admirable position in some way (see Example 41). When used as a pronoun, 人家 refers to the speaker herself, normally a female, with an implication of showing coquetry (see Example 42). Examples:

Example 41
<u>人家</u>小王都走了, 你怎么还在这儿?(showing admiration).
<u>(rén jiā)</u> Xiao Wang was gone already, why are you still here?

Example 42
袭人啐道:'小蹄子,　<u>人家</u>说正经话,　你又来胡拉混扯的了。'　　(showing coquetry).
'Little bitch!' swore Xi Ren. '<u>**We**</u> were speaking seriously, but you go talking such nonsense.

Sometimes, there may be a second Deictic element in a nominal group, which is commonly termed as '**post-Deictic**'. The use of a post-Deictic helps further identify the Thing in terms of such qualities as typicality, similarity, usuality and possibility. Interpersonally speaking, post-Deictics may function similarly as a comment adjunct in a clause, which expresses the speaker's attitude to the thing being talked about. Examples:

Example 43

Post-Deictic as a comment on the reason of the argument

这是个显而易见的道理。

This is such an **obvious** point.

Example 44

Post-Deictic as a comment on the typicality of the case

作者选择了<u>两个**典型**的案例</u>来进一步证明自己的观点。

The author picked <u>two **typical** examples</u> to further demonstrate his point.

Example 45

Post-Deictic as a comment of the accuracy of the decision

你做了<u>一个非常**明智**的决定</u>。(comment of the accuracy of the decision)

You made a **wise** decision.

Many post-Deictic items may also be used to create the sense of modality, such as probability and obligation, which will be discussed in detail in Sect. 5.6.

5.5.4 *Interpersonal Metaphor in Nominal Groups*

Apart from attitudinal Epithet and/or attitudinal Thing, nominal group provides a speaker with another resource to enact attitude: through the use of lexical and grammatical metaphors. The following discussion will be divided into two parts: in Subsection 5.5.3.1, I will discuss the interpersonal lexical metaphor; and in Subsection 5.5.3.2, I will focus on the interpersonal grammatical metaphor.

5.5.4.1 **Interpersonal Lexical Metaphor**

In the case of Chinese nominal groups, mainly two lexical resources, nouns and adjectives, are used to create **interpersonal lexical metaphor**. It happens when a noun, which congruently realises one Thing type, is used to represent another Thing type; or an Epithet, which congruently represents an attitudinal feature, is used to modify a Thing which does not bear this feature in reality. In both cases, the purpose of using these lexical metaphors is to enact an attitude towards the Thing being talked about, with an intention to either appreciate or to depreciate the referent.

Thing and Lexical Metaphor

When the metaphor happens to the position of the Thing, it can be further elaborated according to the Thing Type. Figure 5.4 shows the general tendency of presenting a human referent along the attitudinal cline:

Examples:

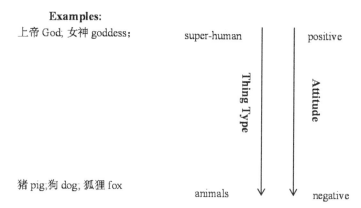

Fig. 5.4 Human referent as animal alone the attitudinal cline

As Fig. 5.4 shows, metaphorically, when human referent is presented as a high-level conscious being, typically a supernatural human, the speaker indicates a high-level admiration of the person being talked about. In contrast, when a human referent is dehumanised as an animal, there is usually a strong indication of dislike about the person being talked about. Certainly, this is only a very general tendency, and further elaboration along the same cline could be presented. For example, within the group of 'superhuman', further categorisation of good and bad superhuman, such as 'God' and 'ghost', would also follow the same attitudinal cline. Similarly, different animals may bear different attitudinal values in a certain culture, and the dehumanisation of human Thing may not always lead to a shift to the negative attitude. In particular, in the Chinese culture, 龙 *dragon* and 凤*phoenix* typically carry highly positive values, and when a human Thing is dehumanised as 龙 *dragon* or 凤 *phoenix*, the attitude is shifted to the extremely positive end. However, more often than not, the cases of animal assimilation of a human referent are driven by the speaker's intention to enact a negative attitude.

The commonly perceived features and behaviours of the selected animals imply the negative characteristics and behaviours that the human referent has, such as the laziness, nastiness, stupidity of a pig, the adulation and abjection of a dog, and the guile of a fox. There is one exception though, which is the case of describing children. It is common to assimilate children to animals, usually harmless and innocent young animals which share some similar characters such as activeness, cuteness and alertness. The purpose of using lexical metaphors in this case would be to express the speaker's adoration about the child being referred to. Below are some examples of animal words being used in lexical metaphor to express the speaker's like and dislike of the referent:

Example 46

Negative: Human adult as animal
你这样反对人民领袖, 就是地主资本家的走狗。

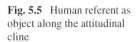 **Fig. 5.5** Human referent as object along the attitudinal cline

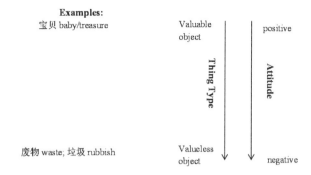

If you are against people's leader, you are **the running dog** (= stooge) of the landlords and capitalists.

人家可千万别被他这个老狐狸给骗了。

Please don't be taken in by this **old fox** (= him).

Example 47

Positive: Children as animal

春天里, 我们是一群快乐的小鸟。

In spring, we are a group of happy little **birds**.

你可真是个小馋猫啊!

You are such a greedy little **cat** (= gluttonous).

Sometimes, a speaker may refer to a human being as an unconscious object. In this situation, the attitude is represented by the value carried by the object. Figure 5.5 shows the general tendency:

Similar to the case of animal assimilation, when a human is referred to as a high-value object, it indicates the speaker's fondness of the person being talked about. On the contrary, if someone is described as a valueless object, it indicates the speaker's strong dislike of the person. Again, there is some difference between the case of an adult referent and a junior referent. For example, when the name of a general object, 东西 *object/thing*, is used to refer to a human, the attitude can be very different in the two cases:

Example 48

Negative: Human adult as 东西 *object/thing*

他这么对我, 真不是个东西!

Treating me so badly, he is not a thing (=a good person)!

Example 49

Positive: Children as 东西 *object/thing*

他可真是个调皮的小东西!

He is such a cheeky little thing!

The discussion above mainly focuses on the human referent. When it comes to a non-human referent, a similar strategy applies: referring to animals as unconscious products (玩意儿 *thing*, 东西 *thing*), and valuable things as valueless things (垃圾 *rubbish*, 废物 *trash/waste*) when the attitude goes down. The tendency seems to be one directional only, which is in the direction of devaluation, rather than the other way around.

Till now I have discussed the major contributions that the nominal group can make to enacting attitude. As a highly significant contributor to expressing interpersonal meanings, nominal groups help create the prosodic attitudinal effect through the 'colours' of different functional elements within the group, which work together harmoniously to create a prosodic effect.

Epithet and Lexical Metaphor

When the experiential function of an Epithet, which congruently construes certain qualities of the Thing, completely concedes to its interpersonal function, a lexical metaphor occurs. In this situation, the speaker expresses his attitude by attaching certain quality to the Thing against reality. For example,

Example 50
趁妈妈还没发现, 赶紧把你的臭袜子穿上!
Before mum finds out, put on your **stinky** socks quickly!

Example 51
不好意思, 这是一点微薄的小礼, 不成敬意。
Excuse me, this is just a **shabby** little gift to show my respect.

Example 52
他可是个大忙人, 哪会有空见我呢?
As he is such a **busy** person, how would he find time to see me?

In the above examples, the socks may not be 'stinky' (Example 50), and the gift may not be 'shabby' (Example 51), and the person may not be 'busy' (Example 52) in reality—the speaker attaches these properties to the Things in order to enact an attitude. Various motives could be behind this type of lexical metaphors, such as to express dissatisfaction towards the listener (as in Example 50), to express modesty of the speaker himself (as in Example 51), which is a virtue highly valued in the Chinese culture, or to sound sarcastic (as in Example 52). In any of these cases, the experiential meaning realised by the metaphoric Epithet has become minimal and the interpersonal meaning has been maximised, as the key purpose of assigning an Epithet to the Thing in these examples is to enact the speaker's attitude. There are some common features shared by the Epithets used in such metaphorical sense: experientially they represent some material features of the Thing, and interpersonally they are attitudinal. In a non-metaphorical context, such Epithets realise meanings in both dimensions. However, in a metaphorical context, the focus has been shifted to the interpersonal dimension, and the experiential meaning realised by the Epithet in this case is insignificant. Compare the examples below:

Example 53

你这是刚从泥巴堆里爬出来吗?瞧瞧你这身脏衣服!

Did you just come out of the muddy puddles? Look the **dirty** clothes you wear!

Example 54

别碰我!把你那脏手从我身上拿开!

Don't touch me! Keep your **dirty** hands off me!

In Example 53, the Epithet construes the experiential feature of 'being unclean', which is one of the properties of the Thing 'clothes'. However, in Example 54, the Epithet is heavily attitudinal, with no such an experiential indication of being 'unclean'—the 'hand' may not look dirty, but it is simply undesirable.

5.5.4.2 Interpersonal Grammatical Metaphor

An **interpersonal grammatical metaphor** uses grammar, rather than lexis, as a resource to create an attitudinal metaphor. In Chapter 4, when introducing the functional elements on the experiential structure of the nominal group, I presented two general tendencies along the 'lexis–grammar' cline, and the 'stable-transient' cline (see Figs. 5.1 and 5.2). These clines indicate that the elements representing the more inherent characteristics of the Thing, such as Classifier and some perceived Epithets (like colour, size and smell), tend to be lexically integrated with the Thing, whereas the elements representing the more transient features, such as Qualifier and mental and evaluative Epithet, tend to be loosely related to the Thing through grammar. In Chinese, a hypotactic structural marker 的 *de* is a strong indicator of the relationship between a functional element and the Thing. From an interpersonal point of view, such tendencies bring a new picture (Fig. 5.6):

When the properties represented by each functional element within a nominal group are viewed as arguable features of the Thing, their arguabilities form a cline as presented in Fig. 5.6. As Thing represents the most basic experiential class that defines a participant as it is, the feature it represents is not open for arguments. In

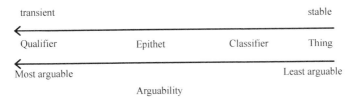

Fig. 5.6 Cline of arguability

contrast, a Qualifier represents features that are the most arguable due to their transient nature. Epithet and Classifier stand in between, with the former representing more arguable features than the latter. In terms of congruent lexicogrammatical organisation, features closer to the 'most arguable' end are loosely related to the Thing, where 的/*de* often comes in between, whereas features closer to the 'least arguable' end are more closely organised with the Thing without *de* 的.

When a more arguable feature is represented by an element that is congruently more closely related to the Thing on the structure, the organisation makes the feature less arguable than it should be. In such a case, an interpersonal grammatical metaphor happens. The motive behind this type of metaphor is to make a certain feature of the Thing less arguable and more defining instead. So the general principle of this type of metaphors is to push the elements on the experiential structure closer to the Thing to reduce the arguability. The extreme case would be to marry the Thing and the modifier into one word or to simply take the Thing's position. Some examples are presented in Table 5.8:

As can be seen in Table 5.8, when the features that are congruently realised by Qualifier or Epithet have been presented as Thing or a part of the Thing, these features become much more defining and therefore less arguable. In fact, many of the most recently emerged new words used in the cyber world are the results of such metaphorical shift of the grammatical positions.

Table 5.8 Examples of interpersonal grammatical metaphor

Congruent Form	Metaphorical Form
Qualifier + Thing: 有钱人的下一代 The younger generation of the rich people 当官的下一代 The younger generation of the officials	*As Thing:* 富二代 The Rich II (=the children of the rich) 官二代 The official II (=the children of these officials)
Epithet + Thing: 神圣的火炬 Holy torch 豪华住宅 Luxury residence	*As Thing:* 圣火 Holy flame 豪宅 Mansion
As Epithet: 她皮肤白皙, 富有美丽 She has fair skin, (and is) rich and beautiful 他高大富有帅气。 He is tall, rich and handsome	*As Thing:* 白富美 The white rich and beautiful (= the young women with these attributes) 高富帅 The tall, rich and handsome (=the young men with these attributes)

5.6 Modality in Nominal Groups

Modality refers to the intermediate degrees, the various kinds of indeterminacy that fall between 'yes' and 'no' (see further in Halliday and Matthiessen 2004:146). In terms of nominal groups, there are mainly two types of functional elements that provide resources for modality: the metaphorical Thing, and the post-Deictic. Both can fall into the two fundamental categories of modality: modalisation and modulation.

The metaphorical Things of modality are realised by two types of nominalisations: metaphorical Things of modalisation are realised by nominalised modal adverbs, and the metaphorical Things of modulation are realised by nominalised modal auxiliaries (for obligations) and nominalised mental verbs (for inclinations). Table 5.9 shows the two types of modality being realised by metaphorical Things, and their agnate congruent forms (see Table 5.9).

The post-Deictics realising modality also falls into the two categories of 'modalisation' and 'modulation'. They are realised either by adjectives construing the features of probability, usuality and obligation, or by nouns representing inclinations. Table 5.10 presents some examples of post-Deictics of modality:

Table 5.9 Metaphorical things of modality

		Examples	
		Metaphorical things	Congruent forms
Modalisation	Probability	发生这种事的可能性极大。 The **possibility** that such thing happens is very high	极有可能发生这种事。 It is very **possible** that such thing happens
	Usuality	当地震成为常态, 我们将何去何从? When earthquake becomes the **norm**, what shall we do?	当地震经常发生的时候, 我们将何去何从? When earthquake happens **often**, what shall we do?
Modulation	Obligation	这些话无不言简意赅地道出了守信重要性和必要性。 These words all simply demonstrate the **importance and necessity** of being trustworthy	这些话无不言简意赅的说明, 守信很重要, 必须要守信。 All these words simply show that being trustworthy is very **important**, and one **must** be trustworthy
	Inclination	同学们, 你们毕业后有出国的打算吗? Dear students, do you have the **intention** to study abroad after graduating?	同学们, 你们毕业后打算出国吗? Dear students, do you **intend to** study abroad after graduating?

Table 5.10 Examples of modality realised by post-Deictic

		Examples
Modalisation	Probability	新事物代替旧事物，是社会发展的<u>必然</u>结果。 The new replacing the old is an **inevitable** result of social development 广东省发现一例人感染H7N9禽流感<u>疑似</u>病例。 One **suspected** case of H7N9 infection was found in Guangdong province 重启野味市场，<u>最可能</u>的结果就是非典卷土重来。 The most **likely** outcome of re-opening the game market is the return of SARS
	Usuality	"多媒体化"，这是目前高中语文课，特别是语文公开课中出现的<u>常见</u>现象。 The use of multimedia materials is a **common** phenomenon in today's high school Chinese classes, especially in those open classes 一场<u>罕见</u>的沙尘暴23日横扫澳大利亚东部地区。 A **rare** sandstorm swept across eastern Australia on 23rd
Modulation	Obligation	想象是学生掌握知识的<u>必要</u>条件。 Imagination is **necessary** condition for students to grasp knowledge
	Inclination	找工作之前，如何了解你的<u>目标</u>行业呢？ Prior to your job hunting, how will you get to know about the **target** industry?

Fig. 5.7 Degrees of inclination

Some modality types realised by nominal group elements may also be graded in terms of degree. For example, in terms of inclination, metaphorical Things provide choices between the high and low ends (see Fig. 5.7):

Till now my discussion has covered all the four major categories on the Interpersonal System of Nominal Groups. In the following section, I will present a case study to demonstrate how the explorations above can be applied in text analysis.

5.7 Case Study

In this section, a case study will be presented. The purpose is to demonstrate how, by using nominal groups, one's attitude can be effectively reflected, and how nominal groups can contribute to the prosodic effect of interpersonal meaning of a text.

5.7.1 Context and Data

The data in this case study were sourced from Zhihu (zhihu.com), China's most influential question-and-answer website (a similar website in the USA is Quora), where questions are asked and answered by its community users. I'm going to focus on the answers to one question that was posted at Zhihu: "如何评价郭德纲?" (*How would you evaluate Guo Degang?*).

Guo Degang is a Chinese crosstalk (相声 xiāng shēng) comedian, widely recognised as China's most successful crosstalk comedian in the twenty-first century. Meanwhile, he is also a celebrity full of controversies—while enjoying a high popularity and having a large group of supporters, Guo is also widely criticised by fellow crosstalk actors and official media for the vulgarity in his dirty jokes (Cai 2016). It is not surprising that, when a question inviting people to comment on Guo is raised at Zhihu, the answers are not always straightforward.

5.7.2 Analysis

Two approaches will be adopted in the analysis of the data, which include 35 answers to the question that were posted at Zhihu since May 2020. Firstly, I will examine nominal groups collected from these answers. This is to investigate how, by using nominal groups, one's attitude can be manifested. Secondly, a sample text will be selected for detailed analysis. This text analysis aims to demonstrate the contributions made by nominal groups in creating the prosodic effect of interpersonal meanings.

5.7.2.1 Analysing Attitude Through Nominal Groups

To analyse how people use nominal groups to express attitudes about Guo, I will focus on the nominal groups that are used to refer to the main subject, Guo Degang, as well as those nominal groups in the relational clauses which realise the participant role of Value when 'Guo Degang' is the Token. Altogether 50 nominal groups were collected for this purpose, sourced from the 35 posted answers. Table 5.11 presents these nominal groups by the attitudinal colours that they carry and by their grammatical functions.

Table 5.11 Nominal groups describing Guo Degang

	When Guo is the referent	As the value when Guo is the token in a relational clause
Positive	郭老师 teacher Guo, 先生 sir, 老郭 Lao Guo, 老郭先生 Mr Lao Guo, 郭德纲先生 Mr Guo Degang, 桃儿 Peach	曾经的不完美勇士 a warrior who once was imperfect, 大师范 a master role, 艺术家 an artist, 绝顶的聪明人 an extremely clever man, 成功的商人 a successful businessman, 社会名流 celebrity, 相声天才 a crosstalk genius, 一个非常有魅力的人 a very charming person, 好人 a good person, 相声的领军人物 the leading figure in crosstalk sector, 一个极其认真的人 an extremely earnest person, 一个很严肃的人 a very serious person, 好艺人 a good performer, 真君子 a real gentleman, 一个真真实实的人 a genuine person, 有使命感的人 a person with a sense of mission, 一代宗师 a grandmaster
Neutral	郭德纲 Guo Degang, 他 he	一个被时代埋葬的理想主义者 an idealist buried by the times, 行业的一方大佬 a mogul in the industry, 成名大腕儿 a big name, 江湖人 a street artist, 有钱的江湖人 a rich street artist, 相声的守墓人 a graveyard keeper for crosstalk, 搞艺术的 someone in the art industry, 说相声的 someone in the crosstalk sector, 很矛盾的人 a contradictory person, 富豪 a rich man, 普通人 ordinary person, 男人 man
Negative	郭这人 this person Guo, 这个人 this person, 其人 this man, 郭某 certain Guo, 郭某刚 Guo Certain Gang	跳不起来的蚂蚱 a grasshopper that cannot hop; 匪气十足的郭德纲 a vulgar Guo Degang; 中国驰名双标 a well-known double-standard in China; 真小人 a real scoundrel; 大尾巴狼 a big-tailed wolf (i.e. a pretentious man)

I would like to make a few comments on the examples presented in Table 5.11. Firstly, in terms of the ways in reference to the major topic Guo Degang, a speaker's choice in realising the reference is a very useful indicator of his/her attitude. When a title comes together with Guo's name or surname, such as 郭老师 *teacher Guo* and 郭德纲先生 *Mr Guo Degang*, it has a strong indication of a positive attitude of the writer as these titles indicate politeness and respect from the writer when talking about the referent. An extremely important context information in this analysis is that, as these are answers posted to a public discussion forum, most writers are unidentifiable and write under their pseudonyms. Such anonymity gives the writers more freedom to express their views in a candid and sometimes bold manner than they would do when writing an authored piece. Such anonymity also gives writers more freedom to choose nominal groups to manifest their attitude towards Guo Degang when they make a reference to him. For example, negative attitude can be detected when the writer mentions Guo without fully identifying him: this is done by avoid using a proper name and instead using a non-specific Deictic item and/or a general noun representing the least specified type. Examples:

Reference to Guo Degang with a negative attitude:
Example 55
这个人 *this person* (Deictic + general name).

Example 56
郭某 *Certain Guo* (surname + non-specific determiner).

Example 57
郭某刚 *Guo certain Gang* (surname + non-specific determiner + partial given name).

By mentioning the topic person without fully identifying him, whose identity is in fact the known information to both the writer and his readers, the writer distances himself/herself from the referent and a sense of disapproval of the referent is highly revealing.

There is also an interesting example in Table 5.11 that is worth mentioning: some Zhihu users refer to Guo Degang as 桃儿 *Peach*, which is a nickname originally used by Guo's wife to address her husband. Understandably, the use of this nickname indicates intimacy and fondness, and by using it, the writers clearly show their positive attitude towards the referent.

The second aspect that I hope to comment on is the way in which attitude is enacted by nominal groups in relational clauses. As Table 5.11 shows, attitudinal colours, positive or negative, are displayed by nominal groups through: (i) an attitudinal Thing; (ii) an attitudinal Epithet; (iii) attitudinal Qualifier; (iv) interpersonal lexical metaphor; (v) interpersonal grammatical metaphor. Examples:

Example 58
Attitude expressed by attitudinal Thing
一代宗师 a grandmaster

Example 59
Attitude expressed by attitudinal Epithet
匪气十足的郭德纲 a **fully vulgar** Guo Degang

Example 60
Attitude expressed by attitudinal Qualifier
曾经的不完美勇士a warrior who once was imperfect

Example 61
Attitude expressed through an interpersonal lexical metaphor
跳不起来的蚂蚱 a **grasshopper** that cannot hop;

Example 62
Attitude expressed through a delicate interpersonal grammatical metaphor.
中国驰名双标 a well-known **double-standard** in China

Note that in Example 61, a lexical metaphor is used to express a negative attitude towards Guo Degang: a conscious human Thing is assimilated into an insect. As discussed in 5.5.4.1.1, when an adult human participant is presented as an animal, it often indicates a strong negative attitude of the speaker to the human participant. Also, the negative sense in Example 61 actually comes from two functional elements: both Thing and qualifier. While the Thing 蚂蚱 (*grasshopper*) realises a lexical metaphor, the qualifier 跳不起来 (*that cannot hop*) brings the indication that the 'grasshopper' has no stamina and won't last long. In addition, in Example 62, a delicate grammatical metaphor is used to express a negative attitude: this time, the element which congruently takes the position of qualifier, 双标 *double standard*, takes the position of the Thing. This is a shift on the experiential structure, from 一个搞双标的人 *a man who is well-known for having double standards* to 驰名双标 *a well-known double-standard*. When a qualifier takes the position of the Thing, the quality that the qualifier construes, 双标 *having double standards*, becomes much less arguable but more defining in describing the real person whom the quality is assigned to.

Many examples in Table 5.11 work with other functional elements to enact attitude, and individual attitudinal items cannot work alone to bring an overall effect of interpersonal meanings. And this brings the third aspect that I would like to comment on.

Thirdly, it is not always the case that a generally positive opinion piece about Guo only uses positive attitudinal items; likewise, not all the generally negative comments use negative items only in the text. Rather, we find that sometimes positive items work together with neutral or negative items in the same text and the colour of the interpersonal meaning is accumulated through the interactions and competitions between these different attitudinal items. For example, in Table 5.11, two nominal groups representing different attitudinal colours, 真君子 *a real gentleman* (positive) and 真小人 *a real scoundrel* (negative), appear in the same sentence of the same text, and the overall attitudinal colour of the text is positive (see the sentence in Example 63):

Example 63
真小人，真君子，这是一个真真实实的人。
A real scoundrel, a real gentleman, this is a real person.

In Example 63, there are three nominal groups in the sentence and the attitude is expressed through different elements: 真小人 *real scoundrel* (neutral Epithet + negative Thing), 真君子 *real gentlemen* (neutral Epithet + positive Thing) and 一个

真真实实的人 *a real person* (positive Epithet + neutral Thing). Note that in the first two nominal groups, the attitudes are expressed by attitudinal Thing (小人 *scoundrel* and 君子 *gentleman*), whereas in the last nominal group, the attitude is expressed by attitudinal Epithet, as the third 真 *real* indicates the quality of 'being genuine'. The first two nominal groups work together to imply that Guo is a complicated character featured with both good and bad qualities, and the third nominal group, which is more like a concluding statement, expresses the writer's real opinion about Guo: despite all his merits and defects, Guo is genuine, not pretentious.

The analysis of Example 63 implicates that, when analysing the interpersonal meanings realised by nominal groups, we need to not only focus on the nominal groups themselves, but also on the text where they are used. In other words, a text-based approach is the way to best capture the realisation of attitude.

5.7.2.2 The Prosodic Realisation of Attitude Through Nominal Groups

Now I will shift to a new perspective to continue with the exploration of nominal groups and attitude. This time, a sample text is selected from the Zhihu answers. The analysis of this sample text aims to explore how nominal groups contribute to the prosodic realisation of attitude of the whole text.

When talking about the realisation of interpersonal meanings, Halliday made the following explanation:

> this interpersonal meaning ... is strung throughout the clause as a continuous motif or colouring ... the effect is cumulative ... we shall refer to this type of realisation as 'prosodic', since the meaning is distributed like a prosody throughout a continuous stretch of discourse ...(Halliday 1979: 67)

The above comment has been further developed by Martin who argues that the same prosodic organisation strategy operates not only at the discourse level, but also at the clause and nominal group levels (Martin 2008).

Based on the views of Halliday and Martin, I would like to use the sample text to demonstrate how nominal groups contribute to the cumulating effect of the attitudinal meanings. Table 5.12 gives the context information of the sample text (Text 1).

Table 5.12 Context of the sample text

Field	The socio-semiotic function of this text is sharing and the situation type is that of a personal opinion shared on a public online forum. The domain is concerned with the writer's evaluation of an artist in terms of his character
Tenor	The institutional roles are a public online forum user to the fellow online forum users; both the writer and readers have equal rights to express opinions on the forum and both parties remain anonymous to each other. The evaluation of the experiential domain is negative
Mode	The text is monologic, written and constitutive of its contextual situation. No technical language is used in the text

Text 1

[1] 说白了, 郭德纲就是一说相声的。[2.1] 他算是业界的顶流, [2.2] 众人仰慕的师傅, [2.3] [[但是到底算不算艺术家]], 这就见仁见智了。

[3.1] 他的嬉笑怒骂, 引人捧腹, [3.3] 论搞笑确实是个高手, [3.4] 是个行家。[4.1] 但是依雅俗而论, 俗倒是肯定了, [4.2] 算不算得上雅, 这恐怕还得争议。

[5.1] 他本身就是个矛盾体, [5.2] 是谦谦君子, [5.3] 也是刻薄小人。[6.1] 现如今他功成名就, [6.2] 跻身名流, [6.3] 却依然撇不开那市井气。[7.1] 正如之前某网友所说, 他是相声天才, [7.2] 但就是没人说他是艺术家, [7.3] 尽管他真就是说相声的。

(retrieved from: https://www.zhihu.com/question/20490485/answer/2420933170).

To be honest, Guo Degang is simply someone doing crosstalk shows (xiangsheng). He can be counted as a superstar in his industry, (and) a master worshipped by many. However, [[whether (he) can be considered as an artist]], this is debatable.

His jokes and curses make people laugh. In terms of being funny, he is definitely a top player, (and) an expert. However, in terms of tastes, he is definitely vulgar, but [[whether he is classy]], this remains controversial.

He himself is a contradiction. He is both a modest gentleman and ungenerous villain. Today he is a successful man and has joined the high society, but he cannot get rid of his vulgar vibe. Just like what someone else has said on this forum, he is a crosstalk genius, but no one considers him an artist, though he is indeed just someone doing crosstalk shows.

Table 5.13 presents the analysis of the text with a focus on nominal groups. Items realising different attitudinal colours have been coded at both the clause and nominal group levels. Furthermore, logico-semantic relations between each clause have been analysed as well, which is to help provide an overall impression of the discursive development of the interpersonal meanings through which a prosodic effect is achieved.

A few comments can be made to the analysis presented in Table 5.13. Firstly, most of the clauses are attributive relational clauses, with nominal groups construing the participant roles of Carrier and Attribute. More specifically, the main topic person, Guo Degang, is predominantly presented as the Carrier, whereas the nominal groups that construe a class of Things, which are typically realised by common nouns, are functioning as the Attribute in these relational clauses, such as 君子 *gentleman*, 小人 *villain*. When a nominal group carries attitude, the attitudinal colour may be found in various functional elements within the group, such as the Thing, Epithet or Qualifier, and such realisation seems to happen randomly wherever appropriate.

Secondly, attitude is expressed in various grammatical manners. For example, attitude can be expressed through the use of an evaluative attribute realised by an

Table 5.13   Interpersonal analysis of the sample text focusing on nominal groups

Logico-semantic relations (between each clause) and attitudinal colours of the clause*	Participant roles and attitudinal colours realised by nominal groups and embedded clauses*					Attitudinal process and adjunct
	relational			material		
	carrier	attribute	attributor	actor	goal/range	
Paragraph 1						
[1] (slight negative)	郭德纲Guo Degang	一说相声的 someone who does crosstalk shows				说白了to be honest 就 simply
[2.1] (positive)	他he=Guo	业界的顶流a superstar in his industry				
+[2.2] (positive)	φ: 他he=Guo	众人仰慕的师傅a master worshipped by many				
x [2.3] (negative) concession 但是however	这=(他)到底算不算艺术家 this=[[whether φ:he=Guo can be considered as an artist]]	见仁见智subject to different opinions				恐怕afraid
Paragraph 2						
[3.1] (positive)				他的嬉笑怒骂his jokes and curses		引人捧腹 make people laugh
+[3.2] (positive)	他he=Guo	高手top player				
=[3.3] (positive)	φ: 他he=Guo	专家expert				
x [4.1] (negative) concession 但是However	φ: 他he=Guo	俗vulgar				肯定的 definitely
x [4.2] (negative) concession	这=(他)算不算得上雅 this=[[whether φ:he=Guo is classy]]	争议controversial				恐怕afraid
Paragraph 3						
[5.1] (neutral)	他he=Guo	一个矛盾体a contradiction				
=[5.2] (positive)	φ: 他he=Guo	谦谦君子modest gentleman				
+[5.3] (negative)	φ: 他he=Guo	刻薄小人ungenerous villain				
[6.1] (positive)	他he=Guo	功成名就very successful				
+ [6.2] (positive)				φ: 他he=Guo	名流high society	
x [6.3] (negative) concession 却依然but still				φ: 他he=Guo	市井气vulgar vibe	撇不开cannot get rid of
[7.1] (positive)	他he=Guo	相声天才crosstalk genius				
x [7.2] (negative) concession 但but	他he=Guo	艺术家artist	没人no one			就是just
x [7.3] (slight negative) concession 尽管though	他he=Guo	说相声的a person doing crosstalk shows				真就是 indeed just

*Attitudinal colour coding: **positive**; neutral; negative

attitudinal nominal group, such as '相声天才' *crosstalk genius* and '艺术家' *artist*. Such nominal groups represent names of a class, and by functioning as Attribute in a relational class with Guo as the Carrier, the person is assigned with a specific membership of an evaluative quality. The second way to express attitude is through the Attributor, which is the participant that assigns the attribute to the carrier. In clause [7.2] of the sample text, 没人 *no one*, functions as a negative Attributor. Through the negative Attributor, it becomes invalid when the Carrier '郭德纲' *Guo Degang* carries a positive Attribute '艺术家' *artist* in the relational clause. Another important grammatical way to express attitude in this text is through attitudinal adjuncts which are realised by adverbs. For example, in clause [1], the nominal groups realising the Carrier ('郭德纲' *Guo Degang*) and the attribute ('说相声的' *someone doing crosstalk shows*) are both neutral in attitude. However, a mood adjunct indicating negative attitude, 就是*simply*, appears in the same clause to indicate counterexpectancy and has therefore shaded the overall attitudinal colour into negative. Other examples of using a negative mood adjunct to muffle the originally neutral or even positive tone of the clause can be found in clauses [2.3], [4.2] and [7.3]. As can be seen, overall, attitude is expressed through various grammatical elements spreading all over the text where possible, which is consistent with Martin's comment that attitude is realised opportunistically, as contexts for evaluation arise (Martin 2008).

Thirdly and most interestingly, as Table 5.13 shows, the attitude realised in each clause may not be the same, and the building-up of an attitude happens gradually and coherently as the text unfolds. Such development can be displayed by the logico-semantic relations between clauses. For example, in paragraph 1, both clauses [2.1] and [2.2] give positive comments about Guo and they are connected through extension. Then the following clause (clause [2.3]) shifts the attitude to negative, and this is realised through a concessive enhancement, indicating a disagreement from the preceding attitude. And in paragraph 2, a similar pattern is repeated: clauses [3.1], [3.2] and [3.3] all confirm that Guo is successful in many ways, but then in clauses [4.1] and [4.2] the tone becomes negative again when the author comments on Guo's taste. Interestingly, such backflip moves of 'first praise then criticise' can be found in all three paragraphs. This recurrent textual pattern contributes to the accumulation of the writer's general attitude towards Guo, and through the repetition, a prosodic structure of the interpersonal meaning is developed.

To sum up, through the analysis of the sample text, we can see that nominal group provides important grammatical resources in expressing attitude and it is also a significant contributor to the prosodic realisation of interpersonal meanings.

5.8 Summary

In this chapter, I have explored the resources that the nominal group can contribute in terms of the interpersonal metafunction. An interpersonal system is presented, based on which my investigation is unfolded to further explore its selections and sub-selections, including nominal mood, the system of Person, attitude and modality. As shown in the investigation, nominal groups make very significant contributions interpersonally in a number of aspects, which reflect the interpersonal metafunction in various strata including context (reflected by the system of person), semantics (reflected by nominal mood and attitude) and lexicogrammar (by attitude and modality).

Some Deictic items are discussed in this chapter, as they represent some important selections in terms of nominal mood, Person and attitude. In the following chapter, Deictic items will be visited again as a major subject for discussion, but from a different angle, the textual metafunctional angle.

References

Cai S (2016) A culture hero: 'Xiangsheng' (Crosstalk) performer Guo Degang. Asian Theatre J 33 (1):82–103. http://www.jstor.org/stable/24737157

Halliday MAK (1979) Modes of meaning and modes of expression: types of grammatical structure, and their determination by different semantic functions. In: Allerton DJ, Carney E, Holcroft D (eds) Function and context in linguistics analysis: essays offers to William Haas. Cambridge University Press, Cambridge, pp 57–79

Halliday MAK, Matthiessen CMIM (2004) An introduction to functional grammar, 3rd edn. Arnold, London

Halliday MAK, McDonald E (2004) Metafunctional profile of the grammar of Chinese. In: Caffarel A, Martin J, Matthiessen C (eds) Language typology: a functional perspective. John Benjamins, Amsterdam, pp 305–396

Luo J (2011) 'Xinge zhi wang' Cao Cao "性格之王" 曹操 [Cao Cao the 'king of characters']. Xi'an: Xi'an Jiaotong University Press

Martin JR (2008) What kind of structure?—interpersonal meaning and prosodic realization across strata. Word 59(1–2):111–141. https://doi.org/10.1080/00437956.2008.11432583

Matthiessen CMIM (1995) Lexicogrammtical cartography: English systems. Tokyo: International Language Sciences

Poynton C (1996) Amplification as a grammatical prosody: attitudinal modification in the nominal group. In: Berry M, Butler CS, Fawcett R, Huang G (eds) Meaning and form: systemic-functional interpretations. Ablex, Norwood, NJ, pp 211–229

Chapter 6
Textual Resources of Chinese Nominal Groups

6.1 Introduction

In this chapter, I will describe the Chinese nominal group in terms of another meta-function, namely textual metafunction. Textually speaking, a text can be regarded as a flow of information. From a textual point of view, nominal groups are impor-tant in that they present the identity information of the Thing in context. Through nominal groups, the identity information of the Thing can be presented either as new, which appears for the first time in a text, or as given, which is identifiable to the listeners. Following this direction, some questions can be further asked in relation to the identity of the Thing:

- How identifiable is the Thing in a text? Is it identified explicitly or implicitly?
- When the Thing is interpreted as an instance in the referential space, how is it related to the here-and-now situation?
- When the Thing is presented as an instance, how specific is it to the addressee?
- How is the quantity information about the Thing presented in the text?

The textual resources that nominal groups provide are not only significant in identifying Things, but more importantly, in creating cohesion in text. For example, Deictic elements provide choices in the referential space, presenting a referent as either specific or non-specific. Also, numeric items, working together with Measure words, provide choices in realising ellipsis where the Thing is absent. Furthermore, different nouns with the potential to construe the same type of Things provide resources in creating lexical cohesions. In the following discussion, I will first present three systems of nominal group in the textual metafunctional domain (see Sect. 6.2), namely the system of NAMING, the system of IDENTIFICATION and the system of NUMERIFICATION, all of which are about the choices in presenting the identity of the Thing. Then in Sect. 6.3, discussions will focus on the contribution of nominal groups to creating cohesion in texts. In Sect. 6.3.1, I will explore the choices that

© Springer Nature Singapore Pte Ltd. 2022
J. Fang, *A Systemic Functional Grammar of Chinese Nominal Groups*,
The M.A.K. Halliday Library Functional Linguistics Series,
https://doi.org/10.1007/978-981-19-4009-5_6

nominal groups provide in realising ellipsis. In Sect. 6.3.2, another important cohesive device, lexical cohesion, will be discussed in relation to nominal groups. Finally, in Sect. 6.4, a case study will be presented to explore challenges faced by machine translation in dealing with nominal groups and their impact on cohesion in text. It is important to note that, the systems to be presented in Sect. 6.2 are not distinguished as separate cohesive devices. Rather, they are system networks that reflect lexicogrammatical and/or semantic choices, which contributes to the realisation of cohesion. So there are frequent and close links between the discussions in Sect. 6.2 and the rest of the chapter: an important type of cohesion, reference, will be discussed in Sect. 6.2 when choices in the system of IDENTIFICATION are explored; and in Sect. 6.3, when another two types of cohesive devices, ellipsis and lexical cohesion, are discussed, I will explain them by looking at the selections on the system of IDENTIFICATION.

6.2   Systems in the Textual Domain

In the previous section, I presented some questions one can ask in exploring the identity of a Thing when the Thing is viewed as an instance of a class. Based on these questions, I will present three systems. The system of NAMING reflects the selections one can make in relation to the explicitness in identifying the Thing–whether to name it explicitly or not. The system of IDENTIFICATION shows the specificity of the referent–how far it is to the here-and-now situation. And the system of NUMERATION is about how an instance of a class of the Thing is presented in terms of order and quantity.

6.2.1   System of NAMING

When the Thing is presented as an instance, nominal groups provide resources to identify it as either an instance with a name or as an unnamed instance. In the case of former, it is an explicit identification as the Thing is given a name, whether an individual name or a class name; whereas in the latter, the Thing is identified implicitly without being named. Figure 6.1 presents the system of NAMING showing the further options in these two categories.

6.2.1.1   Named Things

A **named** Thing can be further distinguished as either a Thing with an **individual name**, that is, a proper name, or with a **common name**, that is a name shared with others of the same class.

Fig. 6.1 System of
NAMING

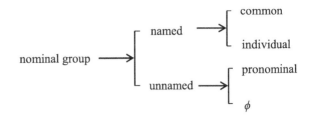

In an unmarked case, there are mainly four types of Things that can bear individual names: human beings and pet animals, institutions, some specific semiotic Things and some complex Things representing specific locations. Being individually named, the Thing is distinguished from others and therefore becomes identified. Table 6.1 presents some examples of individual names of different Thing types:

Normally, individual names of different types of Things have their own lexicogrammatical features, which make the Thing types obvious to the addressees. For example, an institution name is typically realised by a nominal group, where the head noun represents the most basic class name of the institution type, such as 大学 *university* in 清华大学 *Tsinghua University*, 医院 *hospital* in 协和医院 *the Union Hospital*, and so on. Usually, human names in Chinese are highly distinguished in that there are only a few hundreds of characters that are commonly used as surnames and names, and they are widely recognisable to the Chinese speakers. Even in less usual cases where a surname or a name is realised by less common characters, it is still easy to be identified in the text environment, as they are presented together with some other lexicogrammatical features which help identify the Thing type as 'human', such as titles (先生 *Mr.*, 女士 *Ms.*), or participant roles being construed (as senser in a mental process, as sayer in a verbal process, and so on). In an identifying relational clause, an individual human name can also be recognised by the assignment of a human-only identity:

Example 1

桑兰是我国女子体操队中最优秀的跳马选手。

San Lan was the best **vaulter** in the Chinese national gymnastics team.

Table 6.1 Examples of individual names of different Things

Thing type	Examples of individual names
Human	桑兰是我国女子体操队中最优秀的跳马选手。 **Sang Lan** was the best vaulter in the Chinese national gymnastics team.
Institutions	清华大学是中国著名的高等学府。 **Tsinghua University** is a prestigious university in China.
Semiotic Thing	周敦颐的《爱莲说》，读书人不知道的恐怕是绝无仅有的。 No scholars would not know Dunyi Zhou's '**On the love of the lotus**'.
Location	有人从湖北来，带来了洪湖的几颗莲子。 Someone came from **Hubei** and brought a few lotus seeds from **Honghu Lake**.

Example 2
大堰河, 是我的保姆。
<u>Da Yan He</u> was my **nanny**.

Sometimes, domestic animals, especially pets, may also be identified with individual names, which are usually given by their human masters. They are the examples of personification. Children's literature is another example, where animals and even non-conscious beings can be identified individually through naming:

Example 3
鸭先生的小屋前有一条长长的小路。小路上铺着花花绿绿的鹅卵石, 路旁开着五颜六色的鲜花。兔姑娘轻轻地从小路上走过, 说: "啊, 多美的小路呀!"
鹿先生慢慢地从小路上走过, 说:'啊, 多美的小路呀!"
There was a long path in front of <u>Mr. Duck</u>'s cottage. The path was colourfully cobbled with flowers of all kinds of colours on both sides. <u>Miss Rabbit</u> gently passed by the road and said, 'Ah, what a beautiful road!' <u>Mr. Deer</u> slowly passed by and said, 'Ah, what a beautiful road'!

The other type of named Things is those that are given a class name. In this category, the name being presented is a common name shared by a whole class of Things. The names on the system of THING TYPE (Fig. 4.5) are the examples of this type: they are the common names of things that are grouped according to some same experiential features they share. Compared with individual names, common names are on the general end, with a potential to be further specified. Because of the feature of being general, instances with common names can be easily identified in terms of Thing Type. There is not a clear-cut boundary between a common name and an individual name on the cline of instantiation. Rather, the situation can be viewed as a continuum: an individual name can be seen as an instance of a common name; whereas a common name is the most general potential that an individual name represents (see Fig. 6.2).

Sometimes, an instance may be presented as taking the middle position on the specific-general cline: the name is half individual and half common. In realisation, the nominal group typically has the structure of Classifier (individual name) + Thing (common name).

Example 4
去年10月, 湖南桃源出了一个<u>李皇帝</u>; 11月, 四川达县出了个<u>朱皇帝</u>。

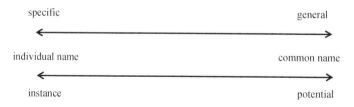

Fig. 6.2 Name and the cline of instantiation

Last October, there was an <u>Emperor Li</u> in Taoyuan Hu'nan Province; and in November, there came an <u>Emperor Zhu</u> in Daxian Sichuan Province.

The potential selections between an individual name and a common name provide rich resources in creating lexical cohesion, which will be further discussed in Sect. 6.4.

6.2.1.2 Unnamed Things

The other major selection in the system of NAMING is '**unnamed**', which represents those Things being talked about in the referential space without an explicit name. They are typically realised by a pronoun, or even completely elliptical. In such a case, these unnamed Things are only identifiable to the interactants, that is, the speaker and the addressee. To someone out of the interaction and out of the context, these unnamed Things cannot be easily identified unless more contextual clues become available. For example,

Example 5

"老栓只是忙。要是他的儿子……"驼背五少爷话还未完, 突然闯进了一个满脸横肉的人, 披一件玄色布衫, 散着纽扣, 用很宽的玄色腰带, 胡乱捆在腰间。刚进门, 便对老栓嚷道: "<u>吃了么?好了么?</u>老栓, 就是运气了你!你运气, 要不是我信息灵……。".

老栓一手提了茶壶, 一手恭恭敬敬的垂着; 笑嘻嘻的听。满座的人, 也都恭恭敬敬的听。华大妈也黑着眼眶, 笑嘻嘻的送出茶碗茶叶来, 加上一个橄榄, 老栓便去冲了水。

"<u>这是包好!这是与众不同的。</u>你想, 趁热的拿来, 趁热的吃下。"横肉的人只是嚷。

"真的呢, 要没有康大叔照顾, 怎么会这样……"华大妈也很感激的谢他。

"包好, 包好!<u>这样的趁热吃下。</u>这样的人血馒头, 什么病病都包好!"

'It's just that Old Chuan's busy,' said the hunchback. 'If his son. . . .' But before he could finish, a heavy-jowled man burst in. Over his shoulders he had a dark brown shirt, unbuttoned and fastened carelessly by a broad dark brown girdle at his waist. As soon as he entered, he shouted to Old Chuan:

'Has (he) eaten (it)? (Is he) getting any better? Luck's with you, Old Chuan. What luck! If not for my hearing of things so quickly'. . . .

Holding the kettle in one hand, the other straight by his side in an attitude of respect, Old Chuan listened with a smile. In fact, all present were listening respectfully. The old woman, dark circles under her eyes too, came out smiling with a bowl containing tea leaves and an added olive, over which Old Chuan poured boiling water for the newcomer.

'This is a guaranteed cure! This is not like other things'! declared the heavy-jowled man. 'Just think, brought back warm, and eaten warm'!

'Yes indeed, we couldn't have managed it without Uncle Kang's help'. The old woman thanked him very warmly.

'(It is) a guaranteed cure! (It is) eaten warm like this. *A roll dipped in human blood like this* can cure any consumption'! (From *The true story of Ah Q* by Lu Sun, translated by Yang Hsien-yi and Gladys Yang)

In the text of Example 5, the topic Thing being discussed in the conversation, 人血馒头*a bread roll dipped in human blood,* which was believed as a cure for tuberculosis, is mentioned for a number of times in the conversation. However, this topic Thing is not explicitly mentioned in the talk: as shown in the underlined sentences, it is presented either by a pronoun or becomes completely elliptical in the sentence. In either way, the topic Thing is not identifiable to the casual audience, but only to the two interactants until it is finally named in the end.

The above example also brings another interesting implication: when it comes to the question of 'identifiability', there are two parallel aspects that one needs to consider.

One is '*explicitness*'–how explicitly the identity of the Thing is presented? Based on the discussions so far, it is obvious that a named Thing, whether with a common name or an individual name, is more explicitly presented than an unnamed Thing. So 馒头*bread roll* is more explicit than 这个*this* in identifying the Thing, and 这个*this* is more explicit than an ellipsis. The matter of 'explicitness' can be viewed from the perspective of a third listener, or typically a casual listener, who is not directly involved in the interaction. So from the perspective of a third listener, if the subject matter is presented as a named Thing, it is explicit in that at least the third listener is able to identify the basic type of the Thing being talked about. However, on the other hand, when a third-person pronoun or an ellipsis is selected to represent the Thing, the identity becomes so implicit that it is very hard for a casual listener to tell what is being discussed unless more clues become available later in the text.

The other aspect is '*specificity*'—how specific the Thing is presented as an instance? This aspect is interpreted from the perspective of the addressee, as the matter of specificity is related to the here-and-now situation where the interaction takes place—how a referent is identified as a specific instance to the listener. 'Explicitness' and 'specificity' are two parallel aspects related to the identification of a Thing. So a specific Thing may not necessarily be presented as explicit. As Example 5 shows, 这 (*this*) in 这是包好 (*This is a guaranteed cure*) represents something with an implicit identity, but also represents something specific to the addressee. In the following discussion, I will focus on the system of IDENTIFICATION, which presents the selections in terms of specificity of an identity.

The two selections under the category of 'unnamed' Things, pronominal and ellipsis, will be discussed separately in the following sections: pronominal choices will be discussed in Sect. 6.2.2, and ellipsis in Sect. 6.3.

6.2.2   System of IDENTIFICATION

Figure 6.3 presents the system of IDENTIFICATION. The two simultaneous selections, SPECIFICITY and DEICTICITY, reflect semantic and lexicogrammatical concerns. Selections in terms of **specificity** are concerned about the identifiability of a particular instance of a general class of the Thing from the addressee's perspective, whereas selections in terms of **deicticity** are concerned with choices in lexicogrammatical realisation, in particular, the use of Deictic elements. In the following discussion, I will investigate each type of selections in detail.

6.2.2.1   Specific + Deictic

When a Thing is presented as a specific instance of a class, an unmarked lexicogrammatical choice in the nominal group is an eligible Deictic element realised by a determiner. Table 6.2 shows the Deictic items in Chinese that make an instance specific to the listener:

In terms of reference, determiners that are demonstrative and determinative, such as 这 *this* and 这些 *these,* are often used anaphorically, when the referent has been previously presented in the text, and the determiner is used to refer back to the referent. In such a way, it becomes identifiable to the listener. The same situation applies to the third-person possessive determiners, such as 他的 *his* and 他们的 *their.* Examples:

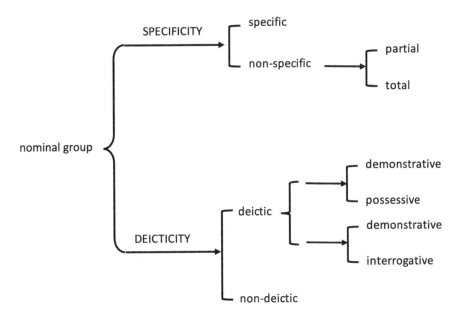

Fig. 6.3 System of IDENTIFICATION

Table 6.2 Specific deictic in Chinese

		Determiners	
Specific deictic	Demonstrative + determinative		这 this, 那 that, 这些 these, 那些 those
	Demonstrative + interrogative		哪 which, 哪些 which (plural), 什么 = 哪 what = which
	Possessive + determinative	first person	我 (的) I *de* (=my), 我们 (的) we *de* (=our)
		second person	你 (的) you *de* (=your), 你们 (的) you *de* (= your plural)
		third person	他 (的) he *de* (=his), 她 (的) she *de* (=her), 她们 (的) they *de* (=their, for female), 他们 (的) they *de* (=their, for human), 它们 (的) they *de* (=their, for non-human)
	Possessive + interrogative		谁的 whose

Determiners realising anaphoric reference:

Example 6

那个学生, 一边揉着自己的中指, 一边看着<u>陈老人的手</u>, 只见**那两只手**确实和一般人的手不同。

That student, rubbing his own middle finger, looked at <u>Lao Chen's hands</u>. Seriously **the two hands** looked different from others.

Example 7

我们这学期又学会了几首新的<u>古诗</u>, 你还记得<u>它们</u>的题目吗?

We have learned a few more <u>ancient poems</u> in this semester. Do you remember **their** titles?

Unlike third-person determiners, possessive determiners that are realised by first- and second-person pronouns, such as 你的 *your* and 我的 *my*, make the Thing identifiable immediately without the need of any anaphoric reference. This is because they are 'interactant' choices, the use of which already involves both the speaker and the addressee.

Interrogative determiners, although unable to give information about a referent but demand instead, make the referent specific by singling it out of a class of Things. In other words, the speaker uses an interrogative Deictic item to demand information about a specific referent. They often come together with other specific Deictic items in a clause:

Example 8

这是<u>谁的书</u>?

Whose book is **this**?

Example 9
<u>哪些花</u>是你种的?
<u>Which flowers</u> were planted by **you**?

Although it is very common to use certain Deictic elements to present a specific instance, there are other strategies that speakers can use to achieve the same textual effect.

6.2.2.2 Specific + Non-deictic

Sometimes, the Thing is presented as a specific instance by other means than a Deictic. In the following discussion, I will investigate three situations where a non-Deictic nominal group is used to present a specific Thing. These situations draw on lexicogrammatical, textual and/or contextual resources to make the Thing identifiable.

A Thing may be presented as specific by means of exophora, where the Thing is part of the specific situation and therefore identifiable. Examples:

Example 10
<u>作业</u>写完了吗?
(The) homework have (you) finished?

Example 11
请把<u>书</u>递给我。
Please pass **(the) book** to me.

In Examples 10 and 11, 作业*(the) homework* and 书*(the) book* are identifiable to both people involved in the exchange–both people know which homework and which book are referred to in these specific settings, and therefore are interpreted as specific in the analysis.

Sometimes, the Thing may be presented as specific by means of homophora, where it becomes identifiable because the identity it represents is a common knowledge shared by both parties in the interaction, and/or it is given a proper name. Examples:

Example 12
你今天见到<u>小张</u>了吗?
Did you see **Xiao Zhang** today?

Example 13
我们去年夏天去参观了<u>"水立方"</u>。
We visited **the Water Cube** last summer.

As demonstrated by Examples 10, 11, 12 and 13, Things being mentioned through exophora and homophora do not need to rely on the grammatical resources to be identified. Instead, this is achieved through the situational and contextual resources.

Table 6.3 Pronouns realising specific Things

		Pronouns
Personal	Interactant	我 I, 你 you, 您 you (honorific), 我们 we, 你们 you, 咱们 we (inclusive)
	Non-interactant	他 he, 她 she, 他们 they (for human), 她们 they (for human female), 它 it, 它们 they (for non-human)
Demonstrative		这 this, 这些 these, 那 that, 那些 those

There is a third type of situation where a non-Deictic nominal group represents a specific instance that is identifiable: by virtue of endophoric lexicogrammatical resources that are provided within the text. This can be achieved in two ways. In the first situation, the Thing is realised by a pronoun, which is either an interactant choice or an anaphoric reference if representing a non-interactant. In the case of anaphoric reference, the referent has been introduced previously in the text, and then is mentioned again through the use of a pronoun. Example:

Example 14

小鹿在门前的花坛里, 栽了一丛玫瑰。他常常去松土、浇水。

Little Deer planted a clump of roses in his front garden. He often loosened the soil and watered the flowers.

Table 6.3 presents the pronouns that realise a specific Thing.

In the second situation, the Thing is identified as specific through the defining elements that modify it in the nominal group. These modifying elements include ordinating Numerative, Epithet, Classifier and Qualifier. The examples below illustrate how each element works to make the thing specific:

Example 15

Ordinating Numerative

从前有一个国王, 他有三个儿子。第一个儿子长得很英俊, 国王建造了一座宫殿给他。第二个儿子很聪明, 国王送给了他一座城堡。第三个儿子长得既不英俊, 也不聪明, 国王一点也不喜欢他。

Once upon a time, there was a king, who had three sons. **The first son** was very handsome, and the king built a palace for him. **The second son** was very bright, and the king gave him a grand castle. **The third son,** neither handsome nor bright, was not at all adored by his father.

Example 16

Classifier

小明家有两个一样大的箱子, 一个皮箱, 一个纸箱。请问是皮箱重还是纸箱重?

Xiaoming has two boxes of the same size, one made of leather, and the other cardboard. Which one is heavier, **the leather box** or **the cardboard box**?

Example 17

Epithet

从前有两个和尚, 一个和尚很有钱, 另外一个和尚很穷。有一天, 这两个和尚碰面了。<u>穷和尚</u>说: "我很想到南海去拜佛, 你看怎麼样?"

<u>富和尚</u>摇头说:"南海离这有多远, 你知道吗? 我早就想去, 只是路途太远, 应该带的东西太多, 一时准备不齐全, 所以到现在没有动身。你什么都没有, 怎么去得成呢?"

Once there were two monks. One was rich and the other poor. One day, the two monks met, and **the poor monk** said, 'I want to worship the Buddha in the Southern Sea. What do you think'?

The rich monk shook his head and said, 'Do you realise how far away the Southern Sea is? I have been thinking of going for a long time, but cannot make it due to the long distance, which requires too much preparation. Being penniless, how can you make it'?

Example 18

Qualifier

一天中午, 三只白鹤在河里捉到了许多鱼。他们吃得饱饱的, 把剩下的一条大鱼埋在地里, 留着明天吃。

......

哪只白鹤能找到<u>埋在地里的大鱼</u>呢?

Once day, three white cranes caught many fish in a river. After the feast, they buried a big fish that was left uneaten in the soil for the next day.

…

Then which crane will find **the big fish buried in the soil**?

In Examples 15, 16, 17 and 18, the underlined parts are the nominal groups with the structure of 'modifier + Thing'. These nominal groups present the Thing as specific in the context, which is identifiable to the readers. It is important to point out that it is only in a given context that these non-deictic modifying elements are able to function in the same way as a specific Deictic. In other words, these non-deictic elements draw on the given contextual information to identify the Thing. An interesting feature shared by these examples is that, when viewed in terms of 'Given/New' information status, the Thing they modify is presented as **given information** in all the four examples: in all the examples, the Thing has been introduced first in the text and then is presented as given information when it is mentioned again. More interestingly, the relevant properties that the modifiers represent are also given information: 三个 *three* in Example 15, 纸箱 *cardboard box* and 皮箱*leather box* in Example 16, 穷 *poor* and 富 *rich* in Example 17, 埋在地里 *buried in the soil* in Example 18, have all been introduced in the texts initially. Except Example 18, all the other examples (Examples 15, 16 and 17) introduce more than one instance of the same Thing type: three 'sons' in Example 15, two 'boxes' in Example 16 and two 'monks' in Example 17. In the texts, these instances fundamentally represent the same Thing Type, but they are different from each other in terms of the qualities that they carry. For example, the two boxes in Example 16 belong to the same Thing type, but they are different from each other in terms of the classifying quality of make, as one is made of leather, whereas the other cardboard. In this situation, the modifier representing this quality can be used to differentiate one Thing from the other of the same type if the differentiating quality has been introduced in the text previously. As can be seen, this identification process can only be made possible as the text unfolds.

Another interesting thing in these examples is that, when translated in English, the non-deictic nominal groups all become deictic in English, typically through the use of 'the'. This simply indicates a difference in terms of lexicogrammatical resources between the two languages: English has the lexical resource to present the Thing as implicitly specific: the subset in question is identifiable, but this will not tell you how to identify it (Halliday and Matthiessen 2004: 314). Chinese, however, does not have such deictic item 'the' to function in this way, and a non-deictic nominal group may represent either specific or non-specific Things, depending on the context. This structural difference creates potential challenges to the Chinese-English-learners as well as translators, as many have trouble in using 'the' properly to present something as specific and given (see further in Huang 1999; Robertson 2000).

6.2.2.3   Non-specific + Deictic

When the Thing is presented as an unidentifiable instance to the addressee, it is non-specific. The use of some Deictic items in the nominal group may enable the speaker to present something as non-specific, and they are typically realised by determiners. Table 6.4 presents the non-specific Deictic items in Chinese.

Based on Table 6.4, I will have a further discussion about the following two points. First, a non-specific instance may represent part of a group or class, and the speaker is not specific about which part of the group/class being talked about. In the case of Chinese, there seems to be only one Deictic item that can function like this: 某 *certain*. Generally speaking, there are two situations where 某 *certain* is used to refer to something non-specific. In one situation, the speaker intentionally chooses not to make the Thing specific due to some reasons, whereas in the other, the speaker presents the Thing as non-specific simply because he is unable to identify it himself.

In the first situation, 某 *certain* plays dual roles in terms of metafunction—it is significant both interpersonally and textually. I will use the example below to illustrate (Example 19):

Table 6.4   Non-specific Deictic items in Chinese

	Determiners	
Non-specific Deictic	Partial	某 certain
	Total	任何 any, 每 every, 哪 whichever, 什么 whatever, 所有 all, 全部 all

Example 19

这是某集团的无耻, 恰是李先生的光荣!李先生在昆明被暗杀是李先生留给
昆明的光荣!也是昆明人的光荣!

The shamelessness of <u>a **certain** group</u> has well demonstrated the glory of Mr Li!
The assassination of Mr Li is the glory that Mr Li left with Kunming! It is also
the glory of the Kunming people.

Example 19 is extracted from a famous political speech, where the speaker
condemned the assassination of his comrade by the government. He chose not to
be specific about who the 'shameless group' was, though he was able to identify
them. The use of the non-specific deictic 某 *certain* simply indicated that it was
obvious and therefore needless to identify who was shameless.

Example 20 illustrates the other situation where 某 *certain* is used to present
something as simply a certain non-specific instance of a kind:

Example 20

安装这个软件之后, <u>某些</u>网站就打不开了。

After installing this software, <u>**some**</u> websites cannot be visited.

Secondly, compared with the partial Deictic, the 'total Deictic' presents the Thing
as a general non-specific instance of a kind and has more options. This is very similar
to English, where determiners like *any, every,* and *all* can be selected to present all
the instances in general. In Chinese, there are another two determiners with the same
function, which only work in a certain grammatical structure: 哪 *which (=whichever)*
and 什么 *what (=whatever)* collocating with 都 *all*:

Example 21

哪个孩子都爱玩游戏。

<u>Whichever kids</u> **all** like playing games.
(= *All kids like playing games.*)

Example 22

什么问题都难不倒他。

<u>Whatever problems</u> **all** can never beat him.
(= *No problems can beat him.*)

6.2.2.4 Non-specific + Non-deictic

Apart from Deictic items, nominal groups also provide some other resources in
presenting a non-specific Thing. This can be achieved in four ways: by presenting
the Thing as the general name of a kind, or as the collection of a group, or simply by
using certain non-specific pronouns to refer to the Thing, or through the modification
of a non-ordinated Numerative.

When the Thing is represented as the general name of a class, it is non-specific
in nature as the name represents all the things of the same kind/type in general.
Examples:

Example 23
松鼠是一种漂亮的<u>小动物</u>, 驯良, 乖巧, 很讨人喜欢。
The squirrel is a beautiful **small animal**, tame, gentle and very adorable.

Example 24
干旱地带的<u>植物</u>都有发达的根系, <u>仙人掌</u>也不例外。
Plants in arid regions have well-developed root systems, and **the cactus** is no exception.

Similarly, when representing a collection of members, the Thing may be realised by a collective noun. In such a case, it is also non-specific in nature. Examples:

Example 25
他死时, <u>人们</u>纷纷赶来吊唁。
When he died, **people** all came to mourn.

Example 26
中华人民共和国中央人民政府主席毛泽东出现在主席台上, 跟<u>群众</u>见面了。
Mao Tse-Tong, the chairman of the central government of People's Republic of China appeared on the platform to meet the **people**.

In Chinese, there are certain number of pronouns which can also represent things that are non-specific. Below are some examples:

Example 27
爱护环境, <u>人人</u>有责。
One one (=Everyone) has the responsibility of protecting the environment.

Example 28
我觉得没有必要<u>事事</u>都向他汇报。
I don't think it is necessary to report **thing thing** (=<u>everything</u>) to him.

Example 29
<u>谁</u>都没有我了解他。
Whoever all (=no one) knows him better than me.

Example 30
他看到<u>什么</u>都不顺眼。
He is not happy with **whatever** he sees.

As Examples 27, 28, 29 and 30 show, these non-specific pronouns in Chinese all come with some interesting lexicogrammatical features: they are either the reduplication of the same noun representing a general name, such as 人人 *one one* (=*everyone*) in Example 27 and 事事 *thing thing* (=*everything*) in Example 28, or only work in a certain syntactic structure: 谁 *whoever* in Example 29 and 什么*whatever* in Example 30 both collocate with 都 *all*.

There is another type under this category: a non-ordinated Numerative is used to modify the Thing in terms of quantity, which makes the Thing non-identifiable. Examples:

Example 31
门口有一位王先生找你。
Outside **a Mr. Wang** was asking to see you.

Example 32
一天中午, 三只白鹤在河里捉到了许多鱼.
One day at noon, **three white cranes** caught quite some fish in the river.

Example 33
朋友送我一对珍珠鸟, 我把它们养在一个竹条编的笼子里。
A friend gave me **a pair of zebra finches**, and I keep them in a bamboo cage.

As Examples 31, 32 and 33 indicate, a non-ordinated Numerative provides quantity information about a referent, and treat the Thing as a general instance. So even when the Thing is a particular instance (as in 王先生 *Mr. Wang* in Example 31), the speaker may present it as non-specific by using a Numerative 'one', as he is unable to identify this particular instance among a group of others.

In his exploration of the use of 的*de* in Chinese nominal groups, Zhang noticed the situations where the subordinating particle 的*de* sometimes has to be used in a nominal group whereas some other times it becomes optional (Zhang 1998). One of Zhang's discussions focused on the identification nature of the Thing (see Zhang 1998: 326), where he tried to interpret the compulsory/optional use of 的*de* as an indication of the identity status of the Thing in people's general cognition. For example, Zhang believed that if an animal's body parts, such as meat or skin, are accepted as of common use to human, *de* tends to be omitted–his examples include 牛肉*ox meat*, and 羊皮*sheep skin*. However, if the body part cannot or is seldom used by human, it is more likely that *de* is needed to connect the Thing (animal) and the partitive (body part) – he gave an example of 老鼠的皮 (a mouse **de** skin, *mouse skin*). However, as his account focused on the context-free grammatical structure, it is hard not to be challenged with some simple examples. Compare Examples 34 and 35:

Example 34
Specific + Non-Deictic
小老鼠的皮是白色的。(**compulsory use of** 的*de*)
The skin of the little mouse (the little mouse de skin) is white.

Example 35
Non-Specific + Non-Deictic

最近, 中药市场上发现一些不法商家用<u>老鼠 (的) 皮</u>冒充鹿茸。(**optional use of** 的*de*)

Recently in the Chinese medicine market, some unscrupulous businesses pass <u>the mouse (de) skin</u> off as the velvet antler.

As illustrated by Examples 34 and 35, even things such as 'mouse skin', which are rarely usable by human, may be realised by a nominal group with or without de. In a given context, the Thing gets an identification status as either specific or non-specific, and it is based on its identification status in the text that a lexicogrammatical selection is made. Therefore, when exploring a grammatical phenomenon, it is essential for one to observe it in a meaningful context.

In the following section, I will have more detailed discussion about 'Numerative'.

6.2.3 System of NUMERATION

The system of NUMERATION provides selections to modify the Thing in terms of order and quantity. It is concerned with how an instance is presented in terms of ordering and quantity. Figure 6.4 presents the system of NUMERATION concerning the Chinese language.

In the following discussion, I will explore the two major selections on the system: Ordination and Quantification.

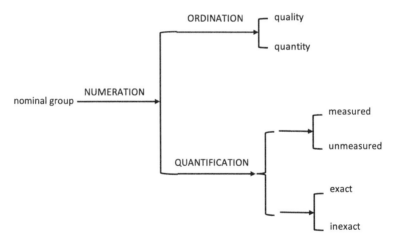

Fig. 6.4 System of NUMERATION

6.2.3.1 Ordination

When an instance is presented in terms of ordination, there are two further choices: it is either ordered in terms of sequence or in terms of certain qualities. As for realisation, the sense of ordination is realised by ordinals. Table 6.5 presents the ordinals used in Chinese.

When an instance is ordered in terms of sequence, the nominal group is typically featured with a 'Numerative (↘ordinal + numeral) + Measure + Thing' structure. And the ordinal used under this category is either a general or a sequential one. The ordering of sequence happens in terms of time, being defined either in exophoric (i.e. out of the text) or endophoric (i.e. inside the text) time reference. Example:

Example 36
Exophoric time sequence
第一次世界大战是一场于1914年7月28日至1918年11月11日间主要发生在欧洲但波及到全世界的世界大战。在1939年第二次世界大战爆发前，这场战争被称之为"世界大战"。

The First World War is a world war which centred in Europe but later spread to the whole world between 28 July 1914 and 11 November 1918. Before the breakout of the Second World War in 1939, this war was referred to as 'the World War'.

Example 37
Endophoric time sequence
从前有一个国王，他有三个儿子。第一个儿子长得很英俊，国王建造了一座宫殿给他。第二个儿子很聪明，国王送给了他一座城堡。第三个儿子长得既不英俊，也不聪明，国王一点也不喜欢他。

Once there was a king, who had three sons. The first son was very handsome, and the King built a palace for him. The second son was very clever, and the King gave him a castle. The third son, neither handsome nor clever, received little favour from the King.

Example 38
Endophoric time sequence
每一件事都很重要，但它有一个顺序，解决头一件事是解决后一件事的前提。

Everything matters, but they need to be put in order of priority. Having the first matter solved is the precondition for solving the next.

Table 6.5 Chinese ordinals

		Ordinals
Ordinative	General	第 di (ordinal prefix)
	Sequential	头 the first 、前 the first、后 the last、下 the next、上 the first
	Superlative	最 the most

As demonstrated in Examples 36, 37 and 38, the sequential ordering may be realised in terms of physical time out of the text: in Example 36, the ordering of the two world wars is based on the physical time as everyone can see; or as illustrated in Example 37, in logogenetic timeframe within the text: the ordering of the 'three sons' is based on the order of the introduction of each of them within the text. In Examples 37 and 38, the referents have been introduced as a general class in the text initially, 儿子 *sons* in Example 36 and 每一件事 *everything* in Example 38, which forms a context for the subset of the instance to be ordered later as the text unfolds.

Apart from sequence, an instance of the Thing can also be ordered in terms of its quality. In this case, the instance is first assigned with a quality and then the ordering is made by comparing the quality of this instance with others of the same class within a certain domain. Unsurprisingly, nominal groups of this type tend to have the following typical structures:

Example 39

Numerative (↘ordinal + numeral) + Epithet + Thing.
广州是中国第三大城市。
Guangzhou is the third largest city in China.

Example 40

Numerative (↘superlative ordinal) + Epithet + Thing.
世界上最高的山是位于中国和尼泊尔交界的喜马拉雅山的珠穆朗玛峰，海拔8882 米。
The world's highest peak is Mt. Qomolangma of the Himalaya Mountains across the border between China and Nepal, at an elevation of 8882 m.

Example 41

Numerative (↘ordinal + numeral) + Qualifier + Thing.
第一个吃螃蟹的人是很令人佩服的, 不是勇士谁敢去吃它呢?
The first-person eating crabs is admirable. Who dares to eat it if he is not brave enough?

Example 42

Numerative (↘superlative ordinal) + Qualifier + Thing.
最先到达山顶的小组获得了一面红旗。
The first group that arrived at the hilltop won a red flag.

As can be seen in Examples 39, 40, 41 and 42, Epithet and Qualifier are used to construe a certain quality of the Thing, based on which the ordering is made by comparing the instance with other instances of the same kind in terms of this quality. I need to point out that in these examples where Epithet or Qualifier are involved, there could be an alternative interpretation of the structure, where the Numerative may be treated as a sub-modifying element of the epithesis or qualification, and therefore not modify the Thing directly.

6.2.3.2 Quantification

When an instance is presented in terms of quantification, selections under this category provide information about the quantity aspect of the instance. As shown in Fig. 6.4, there are two further simultaneous selections to be made under this category: selections in terms of Measure status and Exactness. The former is about whether the instance is measured or not in terms of certain aspect, and the latter is about how exact the quantity is presented. In the following discussion, I will explore each combination of choices in detail.

Measured + Exact

When an instance is measured in exact quantity, the exactness of the quantity is achieved by joint functions of the Numerative and the Measure. In other words, the Measure provides a means by which the instance can be counted in exact numbers. In this sense, the Measure may be considered as an extended numerative, which provides further details about the numerative information. Examples:

Example 43
a. 三只小鸡 three MEA (*for birds*) chickens
b. 两片树叶 two MEA (*slices*) of leaves
c. 一百个学生 one hundred MEA (*for individuals*) students
d. 一滴水 one MEA (*drop*) of water

Measure words used in this category often represent the expository physical features of the instance, such as shape, size, animacy and as on. From a quantitative perspective, they define how the instance is quantified.

Unmeasured + Exact

In Chinese, there are a limited number of nominal groups where the exact quantity information of the Thing is realised through a structure without Measure, but as 'Numerative + Thing'. Note that Measure and Numerative work so closely in Chinese that it is marked that the Thing is modified by a Numerative alone when being quantified. Examples:

Example 44
中国怎么能养活**14亿人**?
How can Chinese feed **1.4 billion** people?

Example 45
该事故共造成**3人**死亡, **5人**受伤。
This accident resulted in **3 people** dead, and **5 people** injured.

In Examples 44 and 45, the same Thing, 人 *people*, is used in the 'Numerative + Thing' structure. It seems that only the most general name of human being, 人 *people*, has the potential to be modified directly by a Numerative without a Measure in presenting the exact quantity about the Thing. If a more specific type of human is construed as the Thing, the Measure becomes obligatory in realising the nominal group structure. Compare the way of presenting quantity of the Thing in the nominal groups in Example 46:

Example 46

全班共**48**人, 包括**20**个女生和**28**个男生。

There are **48** people in the class, including **20** MEA girl students and **28** MEA boy students.

In Example 46, the Numerative 48 modifies the Thing 人 *people* directly, but when the Thing represents a more specific type, such as 女生 *girl students* and 男生 *boy students*, the use of Measure 个 *individual* becomes obligatory to connect the Numeratives 20 and 28 with the Thing.

Measured + Inexact

An instance may also be presented as inexact in quantity while still be measured in a certain manner. The inexactness of the quantity can be achieved in two ways grammatically: it can be realised by an inexact Measure, or by an inexact Numerative. In both cases, one cannot get an answer to the question of 'how many exactly are the instances'. Examples:

Example 47
Numerative + Inexact Measure
a. 一捧玫瑰 an armful (=bunch) of roses
b. 一堆衣服 a pile of clothes
c. 一摞书 a stack of books
d. 一屋子人 a room of people

Compared with the Measure items in the category of 'exact', inexact Measure items are more likely to fall into the category of 'Extension' and 'Enhancement' in relation to the Thing (see further in Sect. 4.7.2). More specifically, the Measure items that are inexact in terms of quantity tend to measure Things subjectively from the Speaker's perspective: Things are measured not according to their physical properties, but according to the Speaker's interpretation of how they are presented. For instance, one Measure word used in the examples above, 捧 *(hold in arms)*, measures the 'roses' according to the manner in which the roses are carried, which can only give a vague indication of how many roses an ordinary person can hold with him arms. In another example above, 堆 *pile* is used to measure a pile of clothes, according to which no one can tell exactly how many clothes the Speaker talks about. It seems that the inexact Measure items make the Things hardly instantiated from its group and therefore make the quantity inexact, even though the Numeratives are still exact.

Below are some examples of the other type, where the Numerative is realised by an inexact numeral and thus the quantity becomes inexact:

Inexact Numerative + Measure

Example 48
参加大会的有三十多个学生。
Thirty-odd MEA students attended the assembly.

Example 49
小白兔采了几朵玫瑰花。
The little white rabbit picked a few MEA roses.

Example 50
一到周末, 他就约上三五个朋友去远足。
At weekends, he would ask three or five (=a few) MEA friends to hike.

Example 51
电话里才说了不到两句话, 就吵起来了。
Talking no more than two (=a few) sentences of words, they started to argue.

Example 52
一眼望去, 水上至少停了十来艘军舰。
At a glance, ten-ish (=a dozen) MEA warships were moored on the water.

Examples 48, 49, 50, 51 and 52 show the commonly used numerals in Chinese that represent an inexact quantity. Some of them, such as 多 (duō) in Example 48 and 来 (lái) in Example 52, are similar to 'some' or '-ish' in English. Others, such as 几 (jǐ) in Example 49, 三五 (sān wǔ) in Example 50, and 两 (liǎng) in Example 51, are close to 'a few' in sense. It is interesting to note that, 两(liǎng) is also be used as an exact Numerative meaning 'two' in many contexts–the exactness is heavily context-based.

Unmeasured + Inexact

There is a fourth type of quantification, where an instance is not measured, and an inexact Numerative makes it inexact in quantity. The situation again is very similar to that in English, where some indefinite Numerative items provide very general quantitative information about the instance. Again, nominal groups in this structure cannot provide an answer to 'how many exactly'. Examples:

Example 53
过了些日子, 玫瑰枝头长出了许多花骨朵。
A few days later, on the branches of the roses many flower buds came out.

Example 54

它们搭窝的时候, 先搬些小木片, 错杂著放在一起, 再用<u>一些乾苔藓</u>编扎起来
。

When building a nest, they first put together some bark flakes they have found, and then bind them together with <u>some dry moss</u>.

Example 55

只要能转变自己找工作的观念, <u>大多数毕业生</u>都能找到工作.

As long as they adjust their job-hunting concept, <u>most graduates</u> will be able to find a job.

Example 56

<u>极少数"藏独"分子</u>企图干扰破坏北京奥运会火炬传递,   是对奥运精神的亵
渎。

<u>An extreme small number of 'Tibetan separatists'</u> were trying to disturb the Beijing Olympic torch replay, which desecrated the Olympic spirit.

As shown in Examples 53, 54, 55 and 56, the inexact Numeratives present a subset of a group of instances in terms of the degree of quantity compared with the total: small quantity (e.g. 极少数 *an extreme small number* in Example 56), median quantity (e.g. 一些 *some* in Example 54) and large quantity (e.g. 许多 *many* in Example 53).

Till now I have completed my discussion about the three major systems in the textual domain. The selections on these systems are significant in creating cohesion and coherence in the text. In the following sections, I will further explore the contributions that nominal groups can make in these aspects.

6.3 Nominal Groups and Cohesion

In terms of cohesion, nominal groups can make significant contributions in mainly three aspects: references, ellipsis and lexical cohesion. Discussion about references realised by nominal groups has been included in Sect. 6.2 when I explored the textual systems. In the following sections, I will focus on the other two aspects in detail, namely ellipsis and lexical cohesion.

6.3.1 Ellipsis in Nominal Groups

When the Thing, sometimes together with one or more other functional elements in a nominal group, becomes omitted, the phenomenon is called ellipsis in nominal groups, or '**nominal ellipsis**' as termed by Halliday and Hasan (Halliday and Hasan

1976: 147). Ellipsis in nominal groups is commonly found in texts, which is an important means to create cohesion. In the following discussion, I will explore Chinese nominal ellipsis in detail. The discussion will be divided into two parts: in Sect. 6.3.1, I will introduce some general features of nominal ellipsis; and in Sect. 6.3.2, I will investigate different types of elliptical nominal groups in Chinese.

6.3.1.1 General Features of Elliptical Nominal Groups

There are three general features of nominal ellipsis that I will discuss here. Firstly, elliptical nominal groups are most often anaphoric and cohesive in texts, and the previous reference in the text makes it possible to recover the omitted part in the nominal group. Below is an example to illustrate this:

Example 57
开国典礼那天, 我同大伯一同到百货公司去买布, 送他和大娘一人一身蓝士林布, 另外, 送给女孩子一身红色的。大伯没见过这样鲜艳的红布, 对我说: "多买上几尺, 再买点黄色的!".

On the inauguration day of PRC, Uncle and I went to buy cloth in a department store, where I bought the blue indanthrene cloth for both him and Auntie. I also bought **a red one** for the girl. Uncle had never seen red cloth in such bright colours, and said to me, 'Get **a few more inches**; get some **yellow ones**'.

Cloth in different colours is the topic Thing in the text (Example 57). The nominal groups construing them appear in the text in the following sequence:

蓝士林布-->红色的-->红布-->几尺-->黄色的
blue indanthrene cloth ---> red one ---> red cloth ----> a few inches ---> yellow one

Nominal groups containing ellipsis have been underlined in the text. The first instance, 蓝士林布 *blue indanthrene cloth*, is non-elliptical. When the second one 红色的 *red* appears in the text, the Thing in the nominal group is omitted, but it is clear to readers as one can recover the missing Thing '布' (*cloth*) by anaphoric reference. Similarly, one can recover a few inches 'of red cloth' in the same way by referring backward to the proceeding instance 红布 *red cloth*. The recovery of 红布 *red cloth* here is significant because it makes the recovered content 'red cloth' a further presupposition for the following instance 黄色的 *yellow*. In a text like Example 57, where ellipsis happens continuously, it is through a succession of anaphoric clues that makes the ellipsis possible. And that is how cohesion is created as the text unfolds.

Secondly, in terms of information status, the omitted part in an elliptical nominal group represents given information, whereas the existing part often represents new information. My second argument is in fact based on my first one: as nominal ellipsis is usually anaphoric, the missing part in the group must have been mentioned previously in the text and therefore represents given information. Meanwhile, the existing elements in an elliptical nominal group often carry new information which makes the instance 'stand out' of the others of the same class. Similar to English, the elements carrying new information tend to carry the tonic prominence in Chinese. In Example 57, if the text is read aloud, the reader will easily notice that the existing elements, such as 红色的 *red* and 黄色的 *yellow*, carry the prominent tones and represent new and differentiating information.

Thirdly, when a nominal group is elliptical, the ellipsis may happen to more than one element in the structure, and when multiple elements become elliptical, the Thing is always one of them. The recoverability of the omitted elements is closely related to two factors: on the one hand, it depends on the integration level of the omitted element with the Thing in the experiential structure; on the other, it is also related to the existing modification structure of the elliptical nominal group. I will use the example below to illustrate this (see Example 58):

Example 58

A: 我新买的两条红色羊毛围巾呢？
Where are the two red wool scarves that I just bought?

Example responses	The non-elliptical response being recovered in brackets	Elements that must be recovered	Elements that may not be recovered
B1: 我只见到你以前买的。I have only seen what you bought before	我只见到你以前买的(羊毛围巾)。I have only seen (the wool scarves) that you bought before	Thing Classifier	Numerative Epithet
B2: 我只看见一条。I have only seen one	我只看见一条(你刚买的红色羊毛围巾)。I have only seen one (red wool scarf that you just bought)	Thing Classifier Epithet Qualifier	–
B3: 我只见到黑的。I have only seen the black (φ: one)	我只见到黑的(羊毛围巾)。I have only seen the black (wool scarf)	Thing Classifier	Numerative Qualifier
B4: 我只见到尼龙的。I have only seen the nylon (φ: one)	我只见到尼龙的(围巾)。I have only seen the nylon (scarf)	Thing	Numerative Qualifier Epithet

Example 58 has two implications. First, it seems that the more integrated the element is with the Thing, the more likely it can be recovered together with the Thing. In Chapter 4 when the functional elements in the experiential structure are introduced, I have discussed the cline of integration (see Fig. 4.2), which shows that classifier is the most integrated element with the Thing, followed by Epithet and Qualifier. This cline is determined by the stability/transiency of the properties they represent–the more stable the property of an element is, the more closely it is

Fig. 6.5 Recoverability of omitted elements in a nominal ellipsis

integrated with the Thing in a nominal group structure. When recovering the omitted elements in an elliptical nominal group, the audience is more likely to recover the elements that are more integrated with the Thing than others. The recoverability tendency can be illustrated like this (Fig. 6.5):

Second, when an elliptical nominal group is made up of only Numerative and Measure as shown in Response B2 in Example 58, all the presupposed functional elements can be recovered. This can be explained by the fact that the Numerative only represents the quantitative aspects of the instance, so the experiential aspects of the Thing are assumed to be the same as they are shared by all the instances of the same class, and therefore recoverable. In general, if the existing elements of an elliptical nominal group are in a partitive logical relation with the Thing, all the experiential functional elements that are omitted can be recovered. More examples:

Example 59

王老汉有两个打光棍的儿子, 一个是木匠, 一个是铁匠。

Wang Laohan has two bachelor sons. One MEA is a carpenter, and one MEA is a blacksmith.

Interpretation of the ellipsis:

一个 = 一个 (打光棍的儿子)

One MEA = One (bachelor son)

Example 60

- 开国上将中, 共有几位国民党的起义将领?

Among the state-founding generals, how many were the insurrectionary generals of Kuomintang?

- 三位。

Three MEA.

Interpretation of the ellipsis:

三位 = 三位 (国民党的起义将领)。

Three MEA = Three (Kuomintang insurrectionary generals)

6.3.1.2 The Structure of Elliptical Chinese Nominal Groups

I have discussed some general features and tendencies of elliptical nominal groups. In this section, I will examine different structures of elliptical nominal groups in Chinese. 'Structure' in this context refers to both logical and experiential structures, which have been discussed in Chaps 3 and 4 separately. Logically speaking, the nominal group has a univariate structure, where all the other elements are the modifiers of the Head forming a hypotactic relation. So from a logical perspective, all the elliptical nominal groups can be categorised into two types: one is those whose Head position is taken by an existing modifier, and the other is those whose Head is elliptical and cannot be filled in by any existing modifiers. I will present each type with examples and discuss them in detail.

The Elliptical Nominal Group with a Head

As discussed earlier in Sect. 6.3.1, when a nominal group is elliptical, the Thing must be omitted. This does not mean that the elliptical nominal group will become a Head-less group, as there might be an eligible existing element which can fill in the position of the Head. In Chinese, apart from nouns and pronouns, there are a few other classes of words which can take the Head position in a nominal group, including numerals, measure words, and determiners. As a result, when a functional element is realised by one of these classes of words, such as Numerative, Measure, and Deictic, it can fill in the Head position in an elliptical nominal group. Below are examples to illustrate how another element may function as Head in an elliptical nominal group:

Example 61
Numerative + Measure: Measure as Head.
- 我买了五条鱼, 吃了两条, 还有几条?
I bought five fish, ate two MEA, how many MEA left?
- 三条。
Three MEA.

Example 62
Deictic + Measure: Measure as Head.
- 哪件衣服是你刚买的?是这件吗?
Which clothes is the one you bought recently? This MEA?
Example 63

Numerative as Head.
- 你一共花了多少钱?
How much money did you spend in total?
- 一千。
One thousand.

Example 64
Deictic as Head.
- 这是谁的书?
Whose book is this?

- 我的。

Mine.

Example 65

Deictic + Numerative + Measure: Measure as Head.

- 哪些是你从图书馆里借来的书?
- 这两本。

Examples 61, 62, 63, 64 and 65 show the most common cases where an elliptical Chinese nominal group still gets a nominal Head. As illustrated above, Deictic, Numerative and Measure all can take the Head position in an elliptical nominal group. However, when all of the three elements exist in an elliptical structure, it is the Measure that functions as the Head (see example 65). Moreover, when functioning as the Head, the three elements show very different potential to be further modified. Generally speaking, the Measure has the best potential for further modification, compared with the other two. This can be illustrated by the above examples: in Example 64, the Head, taken by the Measure, is modified by Numerative; in Example 62, the Head, taken by the Measure, is modified by the Deictic; and in Example 65, the Head, again taken by the Measure, is modified by both Deictic and Numerative. In fact, when the Measure functions as the Head, it can even be modified by an Epithet, such as 大 *big* and 小 *small*, as in 三大条鱼 *three big MEA fishes*, and 一小碗粥 *one small bowl of congee*. Obviously, the other two elements, Deictic and Numerative, cannot be further modified when functioning as Head. The difference is probably caused by the experiential nature of Measure, which makes it more similar to the Thing, and gives it potential to be further elaborated. In comparison, Deictic and Numerative do not have these experiential potentials and are metafunctionally more textual instead.

The Elliptical Nominal Group Without a Head

There is another type of elliptical nominal groups, in which the Head position is left unfilled when the Thing is elliptical. The structure of this type of nominal group is made up of elements which are realised by classes of words that cannot function as Head, such as the Epithet realised by adjectives, the Qualifier realised by adverbs, or adverbial groups, or by rank-shifted embedded clauses and so on. Below are examples of Head-less elliptical nominal groups with different experiential structures:

Example 66

Classifier + de

沙发还是布的好, 不像皮的容易刮花。

As for sofa, a fabric (one) *de* is good, unlike a leather (one) *de* which easily gets scratches.

Example 67

Epithet + de

也许每一个男子全都有过这样的两个女人，至少两个。娶了红玫瑰，久而久之，<u>红的</u>变了墙上的一抹蚊子血，<u>白的</u>还是"床前明月光"；娶了白玫瑰，<u>白的</u>便是衣服上沾的一粒饭黏子，<u>红的</u>却是心口上一颗朱砂痣。

Perhaps every man has had such two women in his life, at least two. Marry a red rose and eventually <u>the red *de*</u> will be a mosquito-blood streak smeared on the wall, while <u>the white *de*</u> is 'moonlight in front of my bed'. Marry a white rose, and before long <u>the white *de*</u> will be a grain of sticky rice that's gotten stuck to your clothes; <u>the red *de*</u>, by then, is a scarlet beauty mark over your heart.

Example 68

Qualifier + de

中国菜流派众多，不同地区的菜肴口味风格差别很大。举例来说，<u>江浙一带的偏甜</u>，<u>广东一带的偏清淡</u>，<u>四川一带的偏辣</u>。

Chinese cuisine has a variety of schools, showing different tastes and styles across different regions. For example, <u>(the cuisines) in Jiangsu and Zhejiang provinces *de*</u> tend to be sweet, <u>(the ones) in Canton area *de*</u> are more delicate and mild, and <u>(the ones) in Sichuan province *de*</u> are generally spicy.

As can be seen in Examples 66, 67 and 68, there is a common feature in these Head-less structures: the subordinate particle 的*de* is used. In Chapter 3, I have introduced 的*de* from the logical perspective, which can be viewed as a hypotactic structural marker connecting the Head with modifiers. In Chapter 4, *de* has been discussed again from an experiential perspective, which indicates the experiential distance between the Thing and other experiential elements. Experientially speaking, Classifier is the closest to the Thing on the structure, and therefore 的*de* usually is not needed between them. However, when looking at the example above, one can see that when the nominal group becomes elliptical, 的*de* is necessary on the structure even with a Classifier. This is probably because that the existence of 的*de* can bring two simultaneous indications which cannot be achieved by any other existing elements: on the one hand, the use of 的*de* makes the structure nominal; on the other hand, it also indicates that the Head is elliptical, as there is nothing after *de*. It may be argued that the first indication does not apply to the 'Classifier + de' case, where the Classifier is also typically realised by a noun, and therefore nominal. In this case, however, *de* is still necessary because, without *de*, it will become a different nominal group where the noun which originally realises the Classifier becomes the Thing in the new group.

There is another interesting feature shared by the Head-less elliptical nominal groups: when a nominal group becomes elliptical without a Head, there is little potential to have additional experiential modifiers in the structure. In other words, the nominal group cannot further expand experientially. For example, one can say 沙发还是布的好 (*A fabric de (φ: sofa) is a good sofa*). However, it is awkward to say *沙发还是黑色的布的好 (*A black fabric de (φ: sofa) is a good sofa*), and it is even more awkward to say *沙发还是新买的布的好 (*A newly bought fabric de (φ: sofa) is a good sofa*). However, head-less elliptical nominal group can generally be further modified by textual elements, such as Deictic, Numerative and Measure.

These elements will not increase the experiential complexity of the elliptical group, but can provide additional information about the instance of the same kind/class. So it is possible to say 沙发还是买一个布的好 (*It is good to buy a fabric de (φ: sofa)*); 我要买这两件红色的 (*I will buy these two red de (φ: ones)*); 那盒我新买的特别好吃 (*That box de (φ: of food) that I bought recently is very delicious*).

6.3.2 *Lexical Cohesion and Nominal Groups*

Apart from reference and ellipsis, nominal groups also contribute to the use of another commonly used cohesive device–lexical cohesion. It refers to the cohesive effect that is achieved by lexical choices. In this section, I will explore the lexical cohesion achieved by the resources of nominal groups, using the previous description of nominal groups to interpret lexical cohesion from a grammatical perspective. As Halliday and Hasan point out (Halliday & Hasan 1976):

> ...because there is no sharp line between grammar and vocabulary: the vocabulary, or lexis, is simply the open-ended and most 'delicate' aspect of the grammar of a language. (p. 281)

In their study of cohesion in English, Halliday and Hasan suggested a framework for the description of lexical cohesion, which involved two types of lexical cohesion: reiteration and collocation (see further in Halliday and Hasan 1976: 288). Reiterative cohesion can be achieved by repeating the same word, using a synonym, or a superordinate word, or a general word that is related to a preceding lexical item. The other type, collocation, achieves cohesion by using related lexical items in the text. The following discussion will focus on these two types of lexical cohesion, interpreting them in the grammatical environment of the nominal group.

6.3.2.1 Reiteration

I will borrow Halliday and Hasan's definition of 'reiteration' when they explore cohesion in English (Halliday and Hasan 1976):

> *Reiteration is a form of lexical cohesion which involves the repetition of a lexical item, at one end of the scale; the use of a general word to refer back to a lexical item, at the other end of the scale; and a number of things in between – the use of a synonym, near-synonym, or superordinate. (p. 278)*

In the environment of nominal group, the most typical reiteration happens when a noun construing the Thing is mentioned previously, and then the same noun, or a synonymous noun, or a superordinate noun, or a general noun, is used in the following sentences to refer back to the same Thing. The following examples illustrate the different types of nominal reiteration in Chinese (Examples 63, 64, 65 and 66):

Example 69

Repetition

春天到了。小鹿在门前的花坛里，栽了<u>一丛玫瑰</u>。他常常去松土、浇水。<u>玫瑰</u>慢慢地抽出枝条，长出了嫩绿的叶子。

Spring is here. Little Deer planted <u>a clump of roses</u> in the front garden. He often loosened the soil and watered the flowers. <u>The roses</u> slowly grew branches and sprouted green leaves.

Example 70

Synonym

<u>宝宝</u>聪不聪明一出生就知道。一个感觉敏锐、反应迅速的<u>婴儿</u>常常很聪明。在你抱他时，你会感觉到这一点。

One can tell if a <u>baby</u> is clever at the time of birth. An alert <u>infant</u> with quick reactions is usually clever. When you hold him, you will notice this.

Example 71

Superordinate

近处的一只小船上，渔人坐在船尾，悠然地吸着烟，<u>灰黑色的鸬鹚</u>站在船舷上，好像列队的士兵在等待命令。渔人忽然站起来，拿竹篙向船舷上一抹，<u>这些水鸟</u>都扑扑地钻进水里去了。

On a small boat nearby, a fisherman was sitting on the rear end of the boat, smoking at his leisure. Some <u>dark grey cormorants</u> were standing on the sides of the boat, like a line of soldiers waiting taking orders. The fisherman stood up suddenly and swiped the sides with his bamboo pole. <u>These waterfowl</u> all dived into the water.

Example 72

General

朋友在新疆给我买了<u>一把匕首</u>，却无法邮寄给我，因为<u>这东西</u>邮局不让寄。

A friend has bought me <u>a dagger</u> in Xinjiang, but cannot send to me because <u>this stuff</u> is not allowed for post.

I will make a few comments based on Examples 69, 70, 71 and 72. Firstly, when the Thing is reiterated, the nominal groups that construe the same Thing may take on different modification structures. This also applies to the case of repetition. As Example 69 shows, the first occurrence of 玫瑰 *rose* appears in the structure of Numerative + Measure + Thing, whereas in the following occurrence it becomes a Thing-only group. One can also change the structure of the second occurrence into 'Deictic + Epithet + Thing', as in 这些幼嫩的玫瑰 *these delicate roses*, and it is still cohesive. Compared with the other functional elements in the nominal group structure, the Thing is the most commonly reiterated item, as the system of THING TYPE provides rich lexical choices along the cline of generality (Fig. 4.6) which can link a preceding Thing with a following reference of the same Thing though the choices between general and specific ends.

However, the reiteration of the other functional elements can also achieve cohesion, but this will fall out of the referential domain. Take a look at Example 73, which presents an extract from the lyrics of a pop song *The blue night and the blue dream* (lyrics by Haining Zhang and Quanfu Zhang 1992).

Example 73

圆圆的月亮	The round moon
悄悄爬上来	quietly climbs up
……	…
蓝蓝的夜蓝蓝的梦	The blue night, the blue dream

In Example 73, different Things, 月亮*moon*, 夜*night* and 梦*dream* are linked together not only because they are semantically close, but also because they are assigned with a quality of either same or similar kind construed by the same or similar Epithets here: 圆圆的 (*round,* attributive Epithet: shape) and 蓝蓝的 (*blue,* attributive Epithet: colour). As said before, the reiteration of elements other than the Thing, such as Epithet, Classifier and Qualifier, is less common, and it often occurs to achieve a rhetorical effect as demonstrated by Example 73.

Back to Examples 69, 70, 71 and 72, as demonstrated in these examples, the use of synonyms, superordinate names and the more general names in the reiteration of the same Thing are all reflecting the choices to construe the same Thing on the system of THING TYPE along the generality cline. The four types of reiteration demonstrated in Examples 69, 70, 71 and 72 actually represent lexical realisations at different degrees of generality in construing a Thing. In Chapter 4, when presenting the system of THING TYPE, I introduced the 'generality cline of the system of THING TYPE' (see Fig. 4.5). This cline shows the tendency of generality/specificity in the system of THING TYPE, providing choices to construe the Thing as either a general type (therefore close to grammar), or a specific instance (therefore close to lexis). Mapping the four types of reiteration onto the cline, one can see that repetition is located on the specific end, and general reiteration is on the general end, with synonyms and superordinates in between (see Fig. 6.6).

In the referential space where a reiteration anaphorically refers to something being mentioned before, then the move of choices on the generality cline becomes one-way only: the initial occurrence is always on the specific end, and the following reiterating choice can only be more general, but not the other way around. For example,

Fig. 6.6 Reiteration on the generality cline

Example 74

a. 小王最近好像有心事, 你该跟这个学生谈一谈。(specific– > general)
   Xiao Wang seems to be worrying about something these days. You should
   have a talk with this student.

b. 小王最近好像有心事, 你该跟这个小伙子谈一谈。(specific– > general)
   Xiao Wang seems to be worrying about something these days. You should
   have a talk with this lad.

c. 小王最近好像有心事, 你该跟这个年轻人谈一谈。(specific– > general)
   Xiao Wang seems to be worrying about something these days. You should
   have a talk with this young man.

e. 小王最近好像有心事, 你该跟这个家伙谈一谈。(specific– > general)
   Xiao Wang seems to be worrying about something these days. You should
   have a talk with this folk.

f. *你该跟这个小伙子谈一谈, 小王最近好像有心事。(general– > specific)
   *You should have a talk with this lad. Xiao Wang seems to be worrying
   about something these days.

Two types of nouns are used in these examples, one representing an individual
name and the other a common name. So 小王 *Xiao Wang,* an individual name, is on
the specific end in terms of identification, and the others, 学生*student,* 小伙子*lad,*
年轻人 *young man,* 家伙 *folk,* all represent instances on the more general end. In
particular, in the first four examples (Examples 74a, 74b, 74c and 74d), the individual
name 小王 *Xiao Wang* presents the instance (the person) as a specific identity, and
when the same person is mentioned again, a common name is used to represent
the same Thing but this common name represents a more general and non-specific
Thing. In other words, when a specific instance of a Thing type is selected in the
first place, a general instance of the same Thing type can be used in the successive
clause for an anaphoric reference, as there is no need to specify the identify again. In
comparison, in Example 68f, when an instance of a more general type of Thing 小
伙子 *lad* comes first in the text, and a more specific instance of the same Thing 小
王*Wiao Wang* comes later, even though the general Thing小伙子*lad* is modified by
a specific Deictic 这个*this*, it is very hard to say that the two instances in Example
68f refer to the same person, unless more context information become available.

In the above examples, whether specific or general, choices of reiteration of the
Thing happen along the horizontal line in the system of THING TYPE: both general
and specific realisations are in the same general category of the THING TYPE system.
So for example, on the general end, all the choices representing 小王 *Xiao Wang,*
such as 学生*student,* 年轻人*young man,* 小伙*lad,* 家伙*folk* in Example 74, belong
to the category of 'Conscious: human'. Similarly, 匕首 *dagger* and 东西 *thing/stuff*
in Example 72, both fall in the category of 'Non-conscious: simple'. On the system
map, the shift of these choices takes place in linearly between the general end on the
left and the specific end on the right.

Apart from the horizontal linear move between the general-specific ends, there
is also a vertical shift of choices in the system of THING TYPE to realise the
reiteration of the Thing, shifting from the most congruent conscious choices on the
top to the less congruent non-conscious choices below–this is my third discussion

point. Sometimes, this transcategorical reiteration happens when the speaker/writer wants to express attitude towards the referent. Look at these examples:

Example 75

你可要提防着老王, 这老狐狸鬼着呢。

You have to beware of <u>Lao Wang</u>. <u>This old fox</u> is wily.

Example 76

今天的桃子都是小猴子采的, 这个小东西动作可快了。

Today's peaches were all picked by <u>Little Monkey</u>. <u>This little thing</u> was really quick.

Examples 75 and 76 involve transcategory reiteration, where a Thing of one category is used to refer back to a Thing of another category: 老狐狸 *old fox* (Conscious: animal) in Example 69 and 小东西 *little thing* (Non-conscious: simple) in Example 70 are used to refer to 老王 *Lao Wang* (Conscious: human) and 小猴子 *little monkey* (Conscious: animal), respectively. Such reiteration across different Thing types often happens with an interpersonal motive: the speaker/writer expresses his attitude towards the referent by connecting the two types of Things, indicating that they have certain qualities in common. As two different Thing types are used to refer the same Thing, to achieve cohesion and avoid confusion, the subsequent reference of the Thing is often immediately after the initial reference, usually in an adjacent clause or sentence, and a specific Deictic item like 这 *this* is used to further the specify the reference.

6.3.2.2 Collocation

Collocation refers to the situation where two or even more lexical items tend to share the same lexical environment and occur in similar contexts. The occurrence of such collocations in adjacent sentences will create a cohesive effect (see Halliday and Hasan 1976). For example,

Example 77

晚饭过后,<u>火烧云</u>上来了。<u>霞光</u>照得小孩子的脸红红的,<u>大白狗</u>变成红的了,<u>红公鸡</u>变成金的了,<u>黑母鸡</u>变成紫檀色的了。

After dinner, <u>the glowing clouds</u> appeared. In the evening glow, children's faces became red, the <u>big white dog</u> became red, the <u>red rooster</u> became gold, and the <u>black hen</u> became purple.

I will focus on two sets of collocations in Example 77: 火烧云 *the glowing clouds* with 霞光 *the evening glow*; 大白狗 *big white dog*, 红公鸡 *red rooster* and 黑母鸡 *black hen*. In the first case, 火烧云 *glowing clouds* and 霞光 *the evening glow* are associated with each other in that they both represent some natural phenomena in the sky. In the second case, 大白狗 *big white dog*, 红公鸡 *red rooster* and 黑母鸡 *black hen* are related because they all represent domestic animals, and more

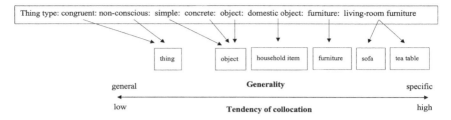

Fig. 6.7 Thing Type and tendency of collocation

interestingly the nominal groups construe these Things all contain attributive Epithet of colour. One may argue that the first pair of words, 火烧云*glowing clouds* and 霞光*the evening glow*, are more likely to co-occur than the latter (大白狗 *big white dog*, 红公鸡 *red rooster* and 黑母鸡 *black hen*), as 狗*dog* may not necessarily co-occur with 鸡 *chicken*, but is definitely more related with 'barking'. However, by the same token, 大白狗 *big white dog* is definitely more related to 红公鸡 *red rooster* and 黑母鸡 *black hen* than to 稀薄的空气 *thin air* or 火红的太阳 *the red sun*. So we can see that collocation is in fact a matter of degrees of proximity between two items—it represents only a relative possibility of one word co-occurring with another. The criterion here is that, as long as this relatedness is strong enough to create a cohesive effect, it is a collocation. In the following discussion, I will try to interpret this proximity in the experiential environment of nominal groups, focusing on two things: the relationship between collocation and the system of THING TYPE, and the collocation achieved between Thing and Facet.

Collocation and Thing Type

Collocational cohesion can be achieved when two lexical items construe the same type of Thing at a specific level. On the generality cline of the system of THING TYPE (Fig. 4.5), the more specific a category is, the more likely the items in the same category will co-occur in the similar contexts. Figure 6.7 illustrates the tendency of collocation in relation to the specificity of Thing Type.

As illustrated in Fig. 6.7, 沙发 *sofa* is most likely to collocate with 茶几 *tea table*, both of which belong to the most specific Thing Type category and are proximate in the system of THING TYPE. The collocation tendency decreases when the common category shared by the two items moves towards the general end. So 东西 *thing* is not as likely to collocate with 沙发 *sofa* in this example due to the decreased proximity, though as a frequently used general noun, 东西 *thing* can be used to anaphorically refer to 沙发 *sofa*, which would still create a cohesive effect. So as Halliday and Hasan point out, the most important principle is to use common sense when analysing a text in respect of lexical cohesion (Halliday and Hasan 1976).

Collocation Between Thing and Facet

Sometimes, the topic Thing of the beginning clause is cohesively tied with the topic Thing of the following clauses because they are in fact the 'Thing' and the 'Facet' in a part-and-whole relationship. Example 78:

Example 78
松鼠是一种漂亮的小动物, 驯良, 乖巧, 很讨人喜欢。它们<u>面容</u>清秀, <u>眼睛</u>闪闪有光, <u>身体</u>矫健, <u>四肢</u>轻快, 非常敏捷, 非常机警。玲珑的<u>小面孔</u>, 衬上<u>一条帽缨形的美丽的尾巴</u>, 显得格外漂亮; <u>尾巴</u>老是翘起来, 一直翘到<u>头</u>上, <u>身子</u>就躲在尾巴底下歇凉。

The <u>squirrel</u> is a beautiful little animal, docile, cute and very adorable. (Its) <u>face</u> is pretty, <u>eyes</u> are bright, <u>body</u> is agile, and <u>limbs</u> brisky, and (it) moves fast and is very alert. With a delicate <u>face</u>, matched with a beautiful bushy <u>tail</u>, (the squirrel) looks very smart. (Its) <u>tail</u> always stands up to (its) head so (its) <u>body</u> can rest in the shadow of the tail.

In Example 78, 松鼠 *squirrel* is the topic Thing of the whole text, which appears in the Theme position in the first sentence. In the following sentences, facet items representing different parts of the body of the squirrel become the centre of description. All look cohesive because this is a smooth shift of topic Things, from the Thing to Facet 1 面容 *face*, and to Facet 2 眼睛 *eyes*, and to Facet 3 身体 *body* and so on. Note that when the Thing is first identified and takes the Theme position in the first clause, the following references realised by the Facet of the Thing become less identified, as evidenced by the ellipsis of the Thing 松鼠 *squirrel* in the following clauses. Here is another example (Example 79):

Example 79
那个学生一边揉着中指, 一边看陈秉正的<u>手</u>。只见那两只<u>手</u>确实跟一般人的<u>手</u>不同: <u>手掌</u>好像四方的, <u>指头</u>粗而短, 而且每个指头都伸不直, 里外都是茧皮, 圆圆的<u>指头肚儿</u>都像半个蚕茧上安了个<u>指甲</u>, 整个看来真像用树枝做成的小耙子。

That student was rubbing his mid-finger, while looking at Chen Bingzheng's <u>hands</u>. Those two <u>hands</u> indeed were very different from ordinary ones: the <u>palm</u> seemed to be square, the <u>fingers</u> were thick and short, none of which can keep straight. Both sides of the hands were covered by thick callus, and <u>the top parts of the fingers</u> looked like half cocoons with <u>nails</u>. The whole hand was like a rake made with tree branches.

As shown in Example 79, the text is unfolded in a cohesive manner, with the topic Things being introduced to collocate with each other: from 手 *hand* (Thing) to 手掌 *palm* (Facet 1) to 手指头 *finger* (Facet 2), to 指头肚儿 *top part of the finger* (Facet 3), to 指甲 *nail* (Facet 4).

So far I have investigated different resources that nominal groups can provide in achieving cohesive effects. The discussion mainly focuses on the contributions made to some commonly used cohesive strategies, including reference, ellipsis and lexical cohesion. In their study of cohesion in English, Halliday and Hasan (1976) also include 'substitution' as another common strategy. However, this is not covered in the present study because Chinese do not have such lexical resources as 'one' and 'ones' to substitute the Head of a nominal group. Therefore, there is no equivalent cohesive device in Chinese as substitution in English. Instead, Chinese seems to be more 'powerful' in using the strategy of ellipsis, which makes it possible to have Head-less nominal groups in a cohesive environment.

6.4 Case Study

In this case study, I will investigate the problems of cohesion caused by the machine-translated nominal groups between English and Chinese. As many can see, with the rapid development of machine translation, nowadays it is common to achieve translation equivalence at the sentence level with the help of the computer. However, in the first decade of the twenty-first century, when the dominant machine translation system was based on the statistical phrase-based machine translation (SMT) paradigm, one major problem remained unsolved: unlike human translators, computers could not recognise the internal links between each sentence, neither could they effectively use grammatical resources to achieve cohesion (cf. Gross 1992; Fox 2002, etc.). In more recent years, a new paradigm, the deep learning-based neural machine translation system (NMT), signals the beginning of a new era for machine translation. Some research has provided evidence that the translation produced by the NMT system has shown a great improvement in terms of both accuracy and fluency compared with the translation produced by the SMT system (e.g. Bentivogli et al. 2016; Toral and Sánchez-Cartagena 2017; Liu 2020). In an updated evaluation of the translation quality of Google Translate, Aiken found that Chinese, among 9 other languages, tended to be the most accurate in the Google translation to and from English, achieving an accuracy rate above 80% (Aiken 2019).

However, it has also been widely acknowledged in these studies that even the NMT systems remain to be improved. For example, for the machine translation from Chinese into English, Liu found that NMT system was better than SMT at handling cohesive ties such as additive, adverbs and pronouns, but both systems under-performed at dealing with demonstratives and lexical cohesion (Liu 2020). However, Liu's study did not provide details about how both systems under-performed in achieving cohesion at the lexical level.

It is against this background that the current case study is designed. I aim to further explore this issue by looking at the following two questions: 1. In solving the cohesion-related problems involving nominal groups, has the current NMT system demonstrated an improvement compared with the SMT system in translation from Chinese into English? And how? 2. What are the cohesion-related problems posed by Chinese nominal groups that remain to be improved in the current NMT system when translating to English?

Table 6.6 Contexts of the sample text

	Field	Tenor	Mode
Text 1: 小鹿的玫瑰花 Little Deer's roses (Chinese text for translation)	The socio-semiotic function of this text is recreating in the form of a short narrative. The domain is concrete and concerned with a little deer and the roses he planted. The protagonist is a personified animal	The institutional roles are a writer to junior school-aged children. The evaluation of the experiential domain is positive and imaginative	The text is monologic, written and constitutive of its contextual situation. It is presented with multimodal features —the text is illustrated with a picture. The story is written in Chinese

6.4.1 Sample Texts and Translation Tool

A sample Chinese text, Text 1, is selected for translation. The context information of the text is presented in Table 6.6.

The next step is to machine-translate the sample text into the English language, using Google Translate, one of the most widely used machine translation tools in the world. Altogether there are two translated texts in the case study: Text 1_SMT and Text 1_NMT are the two English translations of the Chinese sample text 《小鹿的玫瑰花》*Little Deer's roses* (Text 1). The translated texts were collected at two different times: Text 1_SMT was translated by Google Translate in 2013, when Google Translate used the SMT system; Text 1_NMT was translated in 2021 by Google Translate, which was based on the current NMT system.

To investigate the first research question, a diachronic approach will be adopted by comparing Text 1_SMT with Text 1_NMT. By comparing the translations of the same text done by Google Translate at different times, I aim to investigate if the NMT system is better than the SMT system at handling the translation of nominal groups in achieving cohesion. To investigate the second research question, I will focus on Text 1_NMT, which is the translation produced by the current NMT system. The analysis aims to examine the existing problems in the translation of nominal groups, particularly in relation to the achievement of cohesion.

6.4.2 Results and Analysis

After the sample text was translated by Google Translate, the nominal groups in the source language texts (SLT) were compared with their translation equivalents in the two target language texts (TLT). As both research questions are about the translation of nominal groups, my analysis will therefore focus on the translation of nominal groups and the analysis will conduct through the textual lens.

Table 6.7 Text 1 and a literal translation in English

Literal translation in English: *Little Deer's roses* 小鹿的玫瑰花

Spring is here. **Little Deer** (小鹿) planted **a cluster of roses** (一丛玫瑰) in the flower bed in front of his door. He often went to loosen the soil and water (the roses). **The roses** (玫瑰) slowly pulled out branches and grew delicate green leaves. Some days later, **the rose branches** (玫瑰) grew **a lot of flower buds** (许多花骨朵). **Little Deer** (小鹿) and **(his) younger brother** (弟弟) counted together. Altogether there were **12 (buds)** (12个), and **they** (他们) were extremely happy

The flower buds (花骨朵) gradually grew up. When (they) were about to bloom, **Little Deer** (小鹿) accidentally injured (his) foot. **He** (他) had to quietly stay in bed to recuperate. One day, one week, one month (had passed) …**Little Deer** (小鹿) finally could get out of bed and walk. **He** (他) limped to the door. Ah! **The roses in front of the door** (门前的玫瑰) had grown very tall, but among the dense green leaves, not **a single flower** (一朵花) could be seen

Little Brother Deer (鹿弟弟) said regretfully to **(his) elder brother** (哥哥): 'These roses(这玫瑰) you have planted in vain, and **(not) a single flower** (一朵花) you have seen'

At this moment, a yellow warbler flew in. She said, '**Little Deer** (小鹿), I have seen **of your house those red roses** (你家那些红玫瑰). (They) are so beautiful! Seeing **those flowers** (那些花), I want to sing'

A gust of breeze came and said, '**Little Deer** (小鹿), I have smelled **roses of your house** (你家的玫瑰花), (and they are) very fragrant! I blew through the forest with **its fragrance** (它的香味), and everyone praised me as 'the rose fragrance wind'!

Little Deer (小鹿) smiled happily (and) said, 'It turns out that **the roses that I planted** (我种的玫瑰) were red. **They** (它们) were beautiful and scented. Thank you for telling me'

Little Brother Deer (鹿弟弟) smiled happily and said, 'It looks that **your roses** (你的玫瑰) were not planted in vain'!

Table 6.8 presents a literal English translation of the sample text. Note that this literal translation was done by a professional human translator, and the purpose of the human translation is to give the readers an understanding about how exactly the Chinese nominal groups in the SLT are presented. Therefore, some nominal groups in the English translation may seem a bit unnatural as the translation aims to demonstrate the original lexicogrammatical features of the nominal groups in the SLT and serves as a reference translation for readers when I move onto the two machine translation products later.

The nominal groups for analysis have been highlighted in Table 6.7 with the original Chinese nominal groups included in the brackets, which represent the main participants construed in the text, including all the nominal groups concerning小鹿*Little Deer*, 鹿弟弟*Little Brother Deer*, 玫瑰花*roses*, and those representing facets of the roses.

6.4.2.1 Text 1_SMT

Below is Text 1_SMT, the translation done by Google Translate in 2013 using the SMT method.

Table 6.8 SMT versus NMT in translating nominal groups with qualifiers

SLT	Text1_SMT	Text1_NMT
门前的花坛 In front of door *de* flowerbed *The flowerbed in front of the door*	*In front of the flowerbeds	The flower bed in front of the door
门前的玫瑰 In front of door *de* roses *The roses in front of the door*	*In front of the roses	The roses in front of the door
你家那些红玫瑰 Your home those red roses *Those red roses of yours*	*Those red roses in your house	*Those red roses in your house
你家的玫瑰花 Your home *de* roses *The roses of yours*	*Your home roses	Your roses

* ungrammatical and/or inaccurate translation

Text 1_SMT

Spring has come. Deer in front of the flowerbeds, planted a rose bush. He often went to loosen the soil, watering. Rose slowly withdrawn branches, grow a green leaf.

After some days, the branches grow a lot of roses bud. Deer with his brother counted a total of thirty-two, they are very happy.

Bud gradually grown up. Just about to bloom when the deer falls careless feet. He could only lie on the bed to recuperate. Day, a week, a month ...... finally able to get out of bed to walk a deer, he limped to the door. Yeah! In front of the roses have grown very high, but the dense green leaves, a flower cannot see it.

Deer brother regret for his brother, said: 'This is the white rose you planted, a flower never looked at .'

At this time, an oriole flew. She said: 'The deer I've seen those red roses in your house, you can look good look at those flowers, I wanted to sing !.'

Breeze blowing, said: '!! Deer, I heard of your home roses, it can be fragrant with the smell of my blowing forest, everybody Doukua I was 'Rose Wind' it.'

Fawn smiled happily and said: 'It turned out I planted roses are red, they are very beautiful, but also exudes a scent Thank you told me .'

Deer brother smiled happily and said: '! Appears that you do not have white roses planted.'

There are some interesting findings in the translation produced by the SMT-based Google Translate.

Firstly, the translation of the protagonist, 小鹿 *Little Deer*, is very problematic. In the SLT, when 小鹿 (xiǎo lù, *little deer*) was first introduced, it was presented as a named individual, bearing a personal name. This is a very common practice in Chinese to introduce the main characters in the stories for children when the characters are personified animals. By turning an animal's common name, such as 小鹿 *little/young deer*, into an individual personal name, like 小鹿 *Little Deer*, the author is able to fulfil at least two purposes at once: on the one hand, the naming indicates what animal the main character is, through which an identity is given; on the other hand, by presenting the name as an individual name, the author treats the animal character like a human character, through which personification is realised. Note that, graphologically, the common name 小鹿 *young deer* and the individual name 小鹿 *Little Deer* are identical in Chinese, and the difference in naming can only tell in the text environment. For example, the common names for a type of animal usually appear in expounding texts, whereas when used as an individual name of a specific animal identity, it typically appears in a narrative text. When translating these names to English, the translator needs to be aware of the subtle and implicit differences and reflect these differences through case-sensitive choices in English. Unfortunately, in this case study, SMT-based Google Translate failed to distinguish the two different selections on the system of NAMING, as demonstrated by its translation of 小鹿 *Little Deer* as 'Deer' and 'the deer'. The problem was probably caused by the failure to distinguish the personal name from the common name since both have the same presentation in the writing system.

Secondly, SMT-based Google Translate seems to have problems translating those nominal groups that are modified by a Qualifier. Due to the translation error, it makes the identification of the Things difficult. Examples:

Unidentified Qualifier in a Nominal Group

Example 80
SLT: 门前的玫瑰已经长得很高了。
    The roses in front of the door have grown very high.
TLT:*In front of the roses have grown very high.

Example 81
SLT: 原来我种的玫瑰花是红色的。
    It turned out that **the roses I planted** were red.
TLT: It turned out *I planted roses are red.

A possible reason that the SMT system failed to recognise the Qualifier is that there is not a clear structural marker that can help identify such a modifier in Chinese. Although 的 *de* is often used as a marker between a modifier and the Head, it is not an exclusively used marker between the Qualifier and the Head—except Qualifier, 的 *de* can also be a marker for the Epithet, the possessive Deictic, or the Facet. Moreover, it is not a compulsory structural marker, and sometimes there is no marker at all between a modifier and Head. For example, in the SLT, there is a nominal group without 的*de* between the Qualifier and the Head, as in 你家那些红玫瑰 *your home red those roses (=those red roses in your home)*. Meanwhile, in SLT, there are also nominal groups with 的*de* connecting the Qualifier and the Thing, as in 你家的玫瑰花 *your home de roses* (= the roses in your home). As discussed in Sect. 6.2.2.2, the structure 'Qualifier + Thing' may represent a specific instance without a Deictic element (see discussions about 'Specific + non-Deictic). When the Qualifier in this situation becomes unrecognisable in the translation, the specificity of the instance will be inevitably impacted.

Thirdly, there is a significant shift in terms of specificity when the nominal group is non-Deictic in the Chinese text. To be more specific, when a specific instance is realised by a non-Deictic nominal group in Chinese, the SMT-based Google Translate cannot maintain the identifiable status of the instance in the English translation. Rather, it is often translated as a non-specific instance realised by a non-Deictic nominal group. Example:

Example 82
(SLT) Specific + non-Deictic -- > (TLT) non-Specific + non-Deictic
SLT:
小鹿在门前的花坛里，栽了一<u>丛玫瑰</u>。他常常去松土、浇水。<u>玫瑰</u>慢慢地抽出枝条, 长出了嫩绿的叶子。

Little Deer planted a cluster of roses in the front garden. He often loosened the soil and watered the flowers. The roses slowly grew branches and sprouted green leaves.
TLT:
Deer in front of the flower beds, planted a rose bush. He often went to loosen the soil, watering. *__Rose__ slowly withdrawn branches, grow a green leaf.

As Example 82 shows, 玫瑰 *roses* appear in the first sentence as '一丛玫瑰' *a cluster of roses*. When the same Thing appears again later in the text, it is realised by a simple nominal group without any modifiers, '玫瑰' *roses*, though we know through context that it refers to the specific roses planted by Little Deer, as mentioned earlier in the text. As discussed in Sect. 6.2.2.2, the specific status of an instance can be achieved by an item other than the Deictic, such as through exophoric (information through context of situation) or homophoric information (information through context of culture), or through endophoric information (information retrieved through the text) that is given earlier in the text (see further in Halliday and Hasan 1976). In any of these cases, the specific status of the instance is achieved through contextual and textual clues rather than by an explicit lexical marker. Unfortunately, it looks that these context-based reference clues are often something that the SMT-based Google Translate cannot capture.

Fourthly, in recovering the nominal groups that are omitted in the SLT, the SMT-based Google Translate didn't achieve a good result, either. In several cases when a nominal group is omitted, the translation system cannot successfully recover the omitted nominal group, causing an incomplete and ungrammatical clause structure. Examples:

Example 83

SLT:

小鹿在门前的花坛里, 栽了<u>一丛玫瑰</u>。他常常去松土、浇水。

Little Deer planted **a cluster of roses** in the flower bed in front of his door. He often went to loosen the soil and water (**the roses**).

TLT:

*Deer in front of the flowerbeds, planted a rose bush. He often went to loosen the soil, watering.

As Example 83 shows, the topic Thing, 玫瑰 *roses*, appears in the first sentence of the SLT as new information. Then in the following sentence, it is omitted, but it is fully recoverable to Chinese readers based on endophoric clues. However, in English, the omission would make the sentence ungrammatical and therefore should not happen. Unfortunately, the SMT-based Google Translate couldn't recover the omitted nominal group '*the roses*' which functions as Goal in the material process of 'watering'. The omission in the TLT makes the whole sentence ungrammatical.

Finally, in contrast with my third point, the SMT-based Google Translate does well when there is a clear lexical marker for the specificity status. In the sample text, when a lexical item, such as a pronoun, a determiner, or a numeral, is used to clearly mark the specificity status, the specificity status can be well maintained in the machine translation in the same way. Examples:

Example 84

(SLT) Specific → (TLT) Specific.

SLT:

小鹿, 我见过你家<u>那些</u>红玫瑰, 可好看了!

TLT:

The deer, I've seen **those** red roses in your house

Example 85

(SLT) non-Specific → (TLT) non-Specific.

SLT:

这时, <u>一只黄莺</u>飞来了。

TLT:

At this time, **an** oriole flew.

It seems that the SMT-based system can do well if the identifiability status is realised by lexical items. However, if it is achieved through textual and contextual clues, then it is very hard for the computer to identify the status of specificity.

To sum up, it seems that the SMT-based Google Translate cannot achieve a good translation quality when it comes to the translation of the textual meanings realised by Chinese nominal groups. In particular, the system seems to have problems recognising endophoric clues which are significant in helping human translators distinguishing an individual name from a common name, recognising a nominal group modified by a Qualifier, analysing the status of specification of an instance, and recovering the omitted nominal groups. In comparison, the computer cannot utilise the clues which are available as the text unfolds—its sole dependence on the lexical items available in the SLT has determined its disadvantage in dealing with the implicit context-based information.

6.4.2.2 Text 1_NMT

Below is Text1_NMT, the translation done by Google Translate in 2021 using the NMT method.

Text1_NMT

Spring is coming. The deer planted a rose in the flower bed in front of the door. He often goes to loosen the soil and water. The rose slowly pulled out its branches and grew green leaves.

After a few days, many flowers and bones grew on the rose branches. Deer and his brother counted together, and there were thirty-two in total, and they were very happy.

The flower bones gradually grew up. Just when it was about to bloom, the deer accidentally injured his foot. He could only lie in bed quietly to recuperate. One day, one week, one month... The little deer was finally able to get out of bed and walk, and he limped to the door. Ah! The roses in front of the door had grown very tall, but not a single flower could be seen among the dense green leaves.

Brother Lu said regretfully to his brother: 'You have planted this rose in vain, and you didn't look at a single flower.'

At this time, a yellow warbler flew in. She said, 'Xiaolu, I have seen those red roses in your house, they are so beautiful! Looking at those flowers, I want to sing.'

A gust of breeze came and said, 'Xiaolu, I have smelled your roses, but they are fragrant! I blew through the forest with its fragrance, and everyone praised me as 'Rose Fragrance'!'

The little deer smiled happily and said, 'It turns out that the roses I planted are red. They are beautiful and scented. Thank you for telling me.'

Brother Lu smiled happily and said, 'It seems that your roses are not in vain!'

For the sake of comparison, the analysis of Text1_NMT will be focusing on the four aspects in which problems are found when I analysis Text1_SMT, including the translation of 小鹿 *Little Deer* as an individual personal name, the recognition of Chinese nominal groups modified by a Qualifier, the translation of specific instances that are realised by non-Deictic nominal groups, and the handling of omitted nominal groups that need to be recovered in the translation.

In terms of the translation of the name of 小鹿 *Little Deer*, the NMT-based Google Translate is found to have a different practice, compared to the SMT-based system. 小鹿 Little Deer has been translated in three ways in Text1_NMT, including: 'The deer' in its first appearance in the text, 'Deer', 'The little deer' and 'Xiaolu' which is the pinyin form of the Chinese characters 小鹿 *little deer*. It is interesting to note that the specific Deictic 'the' was used in the first instance when the protagonist 小鹿 *little deer* appeared in the text. This makes the identity of 小鹿 *little deer* as given information from the very beginning of the story, which might be confusing to some young English readers. Although it may not seem to be an ideal practice, the use of 'the' in the first appearance indicates that the NMT-based Google Translate is able to work out the identification status of the protagonist as a specific instance. Also, the use of 'Xiaolu' in addressing 小鹿 *little deer*, though does not make sense to English readers, demonstrates the attempt of the machine translation system to give an individual name to 小鹿 *little deer*, indicating that the system has some ability to distinguish an individual name from a common name when both bear the same graphological form in Chinese.

In terms of the recognition of Chinese nominal groups modified by a Qualifier, the NMT-based system also seems to show some advancement compared with the system in 2013. Altogether there are 4 nominal groups in the SLT that are modified by a Qualifier. Table 6.8 shows the translation of these four nominal groups by the SMT and the NMT systems.

As Table 6.8 shows, the NMT-based machine translation system successfully recognised all of the 4 nominal groups that have a Qualifier ahead of the nominal Head in Chinese and produced an equivalent nominal group in English with the Qualifier shifting to the post-modifying position. There is one instance where the English translation is not fully accurate: 你家那些红玫瑰 ('your home those red roses', *those red roses of yours*) was translated as 'those red roses in your house'. This translation is not fully accurate in that, based on the endophoric information provided by the first paragraph, it is clear that the roses are planted outdoor (in front of the door), so the translation, which indicates the roses are 'in your house', is not accurate. Again, this cannot be reflected by the local nominal group structure in the SLT as the Qualifier '你家的 *of your home*' could indicate either indoor or outdoor when viewed out of context. Again, it seems that the endophoric clues, which derive from the surrounding text but are not explicit in the lexicogrammatical realisation, can still pose a challenge to the current neural machine translation system. However, the current system undoubtedly outperforms the statistical machine translation system in 2013 in recognising and translating the Chinese nominal groups modified by Qualifiers.

In terms of the translation of the non-Deictic nominal groups that identify specific instances, the NMT-based Google Translate again demonstrates a better performance than the old system. In the SLT, a topic Thing, 玫瑰 *rose*, appears a few times in the text. In particular, after the first appearance where 玫瑰 *rose* is presented as non-specific new information (一丛玫瑰 *a cluster of roses*), the following appearance of 玫瑰 *rose* in the text should be interpreted as a specific instance since it specifically refers to the roses that Little Deer planted in front of the door. However, the reference of 玫瑰 *rose* in the following mentioning is realised by a non-Deictic nominal group 玫瑰 *rose,* which is made up of the single noun without any modifying element. Unlike the SMT system which failed to capture the specific status of the instance, the NMT system successfully recognises the identification status of 玫瑰 *rose* and reflects its specific identity in the English translation by adding 'the' in front of 'roses'. See example:

Example 86
SLT:
小鹿在门前的花坛里, 栽了一丛玫瑰(a cluster of roses)。他常常去松土、浇水。玫瑰 (*roses*)慢慢地抽出枝条, 长出了嫩绿的叶子。

Little Deer planted **a cluster of roses** in the flower bed in front of his door. He often went to loosen the soil and water (the roses). **The roses** slowly pulled out branches and grew delicate green leaves.
TLT:
The deer planted **a rose** in the flower bed in front of the door. He often goes to loosen the soil and water. **The rose** slowly pulled out its branches and grew green leaves.

As demonstrated in Example 86, the NMT system is able to recognise the specific identity of 玫瑰 *rose* when it appears in the text for the second time, though the graphological presentation cannot indicate its identification status as both specific and non-specific instances can be realised by the same non-Deictic nominal group. By adding 'the' in the English translation, the machine translation manages to maintain the specific identity status in English. Another interesting note about Example 79 is that, although Google Translate manages to reflect the specific identity status of 玫瑰 *rose* in the English translation, the system fails to capture the quantity information indicated by the Chinese nominal group structure in its first appearance in the text: 'Numerative + Measure + Thing' (一丛玫瑰 *a cluster of roses*). As Chinese language generally does not distinguish plural from singular forms in nouns, the plurality of the Head noun is often interpreted through the Numerative and the Measure in the nominal group. In Example 79, when appearing for the first time, the topic Thing 玫瑰 rose was presented as 一丛玫瑰 *a cluster of roses*, and through the Measure 丛 *cluster* (of plants), it becomes clear that there is more than one rose. Unfortunately, the NMT system fails to capture the plurality indicated through the meaning of Measure and instead presents the Thing in translation in singular forms: '*a rose*' and '*the rose*'.

Lastly, in terms of the omitted nominal groups in the SLT, it is found that, again, an improvement in the machine translation system in recovering the omitted nominal groups. Table 6.9 presents a comparison of the translation of sentences with omitted nominal groups between the SMT and the NMT systems:

As shown in Table 6.9, in none of the instances can the SMT system successfully recover the omitted nominal groups. In comparison, the NMT system has shown a better ability in recovering the omitted nominal groups, though not in all the cases. Due to the limited data for analysis, it is not clear what factors might impact the system's capacity in recovering the omitted nominal groups. Given that the recovering

Table 6.9 SMT versus NMT in translating omitted nominal groups

SLT	Text1_SMT	Text1_NMT
他常常去松土、浇水。 He often went to loosen the soil and water (**the roses**)	*He often went to loosen the soil, watering	*He often goes to loosen the soil and water
就在快要开花的时候，小鹿不小心把脚跌伤了。 When (**they**) were about to bloom, Little Deer accidentally injured (his) foot	*Just about to bloom when the deer falls careless feet	Just when it was about to bloom, the deer accidentally injured his foot
小鹿，我见过你家那些红玫瑰，可好看了！ Little Deer, I have seen of your house those red roses. (**They**) are so beautiful!	*The deer I've seen those red roses in your house, you can look good …	Xiaolu, I have seen those red roses in your house, they are so beautiful!

* ungrammatical and/or inaccurate translation

of an omitted element often relies on the context clues, the analysis of which requires a deep analysis of the endophoric information derived from the text, it is not surprising to find that recovering omitted nominal groups still remains a challenge to the current machine translation system, though there has been a great advancement in this regard compared with the statistical machines translation system.

6.4.2.3   Discussion of the Findings

In terms of the first research question, generally speaking, the NMT-based Google Translate has outperformed the SMT system in translating cohesion achieved by the nominal groups. In solving the cohesion-related problems concerning nominal groups, the current NMT system demonstrated a significant improvement compared with the SMT system in translation from Chinese into English in this case study. More specially, the improvement can be demonstrated in at least four aspects concerning nominal groups, including the capability of distinguishing an individual name from a common name, the recognition of Chinese nominal groups modified by a Qualifier, the identification of specific instances that are realised by non-Deictic nominal groups, and the recovering of omitted nominal groups in the translation. These improvements show that, compared to the SMT system, the neural machine translation method is better in detecting the covert cohesion realised by the nominal groups and is more sensitive to the endophoric clues which are derived from the text but are not explicitly displayed in the lexicogrammatical realisations.

In terms of the second research question, the analysis has shown that the NMT system still has space for improvement, especially in distinguishing an individual name from a common name when both types of names have the same lexical and graphological realisation. Also, the NMT system still seems to be weak in determining the quantity status of the Thing in the Chinese-English translation, as far as this case study is concerned. This indicates that, although the NMT system outperforms the SMT system in capturing the implicit endophoric information derived from the text, this system still cannot be comparable to the human translators in detecting the implicit cohesive devices. Therefore, it is essential for human translators to be aware of the gap and explicitate the cohesive choices through the pre-editing of the SLT, as well as the post-editing of the TLT.

6.5 Summary

In this chapter, I have explored the textual resources of Chinese nominal groups. Three textual systems are presented: the system of NAMING, the system of IDENTIFICATION and the system of NUMERATION. All the three systems are related to the identification of an instance, from the perspectives of the explicitness of the identifying process, the specificity of the instance, and the quantity information of the instance. The three systems reflect the choices in lexicogrammar to present the instance, which have been discussed in detail in the chapter. During the discussion of the three systems, 'reference' of different types and their realisations are investigated as well. Following this, another two important cohesive devices, 'ellipsis' and 'lexical cohesion', are introduced. The focus is on how nominal groups can contribute to these strategies and provide resources to achieve the cohesive effects. Finally, a case study is presented, investigating the detailed cohesion problems in machine translation. Again, the investigation concentrates on the translation problems of nominal groups and their impact on cohesion.

References

Aiken M (2019) An updated evaluation of google translate accuracy. Stud Linguist Lit 3(3):253–260. http://dx.doi.org/10.22158/sll.v3n3p253

Bentivogli L, Bisazza A, Cettolo M, Federico M (2016) Neural versus phrase-based machine translation quality: a case study. In: Proceedings of the 2016 conference on empirical methods in natural language processing. Association for Computation Linguistics, Austin, Texas. https://doi.org/10.18653/v1/d16-1025

Fox H (2002) Phrasal cohesion and statistical machine translation. EMNLP, WS, Association for Computational Linguistics

Gross A (2002) Limitations of computers as translation tools. In: Newton J (ed) Computers in translation. Routledge, London, pp 97–131

Halliday MAK, Matthiessen CMIM (2004) An introduction to functional grammar, 3rd edn. Arnold, London

Huang S (1999) The emergence of a grammatical category definite article in spoken Chinese. J Pragmat 31:77–94

Liu J (2020) Comparing and analyzing cohesive devices of SMT and NMT from Chinese to English: a diachronic approach. Open J Mod Linguist 10:765–772. https://doi.org/10.4236/ojml.2020.106046

Robertson D (2000) Variability in the use of the English article system by Chinese learners of English. Second Lang Res 16(2):135–172. https://doi.org/10.1191/026765800672262975

Toral A, Sánchez-Cartagena VM (2017) A multifaceted evaluation of neural versus phrase-based machine translation for 9 language directions. In: Paper presented at the proceedings of the 15th conference of the European chapter of the association for computational linguistics, vol 1, Long Papers. https://doi.org/10.48550/arXiv.1701.02901

Zhang M (1998) Cognitive linguistics and Chinese noun phrase. China Social Sciences Press, Beijing

Chapter 7
Summary and Directions

7.1 Introduction

I have completed the metafunctional description of Chinese nominal groups. In this final chapter, I will summarise the main findings in terms of each metafunction. I will also explore the potential applications of the current research to research projects and propose for further research in nominal groups in the future.

7.2 Summary

In Chaps. 3, 4, 5 and 6, I have used systemic functional linguistic theory to describe Chinese nominal groups. The description is organised according to the three meta-functions for which nominal groups provide resources: ideational (including logical and experiential), interpersonal and textual metafunctions. In each metafunctional description, I focused on detailed examinations of the elements in a nominal group that are relevant to the metafunction concerned, and how they work in the group to contribute to the metafunctional meanings. As a result of each metafunctional exploration, systems and system networks have been presented, which summarise the selections one can make in achieving a particular metafunctional meaning. Table 7.1 presents a summary of the main systems being drawn for each metafunctional strand:

The description starts from the logical exploration, where different structures of nominal groups in Chinese are investigated. The description focuses on three aspects: the complexity of the nominal groups, taxis and logico-semantic relations between the nominal Head and its modifiers. Some complex structures are also discussed, including sub-modification, separate Head and Thing, and rank-shifted clauses as a modifier. I have also presented the logical system of MODIFICATION, which shows a theoretically endless potential for the Head to be modified repetitively, and the

© Springer Nature Singapore Pte Ltd. 2022
J. Fang, *A Systemic Functional Grammar of Chinese Nominal Groups*,
The M.A.K. Halliday Library Functional Linguistics Series,
https://doi.org/10.1007/978-981-19-4009-5_7

Table 7.1 Summary of main systems

Metafunction	System
Logical	MODIFICATION
Experiential	THING TYPE
	EPITHESIS
	CLASSIFICATION
	QUALIFICATION
	MEASURE
Interpersonal	ATTITUDE
	NOMINAL MOOD
	PERSON
	MODALITY
Textual	NAMING
	IDENTIFICATION
	NUMERATION

logico-semantic relation between a modifier and the Head is either an expansion or a projection. In general, the logical structure of a nominal group is always a univariate one, where all the modifiers are in the same kind of relationship with the Head: the hypotactic relationship where modifiers are dependent element on the Head.

The experiential description of nominal groups is the most significant part of this research, which lays the foundation for the description of interpersonal and textual resources. This is because, in the metafunctional description of groups, it is very hard to draw a distinct line for each metafunction, which is different from the description of clauses (cf. Halliday and Matthiessen 2014). Rather, it is based on the clear definition of the elements in an experiential structure that the description of the other two metafunctions becomes possible. Therefore, the arrangement of the metafunctional description in this book is made in such an order that an experiential description precedes the interpersonal and the textual ones.

In Chapter 4, I have given a metafunctional overview of each functional element in the experiential structure, indicating the metafunctional potential of each element. Some important general tendencies along the experiential structure have also been discussed, including the 'instantial-general' cline and the 'grammar-lexis' cline, which are closely related to the modifiability of the Thing. The system of THING TYPE is the most important system in the experiential domain, which has a great impact on the categorisation of the sub-systems, such as the systems for Classifier and Epithet. The major selections on the system of THING TYPE are based on congruency/metaphoric propensity, the consciousness/unconsciousness of the Thing, the concreteness/abstractness of the Thing and the measurability of the Thing. These categories, drawing on semantic distinctions, aim to reflect different grammatical potentials. This has been demonstrated by detailed examples at both group and clause levels, showing how the categorisation reflects modifiability and the potential of construing participant roles. Systems for other important experiential elements have also been presented, including the system of CLASSIFICATION, the system of EPITHESIS, the system of QUALIFICATION and the system of MEASURE. The discussions of these sub-systems have reached one common conclusion: the selections in the Thing Type system is the determining factor influencing the experiential potential of the other experiential elements in the group.

In Chapter 5, I have explored the interpersonal resources of the nominal group. The discussion focuses on nominal groups' contributions in the following aspects: nominal mood, subject person choices, enacting attitude and presenting modality. Nominal groups play a significant role in creating a prosodic attitudinal effect as the text unfolds. This is mainly achieved by the use of attitudinal Epithets, attitudinal Things, as well as lexical and grammatical metaphors. The interpersonal system allows a speaker to play with the choices to value or devalue the Thing, to humanise or to de-humanise a referent, in which way the attitude is enacted. Nominal groups also provide resources to create modality, which is mainly achieved through the use of metaphoric Things and post Deictics. The modality realised by nominal groups also corresponds to the two categories of modulation and modalisation.

The exploration of the textual resources in Chapter 6 includes two parts. First, I have discussed the lexicogrammatical choices on the three textual systems: the system of NAMING, reflecting how things are named; the system of IDENTIFICATION, reflecting choices to present the Thing as specific or non-specific, as identifiable or unidentifiable; the system of NUMERATION, reflecting choices to present an instance as ordinated or quantified. These systems indicate how reference, which is an important cohesive device, works in the text to create cohesion. Analysis of examples indicates that, when investigating the contribution made by nominal groups to cohesion, one needs to base the observation on the context and textual information. Apart from reference, another two important cohesive strategies, ellipsis and lexical cohesion, are also discussed. The discussion has mainly focused on how nominal groups provide resources in adopting these strategies to create cohesion. When ellipsis occurs to a Chinese nominal group, the Thing must be omitted, and numerative, measure and deictic could all fill in the vacancy and take the Head position. The discussion of lexical cohesion mainly has focused on two strategies: reiteration and collocation. It has been found that both strategies are closely related to the specific-general cline of the THING TYPE system, which allows for lexical choices along the cline to achieve reiteration and collocation of various kinds.

In this book, the metafunctional descriptions of nominal groups are text-based, and all the examples come from genuine texts. A trinocular vision has been adopted as much as possible to ensure the observation of the data is comprehensive and effective. This is demonstrated by the fact that all the examples in the discussions come from texts and text types are always considered as an important factor influencing the lexicogrammatical choices. The contextual concerns have been well demonstrated by the case studies at the end of each major chapter. And semantic motives behind each major selections in a system have also been discussed wherever relevant. As from below, the categories below the rank of group that realise the nominal groups are also considered in the descriptions wherever it becomes a significant issue, such as in the descriptions of 'metaphorical Things' and the system of NUMERATION.

From above:

- Case studies

- Semantic discussions

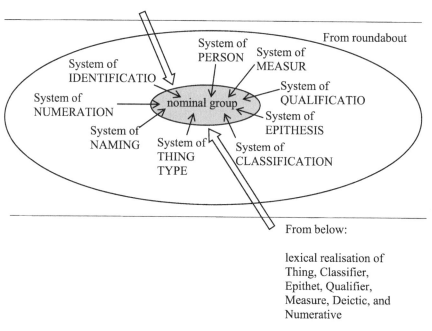

Fig. 7.1 Trinocular vision being achieved

And from the perspective of roundabout, systems and system networks have been presented in terms of each metafunctional dimension of nominal groups, reflecting selections that one can make in achieving the metafunctional meanings concerned. Figure 7.1 illustrates how nominal groups have been approached trinocularly in the current study.

7.3   Using Functional Grammar of Nominal Groups in Research Projects

The metafunctional description of nominal groups can be applied to many areas of research, including text analysis, language typology, language teaching and translation studies. At the end of each metafunctional description in Chapters 3–6, a case study is presented, demonstrating how the metafunctional description could be used in different areas.

In Chapter 3, the case study focuses on the logical complexity of the nominal groups used in two texts of the same domain targeting audience of different age groups. The logical analysis of the two texts finds that sub-modification seems to have a great impact on the complexity of the logical structure of a text, whereas other logical features, such as the number of modifiers, the status of the group complexing (as a group simplex or a complex), seem to have limited impact on the logical complexity. This brings potential lexicogrammatical indications for people intending to design texts for language tests targeting different competency levels. The logical complexity of the nominal groups should also be considered when people conduct research in children's books. It may also bring insights into the choice of texts in translation training: for example, those texts with high logical complexity tend to present more challenges in translation than those without. The study of logical complexity of the nominal groups can provide lexicogrammatical evidence showing how and why one text is more difficult than another. It is hypothesised that the complexity of sub-modification is an important indicator of translation difficulty of a source language text. Certainly, a large parallel corpus covering different text types is needed to provide evidence to test this hypothesis.

In Chapter 4, the case study presents a corpus-based investigation of the experiential modification environment of different types of Things. The case study aims to compare the modification potential of the four types of Things in terms of classification, Epithesis and Measure. Findings show that Thing type plays a decisive role in determining the potential of the nominal group in expanding its experiential structure and how it can be expanded. The experiential analysis of the modification potential of the Thing provides a new perspective of doing text analysis: instead of focusing on clauses, one can also conduct delicate analysis of the nominal groups focusing the Thing type, which provides a picture of how the Thing of a given Thing type can be depicted through different modifications. Such analysis can also open new channels in contrastive linguistics, especially when a corpus-based approach is adopted, as it is able to examine the similarities and differences between two languages in construing the Thing as well as its potential qualities. The system of THING TYPE also makes it possible to profile the general tendency in Thing type choices in different types of texts, which is expected to add depth and new perspectives to conducting text analysis.

In Chapter 5, the case study presents an alternative angle of analysing the attitudinal colour of a text by focusing on nominal groups. The case involves genuine data retrieved from an online Q&A forum on a controversial celebrity figure in China. The interpersonal analysis of the nominal groups demonstrates the use of various strategies at the level of nominal groups in expressing complex attitudes, including the use of very delicate interpersonal grammatical and lexical metaphor, the use of different types of attitudinal Epithets and the choice of references realised by nominal groups to tune up or down the intended effects. Again, the case study is presented as another piece of evidence showing how doing delicate text analysis may help people zoom in the details in the text which accumulate to achieve the interpersonal effect in a prosodic manner. The interpersonal exploration of nominal groups is able to produce rich data in appraisal analysis, which can be adopted in both quantitative and qualitative approaches.

In Chapter 6, the case study focuses on a problem faced by a rather popular area in translation studies—machine translation. The case study compares two machine translation systems, the statistical and the neural machine translation systems used by Google Translate. The purpose is to investigate how machine translation deals with the challenges of cohesion that involve nominal groups. Findings show that, in solving the cohesion-related problems concerning nominal groups, the current neural machine translation system demonstrated a significant improvement compared with the statistical translation system in translation from Chinese into English. However, the current neural translation system still cannot be comparable to the human translators in detecting the implicit cohesive devices, which are closely related to the implicit endophoric information that is not displayed in lexicogrammar. The study of cohesion achieved by nominal groups provides good insights into the challenges faced by the current machine translation systems and brings new perspectives for exploring the topics related to translation-based pre- and post-editing. Also, by examining the selections in the textual systems of NAMING, IDENTIFICATION and NUMERATION, researchers are able to conduct contrastive studies between Chinese and another language in terms of textual metafunction at a level below clause.

To sum up, the metafunctional study of nominal groups will provide researchers with an alternative to clause grammar when they conduct research in areas including discourse analysis, language teaching, contrastive linguistics and translation studies. It makes delicate text analysis a potential tool for projects in multiple disciplines and enables researchers to give a microscopic study of the important nitty-gritties below the level of clause.

7.4 Future Directions

Although this book provides an overall metafunctional description of Chinese nominal groups, there are a number of aspects where further studies are needed. Due to the limit of space and time constraints, these issues have gone beyond the scope of the current project and need to be addressed in the future studies. I will briefly talk about them based on the trinocular vision in relation to stratification.

Firstly, from the angle of 'above', to get a more comprehensive picture of nominal groups functioning in different contexts, a well-balanced corpus of different text types should be included for observation. In the current study, although texts of all the major text types have been collected, each text type is not evenly represented in the working corpus. The distribution of the current corpus shows a high proportion of recreating texts that come from the working corpus (collection of Chinese textbooks), whereas the proportions of expounding, exploring, enabling and doing texts are considerably lower. This uneven distribution simply reflects the current choice of text types used in China's schools. For future studies, if all the text types are evenly distributed across the corpus, the researchers may get interesting examples demonstrating more comprehensive and delicate selections on the grammatical systems. For example, an increased collection of expounding texts like scientific articles may present researchers opportunities to conduct a delicate investigation of the metaphorical Thing type.

Secondly, from the angle of 'roundabout', more work should be done to extend the delicacy of the system networks of nominal groups. In the current study, the system networks being presented still leave quite some space for further development along the cline of delicacy. Take the system of THIING TYPE for example. The current system can be viewed closer to the 'grammar' end than to the 'lexis' end. To further elaborate the system and develop towards the more delicate end, it is essential for the future researchers to base their investigations on a paradigmatic foundation, which brings the grammatical description closer to the meaning potential, and therefore makes it both powerful and elastic. Meanwhile, a topological account should also be brought in as a continuation of the typological description to further elaborate the system network towards the delicate end (cf. Martin and Matthiessen 1991; Matthiessen 2007a). For example, in the case of the system of THING TYPE, taxonomic elaborations may fit in for a topological description of a primary Thing type.

Thirdly, from the angle of 'below', the resources of phonology should also be taken into account in the future descriptions. In the current study, all the texts involved are written, due to the fact that onerous workload of transcribing spoken texts is beyond the management of the current author. As a result, the potential impact that could have been brought by the phonological resources may not be covered in the description. For example, tones and intonations usually carry important attitude clues in spoken texts, and it would be interesting to investigate the relations between the tone movements and their representations of attitudinal Epithets in the nominal group structure. Also, in the textual exploration concerning information status, tone prominence plays important roles in presenting given/new information. As the existing elements in an elliptical nominal group typically represent new information, they tend to carry the prominent tones. It would be interesting to further examine which element among others carries the prominent tone, and how this is related to its metafunctional role in the nominal group structure.

As arguably the first attempt to give a comprehensive and overall account of the metafunctional resources of Chinese nominal groups, this book is expected to make its contribution to the metafunctional study of Chinese language, and to fill in the blank of metafunctional description of nominal groups in Chinese. It is hoped that this project, through its demonstration of the significance of nominal groups in construing experiences, enacting attitudes and creating cohesion, will attract more research interests in exploring systemic functional grammar at levels below clause.

References

Halliday MAK, Matthiessen CMIM (2014) Halliday's introduction to functional grammar. Routledge, London

Martin JR, Matthiessen CMIM (1991) Systemic Typology and Topology. In Christie F (ed) Literacy in social processes: papers from the inaugural Australian systemic functional linguistics conference. Deakin University, pp 345–384

Matthiessen CMIM (2007) The 'architecture' of language according to systemic functional theory: developments since the 1970s. In: Hasan R, Matthiessen CMIM, Webster J (eds) Continuing discourse on language. London: Equinox, pp 505–561

Printed by Printforce, the Netherlands